Derrida's Legacies

This volume brings together some of the most well-known and highly respected commentators on the work of Jacques Derrida from Britain and America in a series of essays written to commemorate the life, and come to terms with the death, of one of the most important intellectual presences of our time.

Derrida's thought reached into nearly every corner of contemporary intellectual culture and the difference he has made is incalculable. He was indeed controversial but the astonishing originality of his work, always marked by the care, precision and respect with which he read the work of others, leaves us with a philosophical, ethical and political legacy that will be both lasting and decisive.

The sometimes personal, always insightful essays reflect on the multiple ways in which Derrida's work has marked intellectual culture in general and the literary and philosophical culture of Britain and America in particular. The outstanding contributors offer an interdisciplinary view, investigating areas such as deconstruction, ethics, time, irony, technology, location and truth. This book provides a rich and faithful context for thinking about the significance of Derrida's own work as an event that arrived and perhaps still remains to arrive in our time.

Contributors: Derek Attridge, Thomas Baldwin, Geoffrey Bennington, Rachel Bowlby, Alex Callinicos, David E. Cooper, Simon Critchley, Robert Eaglestone, Simon Glendinning, Marian Hobson, Christopher Johnson, Peggy Kamuf, Michael Naas, Nicholas Royle

Simon Glendinning is Reader in European Philosophy at the European Institute, London School of Economics and Political Science. His publications include *On Being with Others: Heidegger, Wittgenstein, Derrida* (Routledge, 1998) and *In the Name of Phenomenology* (Routledge, 2007).

Robert Eaglestone is Professor of Contemporary Literature and Thought at Royal Holloway, London. He is the author of *Doing English: A Guide for Literature Students* (Routledge, 1999, 2nd ed. 2002) and books on ethical criticism, postmodernism and the Holocaust. He is the series editor of *Routledge Critical T*

Derrida's Legacies
Literature and philosophy

Edited by Simon Glendinning and Robert Eaglestone

Routledge
Taylor & Francis Group

LONDON AND NEW YORK

First published 2008
by Routledge
2 Park Square, Milton Park, Abingdon, Oxon OX14 4RN

Simultaneously published in the USA and Canada
by Routledge
270 Madison Ave, New York, NY 10016

*Routledge is an imprint of the Taylor & Francis Group, an
informa business*

Typeset in Baskerville by
Keyword
Printed and bound in Great Britain by
Antony Rowe Ltd, Chippenham, Wiltshire

British Library Cataloguing in Publication Data
A catalogue record for this book is available from the British Library

Library of Congress Cataloging in Publication Data
Eaglestone, Robert, 1968–
Derrida's legacies : literature and philosophy / Robert Eaglestone
and Simon Glendinning.
p. cm.
Includes bibliographical references and index.
1. Derrida, Jacques. I. Glendinning, Simon, 1964– II. Title.
B2430.D484E24 2008
194—dc22
2007028589

ISBN 10: 0-415-45427-1 (hbk)
ISBN 10: 0-415-45428-X (pbk)
ISBN 10: 0-203-93328-1 (ebk)

ISBN 13: 978-0-415-45427-8 (hbk)
ISBN 13: 978-0-415-45428-5 (pbk)
ISBN 13: 978-0-203-93328-2 (ebk)

Contents

Notes on Contributors

Derek Attridge is Professor of English at the University of York, U.K. His recent publications include *How to Read Joyce* (Granta, 2007), *The Singularity of Literature* (Routledge, 2004), and *J. M. Coetzee and the Ethics of Reading: Literature in the Event* (Chicago, 2004). He is the editor of *Acts of Literature* (Routledge, 1992), a collection of Derrida's essays on literature, and the author of a number of essays on Derrida.

Thomas Baldwin is a Professor of Philosophy at the University of York. His publications include: *Contemporary Philosophy* (Oxford UP 2001), *The Cambridge History of Philosophy 1870-1945* (Cambridge UP 2003), *Reading Merleau-Ponty* (Routledge 2007). He is currently editor of MIND, the main British philosophy journal.

Geoffrey Bennington is Asa G. Candler Professor of Modern French Thought at Emory University. He is the author of a dozen books in philosophy and literature. He is currently working on a book of deconstructive political philosophy.

Rachel Bowlby is Northcliffe Professor of English at UCL. She has translated work by Derrida including *Of Hospitality* and *Paper Machine*. Her own books include *Shopping with Freud, Carried Away: The Invention of Modern Shopping*, and *Freudian Mythologies: Greek Tragedy and Modern Identities*.

Alex Callinicos is Professor of European Studies at King's College London. He previously taught political philosophy at the University of York. His books include *Althusser's Marxism, The Revolutionary Ideas of Karl Marx, Making History, Against Postmodernism, Social Theory, Equality, An Anti-Capitalist Manifesto, The New Mandarins of American Power*, and *The Resources of Critique*. He is currently working on a book on the theory of imperialism.

David E. Cooper is Professor of Philosophy at Durham University. He has been a visiting professor at universities in the USA, Canada, Germany, Malta, and Sri Lanka. His several books include *Metaphor* (1986), *The Measure of Things: Humanism, Humility and Mystery* (2003), and *Meaning* (2004).

Simon Critchley is Professor of Philosophy at the New School for Social Research and at The University of Essex. He is author of many books, most recently *Infinitely Demanding* (Verso, 2007). *The Book of Dead Philosophers* is forthcoming from Granta in 2008.

Robert Eaglestone is Professor of Contemporary Literature and Thought at Royal Holloway, University of London. His publications include *Ethical Criticism* (1997), *Doing English* (1999, 2002) and *The Holocaust and the Postmodern* (2004) and articles on contemporary European writers and philosophers. He is the series editor of Routledge Critical Thinkers and Deputy Director of Royal Holloway's Research Centre for the Holocaust and Twentieth Century History.

Simon Glendinning is Reader in European Philosophy in the European Institute at the London School of Economics and Political Science. He is the author of *On Being with Others: Heidegger-Wittgenstein-Derrida (1998) The Idea of Continental Philosophy* (2006) and *In the Name of Phenomenology* (2007) He is editor of *Arguing with Derrida* (2001) and *The Edinburgh Encyclopedia of Continental Philosophy* (1999).

Marian Hobson is a Professorial Research Fellow at Queen Mary, University of London and a Fellow of the British Academy. She is a specialist both of the European Enlightenment and of the work of Derrida. Her book, *Jacques Derrida: Opening Lines* (Routledge,1998) is being translated into Turkish. She translated his dissertation, *The Problem of Genesis in Husserl's Philosophy* (Chicago, 2003) and is the author of several articles on Derrida, including "Mimesis, presentation, representation", in *Derrida and the Humanities*, ed. Tom Cohen (CUP, 2001) which was translated into French for *Europe* (mai 2004); "L'exemplarité de Derrida" (Cahiers de l'Herne, 2004); "Hostilites and Hostages (to Fortune): on some part of Derrida's reception" (*Epoché*, 2006). Her book on eighteenth-century aesthetics (CUP, 1982) has just been published in a French translation (*L'art et son objet: Diderot, la théorie de l'illusion et les arts en France au XVIIIe. Siècle* (Champion, 2007).

Christopher Johnson is Professor of French at the University of Nottingham, specializing in contemporary French thought and the philosophy of technology. He is the author of *System and Writing in the Philosophy of Jacques Derrida* (1993), *Jacques Derrida. The Scene of Writing* (1997) and *Claude Lévi-Strauss: the Formative Years* (2003). He is a member of the editorial board of *Paragraph: A Journal of Modern Critical Theory* and a founding member of the Science Technology Culture Research Group at Nottingham.

Peggy Kamuf is Marion Frances Chevalier Professor of French and Professor of Comparative Literature at the University of Southern California. Her latest book is *Book of Addresses*, which received the René C. Wellek Prize for Literary and Cultural Theory in 2006 from the American Comparative Literature Association. She has translated a number of works by Derrida, including *Specters of Marx* (Routledge, 1994) and edited several collections of his essays, most recently *Psyche: Inventions of the Other* (with Elizabeth Rottenberg).

Michael Naas is Professor of Philosophy at DePaul University in Chicago. He is the author of *Turning: From Persuasion to Philosophy* (Humanities Press, 1995) and *Taking on the Tradition: Jacques Derrida and the Legacies of Deconstruction* (Stanford University Press, 2003). He is the co-editor of Jacques Derrida's *The Work of Mourning* (University of Chicago Press, 2001) and the co-translator, with Pascale-Anne Brault, of several works by Derrida, including *The Other Heading* (Indiana University Press, 1992), *Memoirs of the Blind* (University of Chicago Press, 1993), *Adieu—to Emmanuel Levinas* (Stanford University Press, 1999), *Rogues* (Stanford University Press, 2005), and *Learning to Live Finally* (Melville House, 2007).

Nicholas Royle is Professor of English at the University of Sussex. His books include How to Read Shakespeare (2005), Jacques Derrida (2003), The Uncanny (2003), After Derrida (1995), and (with Andrew Bennett) An Introduction to Literature, Criticism and Theory (3rd edition, 2004). He is editor of Deconstructions: A User's Guide (2000) and co-editor of the Oxford Literary Review. He is currently completing a book, In Memory of Jacques Derrida, forthcoming from Edinburgh University Press.

Preface

Simon Glendinning

A preface to what remains to come: I

One of the contributors to this volume has recently suggested that Derrida's work has an impact akin to 'something that goes bump in the day'.[1] Perhaps this explains why his work has been so prominently marked by responses ranging from the derogatory to the adulatory, explains why he was both 'excluded *and* favourite'.[2] There is a resistance and an attraction on the part of us all finding enigmatic and uncanny what we usually find unproblematic and familiar. In responding to Derrida, one of these reactions tends to come to the fore at the expense of the other. Those who take the line of greatest resistance tend to find him digestible at all only by first re-processing his thought into something more immediately tractable and digestible – more often than not something sceptical or relativistic or nihilistic.

However, even those who have found themselves drawn to Derrida will acknowledge that his writings are stubbornly difficult to read. To take a term from Roland Barthes, his texts are of a profoundly '*writerly*' type.[3] This term characterizes texts which are particularly demanding on the reader, texts which do not conform to a reader's ordinary expectations concerning what well-disciplined writing of a certain type or genre (a *classic* 'philosophical text', for example) should look like. Of course, badly written texts might equally have these non-conformist characteristics – and to be asked to accept that the inherited resources typically available to even the most well-educated of readers might provide only limited competence, or even a kind of structural incompetence, in coming to terms with what is going on in Derrida's work, is, again, as likely to produce exasperation as attraction. Indeed, people who are seeking clarity on 'what Derrida really means' are typically infuriated by the mere sight of his texts, and infuriated even more by well-meaning and otherwise intelligent people who defend him but cannot themselves provide unproblematic summaries of 'what Derrida really means'.

Derrida is not the only philosopher who always somehow seems to evade our best, or even 'least worst', attempts at coming to terms with his work.[4]

With all the obvious risks that go with the suggestion, I know I am inclined to take that difficulty – that his writings still lie far ahead of us – as a definite virtue. Similarly, I cannot say why, in the face of the fact that I felt that I understood almost nothing, I continued to read and re-read Wittgenstein when I was a student. I would still feel very uncomfortable suggesting that 'now I understand' his way of thinking and his writings. Reading Wittgenstein is not over for me, not at all. Nor, for me, is reading Derrida. And one thing I am quite sure about is that finding it hard to make headway in the remarkable textual environments that Derrida (like Wittgenstein) left us is internal to their formation. As a reader you have to learn to endure ongoing struggles of not knowing your way about, of not knowing 'what it really means' and of re-learning what wanting to know that might mean.

Naturally, one has to find some kind of worth in them, one has to find one's time for some reason well-spent, to go on and on with such demanding texts. The infuriated may find it baffling, but I have to accept that the fact that my ongoing education in philosophy has involved reading and reading and reading and reading again the writings of Derrida is inseparable from finding in the details of its turns and steps a kind of reading pleasure. This is a pleasure akin to the kind of pleasure one can get from listening to a piece of music again and again, and finding a certain theme or sequence or movement within it irreplaceably fitting.

Before moving more directly to explore an example of his writings I want first to examine the case of a reader who found a way to *stop* reading Derrida's way of doing philosophy, a way of interrupting the kind of faithful willingness to go on with it that has marked my own encounter. In a recent book in which he openly exposes the bumpy path of his own ongoing education in philosophy, Gavin Kitching recounts and accounts for how he came to see what he found in Derrida as a sort of paradigm of conceptual errancy.[5] Derrida's writing is not the philosophical pleasure dome that I have cast it as but, and here Kitching calls on a certain Wittgensteinian teaching, an exemplary instance of writing that has lost its connection to our ordinary life with language. Indeed, for Kitching it is an error to suppose that there is anything like a 'way' in Derrida's way of doing philosophy at all. There is instead, he argues, a peculiar emptiness or idleness. And this is something that can be exposed when we realise that 'we do not know what to say in response'.[6]

I think that Kitching's effort at making vivid this sense of the 'fog' surrounding Derrida's thought inadvertently helps us to lift some of it. And since fog has served to isolate the Derridean continent from many readers, this is also a good place to start. The discussion will ultimately conjoin Derrida with Wittgenstein again in a way I find congenial, and which might also give Kitching (indeed anyone, me for example) pause for further thinking.

According to Kitching, the central feature of Derrida's approach is a generalisation concerning linguistic meaning. It is the idea that meaning in language is everywhere and inherently ambiguous and hence that we can never establish with certainty what a text (for example, what someone says) means. To try to show how radically unclear this generalisation is Kitching imagines two cases that he is confident he does understand: on the one hand, a case where someone really is unsure what another person means, and in contrast to this, and what he insists is also 'more commonly' the case, an occasion when someone is 'absolutely clear' what another person means.[7] In the latter kind of case there is 'no ambiguity of meaning there at all' and the listener typically grasps the speaker's meaning 'immediately'.[8]

Kitching supposes then that while some examples of uses of language seem to speak for Derrida's generalisation others – many, many more others – would seem equally to speak against it. What remains totally unclear – and this is Kitching's point – is Derrida's generalisation itself. It is a 'form of idling language' that, try as one might, one cannot but fail to get one's head round.[9]

I think Kitching is right to suppose that Derrida affirms something like a *general* ambiguity of meaning. I want to stress the 'something like' qualification, however, since Derrida explicitly *contrasts* what he calls 'dissemination' (the dispersal of the 'seme' or unit of meaning) with the traditional concept of 'polysemia'.[10] Nevertheless, the idea that the sense of an expression is *always susceptible* to 'internal shifting' in different contexts does seem to capture something that, as Kitching puts it, 'Derrida insists' on.[11]

So let us closely examine the example that Kitching gives with respect to which, he conclusively concludes, 'Derrida [is] clearly wrong'.[12] It is a wonderful example, one that Derrida, given his deep interest in the writings of Emmanuel Levinas, would have wanted to examine at far greater length than I can here.

> I think, for example, of holding the door open for an elderly female colleague and saying "After you". She walked through the door ahead of me. She did not say, for example "After me? I'd be surprised. Nobody's been after me for years." She got my meaning immediately, but she might not have done. After all, the latter might have been an appropriate, even witty or flirtatious, reply to my words. But on the other hand, no. Such a reply would precisely have been witty because she knew, as I knew, that "after you" said in that context is an invitation to precede the speaker through the door. No ambiguity of meaning there at all. The "action context", as it were, clarified all in that case. Derrida clearly wrong.[13]

The example is, I should think, of a fairly 'common' type. The phrase 'After you' is, as one might put it, a very everyday little text-machine, and it is clear that Kitching knows how to operate with it. In particular, he knows – and his elderly female colleague knows too – that it can be used as 'an invitation to precede the speaker through the door'. Moreover, in the 'action context' we are presented with here that is exactly how it is used. Kitching knows this little text-machine well enough to know how it might be wittily taken, in addition, as a version of the similar sounding 'I'm after you'. And no doubt he could have himself invented an 'action context' in which an even more similar sounding – indeed to the ear indistinguishable – machine still could have functioned quite differently. A rather different contextual chain, for example between two elderly farming colleagues, might end with someone agreeing to take 'arf der ewe'. But, as Kitching says, no. In the 'action context' he is imagining the little machine functions as 'an invitation to precede the speaker through the door'. Other machines might have done that job for him too. He could have said, for example, 'You go first' or 'Do precede me through the door' or 'I invite you to precede me through the door'. In this case he used the rather more elegant 'After you', and there was no misunderstanding: 'she got my meaning immediately'. 'Derrida clearly wrong', right?

I don't think so. What I think Kitching's example shows is that Kitching wants to regard *his own concept* of 'understanding a sentence' as *exhausted* by this idea of knowing how it might be used. Indeed, according to Kitching, saying 'After you' in this context, *is* nothing over and above 'an invitation to precede the speaker through the door'. That is why it can be so immediately understood. There's nothing else to *get* about it. And I do think Derrida's affirmation of dissemination fundamentally challenges that construal of meaning and understanding. He will want to say that there *is always* something else to get. And getting at that, getting at *what it's about*, 'more commonly' requires a sensitivity that is not reducible to the know-how of 'knowing how the sentence might be used'. I will try to explain this.

To get at what Derrida wants to affirm in the affirmation of dissemination, I want to consider the following sentence: 'Professor Kitching held a door open for an elderly female colleague and said "After you"'. Do I understand *this* sentence? Surely it would make a difference to my understanding of what is going on here if it transpired that the elderly female colleague addressed by Professor Kitching was a charmless misanthrope. Or if it transpired that she had just publicly criticised Kitching in a meeting. Or if it transpired that she was really Kitching's fantasy of an elderly female colleague. Or if it transpired that she was Kitching's fantasy of himself as such a female colleague. I am not introducing any ambiguity here. In the sense in which Kitching understands it, there is none. But I think it is clear that each of these variations might lead us *to understand what this sentence is about* differently. Indeed, we can affirm that *and* accept that the expression 'After you' could, in each case, be replaced by some other kind of invitation to precede him through the door. What is no longer so clear or obvious, however, is that we want to say that she 'immediately understands' the sentence on that account alone.[14] To sharpen that point, let's imagine a brief continuation of the narrative: 'Professor

Kitching held a door open for an elderly female colleague and said "After you". After he had said this, he left her as he did the day before'. Are you now so convinced that we should agree that when he said 'After you' 'she got my meaning immediately'? And what about the following continuation? 'Professor Kitching held a door open for an elderly female colleague and said "After you". After he had said this, he followed her as he did the day before.' Again, can we affirm that when he said 'After you' to her it is 'absolutely clear' that 'she got my meaning immediately'?

These are just two paths, and as I have already indicated there are a multitude of 'action contexts' into which one might graft this little text-machine. And in each case, without exploiting any (countable) semantic ambiguity or polysemy in the sense of the expression, we might want to say we understand it differently. This is what Derrida calls dissemination and it is not, in Derrida's view, just a (happy or unhappy) fact of linguistic life that we have to put up with and which someone might now and then exploit with an independently specifiable linguistic instrument. On the contrary, this possibility of grafting a textual form into (strictly *countless*) different textual or contextual chains is, according to Derrida, fundamental to its *being* the singular textual form it is. Here the emphasis is on the openness of the grafted material to expressing something new, something that is, in particular cases, sufficiently singular that it might resist 'immediate understanding'. By contrast, Kitching's approach to someone operating with the words 'After you' is one which would rather construe the scene as a 'more commonly' one in which 'I am absolutely clear that you mean this and not that in language and that they meant this and not that in language'.[15] It is a construal which wants to leave nothing in this text to be desired, nothing singular in it is *yet to come.*

And in construing things this way Kitching also passes over that which, in *his own concept* of understanding, he might have sometimes preferred to affirm. One might also note that this passing over is something that Wittgenstein himself tried to teach us to avoid:[16]

> "After he had said this, he left her as he did the day before." — Do I understand this sentence? Do I understand it just as I should if I heard it in the course of a narrative? If it were set down in isolation I should say, I don't know what it's about. But all the same I should know how this sentence might be used; I could myself invent a context for it.
>
> (A multitude of familiar paths lead off from these words in every direction.)
>
> We speak of understanding a sentence in the sense in which it can be replaced by another which says the same; but also in the sense in which it cannot be replaced by any other. (Any more than one musical theme can be replaced by another.)
>
> Then has "understanding" two different meanings here? — I would rather say that these kinds of use of "understanding" make up its

meaning, make up my *concept* of understanding. For I *want* to apply the word "understanding" to all this.

> *Hearing* a word in a particular sense. How queer that there should be such a thing!

> Phrased *like this*, emphasized liked this, heard in this way, this sentence is the first of a series in which a transition is made to *these* sentences, pictures, actions.

> ((A multitude of familiar paths lead of from these words in every direction.))

I have contracted the sequence of Wittgenstein's remarks somewhat, in part for the sake of brevity. However, I hope that there is enough here to engage in a work of reading Kitching's wanting to apply the word 'understanding' to only part of his concept.

But I have also contracted the sequence of Wittgenstein's remarks enough to see at a glance the recurrence of *the dissemination affirming phrase* 'A multitude of familiar paths lead of from these words in every direction'. What is achieved by the repetition of the very same sentence? Does Wittgenstein find it irreplaceably fitting? Does it function in the same way in both remarks or make the same point? Why the doubling of parentheses in the second case? Is this just a question of style? I do not raise these questions because I know already how to answer them confidently or authoritatively, but because, honestly, I don't. And I am drawing attention to Kitching's reductive conception of what is 'more commonly' the case precisely because one would think that his own faithful willingness to go on with Wittgenstein's work might have itself invited a consideration of this common faithful willingness to go on with 'ordinary language'. Why does he overlook the fact that what he calls his 'Wittgenstienian education'[17] involved reading and reading and reading and reading again the writings of the later Wittgenstein? Kitching describes the 'journey' he has made with Wittgenstein as 'quasi-autobiographical',[18] a point which he pointedly connects to the fact that the bumpy movements of orientation and re-orientation which have marked his journey matter to him sufficiently deeply that he can 'wince' and be 'embarrassed' by the forms of 'thinking and feeling' he formerly accepted.[19] At issue here is precisely not a matter of 'getting the meaning immediately' but a movement in which Kitching developed, changed and worked over an *understanding* of Wittgenstein's text that was, in his view, frequently 'at least to some degree … a *misunderstanding*'.[20] Has the journey of this quasi-autobiographical movement nothing to do with the way the *Philosophical Investigations* is written? And if the objection is that such a text is radically atypical and far from common, and that 'more commonly' one is 'absolutely clear' that others 'meant this and not that' by their words,[21] I would wonder who was more attracted to what, after Wittgenstein, we might want to call 'metaphysical' construals (for example, of wanting to speak 'absolutely') of what 'more commonly' goes on '*in* language, *in* life, *in* context'.[22]

In my view it is precisely this kind of 'metaphysical' construal of the everydayness of one's life with language that Derrida wants to call into question. As we shall see later in this preface, Derrida identifies his 'final intention' in the work undertaken in his text from 1967, *Of Grammatology* (but certainly not only there), 'to make enigmatic what one thinks one understands by the words "proximity", "immediacy", "presence"'.[23] Perhaps especially to make enigmatic what, proximally and for the most part, we like to think we presently understand by these words immediately. Bump.

Derrida's intention here is not the radically 'ineffectual' and 'inconsequential' work of 'philosophical metaphysics' that Kitching supposes,[24] but nor is it, I would suggest, an effort to *deny* (or indeed to *affirm*) the correctness of what Wittgenstein calls 'our naïve, normal way of expressing ourselves'.[25] What Derrida does attempt is to come reflectively to terms with something that – in part because of our naïve normal way of expressing ourselves – he finds us (naively) finding insufficiently enigmatic and remarkable, and so something which he thinks we would do well to resist a desire to interrupt thinking about. At issue here is an ongoing effort reflectively to endure what we already more or less naively endure everyday, indeed as our everyday itself: a life with language. Of course, this reflection on naivety is itself a movement within that life, a moment (one would hope) of some kind of enlightenment or awakening with respect to a previous naivety, and so, as Kitching's recounting of his journey with Wittgenstein nicely illustrates, it also involves an internal transformation of (oneself with respect to) a life with language. What one previously took for sure or took for granted can now make you wince.

A preface to what remains to come: II

Having given an illustration of what someone might want to bring to bear in an effort to stop reading Derrida, I want now to engage in a bit of reading that might encourage others to go on. The text by Derrida I want to go through prepares for a critical examination of the dominant Western conception of the history of writing, a critical examination which quite rapidly develops into a problematisation of the modern Western conception of the linearity of human history in general. The conception of the history of writing in question is one which configures it as moving through a series of distinctive stages: there were, first, primitive pictures, then symbols, then hieroglyphics, then characters, and then finally a phonetic alphabet which, for the first time, properly 'represents' spoken words. The history of writing is thus conceived as a linear history in which we move from non-linear, non-phonetic marks to a linear and purely phonetic script. Derrida's work of reading the tradition on this theme often aims to retrieve an acknowledgement of an essential or structurally necessary non-linearity within the very texts which have sought most vigorously to affirm the purely linear *telos* (goal) of the history of writing, the disclosure within such texts of another trajectory or of more than one trajectory or even something other than a trajectory, a work of reading that opens reading itself out onto something other than the specification of 'the-meaning-of-the-text'.

However, if (as that acknowledgement suggests) we already recognise, at least in a certain way (as Derrida often puts it), that no actual writing can attain the purely linear ideal why are we inclined to look at the history of writing as a movement towards this ideal? One powerful influence (not the only one) has been an appeal to an analogy with a picture of an individual's mental development to understand the development that we call 'the history of humanity'. Indeed, traditional anthropology used to talk blithely of 'the childhood of mankind', of 'man' then passing through its adolescence and now, at last (hooray/boo) reaching (round here anyway) full rational and scientific maturity. And as a modern child learns to write properly, so – we like to think – did (Western, rational, scientific) 'man'. The linearity presumed by the dominant history of writing thus segues seamlessly into the ethnocentrism of the modern Western self-understanding of the history of humanity in general.

But what if we begin to read the non-linear remains left between the lines of this linear picture? This requires, Derrida suggests, a form of rationality and scientificity that neither simply conforms to nor simply rejects the rationality and scientificity of Western modernity. With ethnocentrism embedded in the 'mythography' of Western conceptions of history becoming legible, we are, Derrida suggests, entering a new age of writing: an age in which we are not only starting to conceive the history of writing differently but in which 'we are beginning to write differently' too.[26]

It was never going to be easy to defend such a turn in our time. However, I want to give readers a sense or taste of Derrida's writing by attempting (to borrow Stanley Cavell's apt ambition with respect to reading Wittgenstein) to 'acknowledge from the commencement, anyway leave open at the opening, that the way this work is written is internal to what it teaches'.[27] While this does not require that one spends one's time only on considerations of the way the work is written, at least some attention to it is due, if only at the commencement. In what follows I want to take the opportunity to do so by looking at one of Derrida's most audacious commencements: the opening of *Of Grammatology*.

Of Grammatology begins with a preface, just over a page long. It is quite a traditional preface in that it states without more ado what the author intends to do. Yet that conformity to the norm also makes it engage with a more or less traditional philosophical problem with prefaces, at least since Hegel asked his readers not to take him seriously in his.[28] The supposed problem with prefaces is that the '*prae-fatio*' is a 'saying-before-hand' that is actually written after the fact, after the work, and as standing outside the (real) work of the work, that real work thus being the essential '*prae-fatio*' of the preface. Derrida does not dwell on this out-of-joint logic of the preface in the preface to *Of Grammatology*. However, in an over 50-page-long preface to a text published five years later the status of the preface does become an explicit theme, and Derrida's later remarks helpfully preface the earlier apparently traditional ones:

> The preface announces in the future tense ('this is what you are going to read') the conceptual content or significance of what will already have been written. And thus sufficiently read to be gathered up in its semantic tenor and proposed in advance. From [this] viewpoint, which re-creates an intention-to-say after the fact, the text exists as something written – a past – which, under the false appearance of a present, a hidden omnipotent author (in full mastery of his product) is presenting to the reader as his future. Here it is what I wrote, then read, and what I am writing that you are going to read. After which you will again be able to take possession of the preface which in sum you have not yet begun to read, even though, once having read it, you will have already anticipated everything that follows and thus you might just as well dispense with reading the rest.[29]

The 'pre' of the preface makes the future present, a future which is in fact already written and past. One might wonder then whether there can be *a preface to what remains to come* that does not render what remains to come everything but to come. Perhaps only if what remains to come will have always already resisted the idea of '*complete* gathering up' that a writer of a preface or indeed a writer of a metaphysical system might, beyond the preface, yearn for. Derrida will affirm that resistance.

Of Grammatology begins, as I say, with a short preface. In it Derrida tells us, very straightforwardly, what we will read and announces 'the guiding intention' of the book. This he then describes in terms of the problematisation (or making problematic) of traditional approaches to the 'critical reading' of texts (consequent, as I have noted, on considerations surrounding the status of writing throughout the history, especially, of philosophy), a problematisation which will require, he states, a radical adjustment in 'classical' conceptions of the shape of human history. Indeed, it will 'demand that reading should free itself ... from the classical categories of history'.[30] Derrida does not take this to involve an abandonment of 'classical norms' concerning, for example, the necessity of periodisation in historical research. On the contrary, Derrida himself is concerned in part with coming to terms with a vast 'age' or 'epoch' ('at least some twenty centuries') as a distinctive historical configuration, a configuration with various more or less differently configured contributions. But, as I have already indicated, a major result of Derrida's engagement with that historical material is to disrupt the feeling for linear historical sequence and for clearly separate and distinct stages which readers in our time have come to regard as obligatory in historical scholarship. Indeed, in contrast to modern philosophers or scientists who regard the contributions of their historical predecessors, particularly those they regard as 'historically remote' ones, as of merely historical interest only, Derrida retains something of the more classical conviction that a philosopher is under 'the obligation to study the ancients'.[31] The dead, even the long dead, are not finished, not simply dead and gone and so do not belong to a past that we can simply separate off and leave behind us. Moreover, even though, we in our time have come to regard the classical tradition as a primarily literary tradition, Derrida is (again up to a point classically) engaging with the more classical sense of the classical as a philosophical tradition, albeit one that is premised on a distinctive historical understanding: a philosophical tradition which constantly revives a sense of human history as having a distinctive sense or meaning, with an origin and end. As I have suggested, *Of Grammatology* is an attempt to show that this conception of human history is pre-programmed by a particular interpretation of human writing. His fresh look at the classical conception of writing thus aims to intervene at the very heart of the classical tradition as he reads it.

There is another classical aspect to this. Derrida's 'guiding intention' may be to go back behind that classical tradition to produce a new reading of it, but there is also a very strong, if implicit, criticism of the contemporary so-called 'modern' obsession with the contemporary. Derrida's resistance to the linear norm – what one might call his deperiodisation of classical history – gives him a sharp and (up to a point still) classical sense that one's most relevant predecessor, what remains to be thought, can be historically remote. Texts are seen here as events (something that unfolds in time) not, as it were, meaning-objects. Great texts reverberate and make their way through passages of writing and reading. They are not over – they lie ahead of us.

None of this is separable from Derrida's 'final intention' 'to make enigmatic what one thinks one understands by the words 'proximity', 'immediacy', 'presence'.[32] The point here is not to affirm that our memory of the past informs our inhabitation of the present. On the contrary and more radically, Derrida affirms that what is most alive and active in a time is not always something alive and available (at least not available without more ado) to those who live in it. Indeed, according to Derrida the 'trace' of something that cannot be reduced to anything present (for example, irreducible to the memory of a past present or to the anticipation of a future present) belongs to the very structure of what we too uncritically understand by 'consciousness',[33] an understanding that Derrida finds always to be 'thought only as self-presence'.[34]

That is how many have liked to think of it, and how many still do. However, Derrida also finds resistance to it everywhere too, resistance that has, if anything, been gaining momentum. And while he certainly displays a distinctive and singular initiative in that resistance movement, he does not at all suppose that he is alone in trying to think against the grain of our heritage. Indeed, at a certain point in his discussion of 'the trace' in *Of Grammatology* he turns gratefully to acknowledge that his appeal to this concept in a 'deconstruction of presence' does not serve to distinguish his work from everything else going on today, and he positively welcomes that his discussion will bear the trace of the 'force' of texts and demonstrations of others: for example, from Emmanuel Levinas's discussion of the presentation of the Other as the presentation of an alterity that can never 'be lived in the originary or modified form of presence'; and this reconciled with (and so generalised through) Martin Heidegger's identification of the history of ontology as one which determines 'the meaning of Being as presence and the meaning of language as the full continuity of speech'. And since, as we have just noted, this all opens onto a 'deconstruction of consciousness' as philosophy has traditionally grasped it (as 'self-presence'), the analysis of writing as 'trace' will refer also to the work of Nietzsche, of Freud and, indeed, of various contemporary scientific fields, 'notably biology'.[35]

The 'deconstruction of presence' (the work aimed at by the 'final intention') will in this way call for a kind of thinking and writing that, situated rather boldly within some of the most radical textual and theoretical environments of our time, goes back behind the oppositions through which we have typically understood ourselves for centuries hitherto. Indeed, it will disturb even the most stubborn and radical of all classical period breakers, the break which would have traditionally marked the coming to presence of self-presence itself: 'the opposition of nature and culture, animality and humanity, etc.'.[36]

The scope of this analysis is unbelievably wide. And yet, it is tempered with a modesty that deserves stressing. Wanting to 'respect classical norms' while at the same time endeavouring inventively to strike a path which will make enigmatic the founding resources of Western thought is not something Derrida claims to be able to pursue 'without embarrassing [himself] in the process'.[37] And as I hope to show in the rest of this preface, Derrida's work of re-reading the classical Western heritage cannot avoid this embarrassment. Not simply because his work of re-reading the classical tradition produces hard-to-bear conceptual tensions and torsions (which it does) but rather because these tensions and torsions inevitably multiply and accumulate in a text that can only be written as a kind of preface to what remains to come. For, as we shall see, Derrida's interruption of Western thought has as what might be called its guiding light a 'relation' to a future that simply cannot be reduced to anything present (irreducible, for example, to a present expectation or anticipation). Indeed, it is not something presently alive and immediately available to those who are comfortably at home in the contemporary world or who live, as one says, in our time. How that future to come can serve as a guide or a light to thinking today is not something that such thinking will be able unproblematically to articulate in the terms of philosophy's traditional guidance on guidance and light.

Of Grammatology is divided into two parts. Part I is entitled 'Writing Before the Letter' and 'outlines a theoretical matrix'.[38] This matrix is intended to serve to justify, as far as is possible, the effort at a rehabilitation of writing. Part II is entitled 'Nature, Culture, Writing' and engages with the task of going back behind traditional Western thinking about writing in its exemplary expression in the work of Rousseau. Part I begins with a short text of just over two pages rather enigmatically (for me at least when I first read it) entitled 'Exergue', a text which is led off by the following series of three numbered quotations, forming, Derrida says, 'a triple exergue':[39]

1. The one who will shine in the science of writing will shine like the sun. A scribe (EP, p. 87) O Samas (sun-god), by your light you can scan the totality of lands as if they were cuneiform signs (ibid.)
2. These three ways of writing correspond almost exactly to three different stages according to which one can consider men gathered into a nation. The depicting of objects is appropriate to a savage people; signs of words and of propositions, to a barbaric people; and the alphabet to civilised people. J.-J Rousseau, *Essai sur l'origine des langues*
3. Alphabetic script is in itself and for itself the most intelligent. Hegel, *Enzyklopadie*

The first numbered 'exergue' of the triplet is formed from two sayings which originate from sources even before classical antiquity. They are sayings of the (very ancient) ancients that Derrida sourced from one of the books by the pre-historian André Leroi-Gourhan (entitled *L'Écriture et la psychologie des peoples* and referred to in Derrida's text just cited as 'EP') that were in view in a review essay from which *Of Grammatology* was, in its first part, worked up. Together the two ancient sayings anticipate the project of Derrida's own grammatology, mark his interest in what is historically remote, and, since we have just noted a moment of modesty, indicate the frankly astonishing extent of his ambition.

The second numbered 'exergue' of the triplet represents a profoundly *ethnocentric* (by which Derrida intends to pick out analyses which affirm a certain superiority of what is called 'Western Man') and *phonocentric* (by which Derrida intends to pick out analyses which affirm a certain priority of what is called 'speech') conception of the history of writing, anticipating what Derrida will present as Rousseau's exemplary position in the epoch that he (Derrida) wants to delimit.

And if we anticipate that the kind of *intelligence* supposedly unique to 'man' has been determined over and over again in the history of Western philosophy as the capacity for grasping a *purely* intellectual order or an ideal *logos*, then the third numbered 'exergue' in the triplet, from Hegel, anticipates that the *ethnocentric* and *phonocentric* conception is also *logocentric* (by which Derrida intends to pick out analyses which affirm a certain irreducibility of what are called 'ideal meanings').

But what is an 'exergue'? According to the *Oxford Compact English Dictionary* an 'exergue' is … But the word is not listed there. Many readers of analytic philosophy were prepared by J.L. Austin to do philosophy with a dictionary ('quite a concise one will do'[40]) – with Derrida you often need a fairly good dictionary to read him at all. Trying again, then, what is an 'exergue'? According to the *Chambers Twentieth Century Dictionary* an 'exergue' is 'part of the reverse of a coin, below the main device, often filled up by the date, etc.'. That doesn't seem to help much either. However, the subsequent etymology does: '[Fr., — Gr. *ex*, out of, *ergon*, work.]'. So those like me who are initially perplexed by the title would have been better off had they been competent users of French (the singularities of a language are a favourite theme of Derrida's), and better still had they been attentive to the Greek root of the French word which indicates that we are concerned with something on the edge of or outside the main 'work', an outwork. So the 'Exergue' is in fact another preface, another *prae-fatio*; only this time Derrida reaches for a term for it that goes back to a 'saying-beforehand' which goes back behind (or goes on behind the back of) the Latin 'saying-beforehand'.[41]

Following the triplet of quotations Derrida tells us what his point is in quoting them, or what they are 'intended … to focus attention on'.[42] We need to read the rest of the 'Exergue' carefully because Derrida spells it out very slowly. What the 'triple exergue' announces or is intended to focus attention on is:

(a) '*not only*' a marked *ethnocentricism* connected with the concept of writing and

(b) '*nor merely*' a marked *logocentrism* (or 'the metaphysics of phonetic writing') which, he claims controls (and yet is *also* – in a certain way – constantly challenged by)

   (i) *the concept of writing* in a world where the phoneticization of writing must dissimulate its own history

   (ii) *the history of metaphysics* which has always assigned the origin of truth in general to the *logos*, and

   (iii) the concept of science and

(c) '*must not only*' announce that a science of writing, grammatology, is showing signs of liberation all over the world but, with this 'triple exergue', finally

(d) '*I would like to suggest above all*' that a science of writing runs the risk of never being established as such (there could be for it, for example, no unity of a project, no statement of method, no statement of limits and so on). And that is because the very idea of such a science as one which would liberate us from the epoch dominated by the metaphysics of phonetic writing, the very idea of this science 'is meaningful for us' only *within* that epoch and that domination.

Despite this limitation, however, the fact that Derrida had his days (his 'here and now') in that epoch too did not stop him attempting to make more or less systematic steps; it did not simply stop him in his theoretical tracks with regard to a new grammatological project. He concludes the 'Exergue' with a final (and very characteristic):

(e) '*Perhaps*' a 'patient meditation and painstaking investigation on and around what is still provisionally called writing' may still be a way of being 'faithful to a future world', a future beyond the present horizon of determinate anticipation or foresight, but which nevertheless has a kind of *imminence* such that it 'proclaims itself at present'.[43]

This 'future world' would be one in which the 'the values of sign, word, and writing' which have dominated our epoch will have been 'put into question' in a radically new way.[44] However, in so far as this future remains precisely beyond the horizon of every presently anticipatable future present we also remain in the (theoretically embarrassing) situation of being guided by a future world we do not *know* and hence have to admit that 'for that future world ... for that which guides our future anterior, there is as yet no exergue'.[45]

The logic of the preface was at work all along. However, with *Of Grammatology* we have a case of a preface-like work that aims to be faithful to a future which (Derrida can only, 'here and now', hope) *will have been* prefaced by his initiative. This is Derrida's 'messianism *without* messianism': an affirmation of a 'to come' that he does not claim to *know* what.

The future, the future that is beyond the present horizon of anticipation of the future, can, Derrida concedes, 'only be anticipated in the form of an absolute danger' since it implies a break beyond the 'constituted normality' of our being-in-the-world.[46] However, the normality of our world is one that has been constituted by a 'heritage'[47] which is, Derrida anticipates in the exergue, thoroughly *ethnocentric* and, since it is dominated by 'values of sign, word, and writing' that are fundamentally tied to the *phonocentric* and *logocentric* tendencies that mark 'the epoch of Christian creationism ... when these appropriate the resources of Greek conceptuality',[48] it is a normality that has been through and through (though often insensibly) *theocentric*. Without affirming an anti-ethnocentrism (in the manner of Rousseau, for example) and without being an 'enemy of religion' as such either,[49] Derrida seeks not only a formal clarity with respect to this heritage but wants to prevent it from closing itself off from the movements within itself through which, beyond our 'today', it can have a future worthy of the name. For the sake of our heritage, out of love for it, he believes it to be *better* that one tries – embarrassing oneself along the way no doubt – to be faithful to its future here and now: to welcome it.

The future, as such, is, one might say, the 'nothing' outside of the text that is the world of our today. Nevertheless, what in that today 'proclaims' the future can be read and attended to in the heritage of that text, as an alteration in it. And this is precisely what Derrida tries to do within the limits of the enlightenment granted over time. As slow as can be, he began in the text that brought about his landing in our time, an alteration is taking place whose necessity is, for us, 'perceptible', if only just or 'hardly'. It is this: 'everything that for at least some twenty centuries tended towards and finally succeed in being gathered under the name of language is beginning to let itself be transferred to, or at least summarized under, the name of writing'.[50] That was Derrida's point of departure in forging an opening for the future of our heritage. And now, today, because of the force of Derrida's singular way of inhabiting it, the future of our heritage is not weakened, not destroyed, but positively and faithfully welcomed by others too. That is the beginning of Derrida's legacies.

Notes

1. Nicholas Royle, *Jacques Derrida*, London: Routledge, 2003, p. 149.
2. In the text that is presented as 'Circumfession', beneath Geoffrey Bennington's 'Derridabase' in their jointly composed text *Jacques Derrida* (Chicago: Chicago University Press, 1993), Derrida tells of the death, 'a few months before I was conceived' of a brother he never knew, Paul Moïse, a brother who had been the youngest son before Jackie (as Jacques Derrida was named) became, again, the youngest son. Jackie Derrida then became the youngest son who took the place of the youngest son: 'from this I always got the feeling of being an excluded favorite, of both father and mother,...excluded *and* favorite at two juxtaposed moments...and it is still going on, read the papers' (pp. 279–80).
3. See, for example, Roland Barthes, *S/Z* trans. R. Miller. New York: Hill and Wang, 1974, p. 4.
4. Nicholas Royle, *Jacques Derrida*, p. 149.
5. Gavin Kitching, *Wittgenstien and Society: Essays in Conceptual Puzzlement*, Aldershot: Ashgate, 2003.
6. Kitching, *Wittgenstein and Society*, p. 129.
7. Kitching, *Wittgenstein and Society*, p. 129.
8. Kitching, *Wittgenstein and Society*, p. 128.
9. Kitching, *Wittgenstein and Society*, p. 132.
10. Derrida, *Limited Inc*, G. Graff (ed.), Evanston: Northwestern University Press, 1988, p. 9.
11. Kitching, *Wittgenstein and Society*, p. 124.
12. Kitching, *Wittgenstein and Society*, p. 128.
13. Kitching, *Wittgenstein and Society*, p. 128.
14. This kind of contrast is invoked in the early part of Kitching's discussion where he cites Stanley Cavell saying 'we can understand what the *words* mean apart from understanding why you say them; but apart from understanding the point of your saying them we cannot understand what *you* mean' (Kitching, *Wittgenstein and Society*, p. 125). Kitching wants to bring this sort of point against Derrida – but I find that it is powerfully telling against his own example.
15. Kitching, *Wittgenstein and Society*, p. 129.
16. Wittgenstein, *Philosophical Investigations*, trans. G.E.M. Anscombe, Oxford: Blackwell, 1958. The remarks quoted here are between §§525-534.
17. Kitching, *Wittgenstein and Society*, p. 121.
18. Kitching, *Wittgenstein and Society*, p. 2.
19. Kitching, *Wittgenstein and Society*, p. 3.
20. Kitching, *Wittgenstein and Society*, p. 120.
21. Kitching, *Wittgenstein and Society*, p. 129.
22. Kitching, *Wittgenstein and Society*, p. 130.

23. Derrida, *Of Grammatology*, trans. Gayatri Chakravorty Spivak, Baltimore: Johns Hopkins University Press, 1974, p. 70.
24. Kitching, *Wittgenstein and Society*, p. 138.
25. Wittgenstein, *Zettel*, trans. G.E.M. Anscombe, Oxford Blackwell, 1984, §223. My effort to bring Wittgenstein and Derrida into some kind of conjunction is evident again here since I take it that it is a serious misunderstanding of Wittgenstein to think he wanted to affirm or deny the correctness of the ordinary use of words either.
26. Derrida, *Of Grammatology*, p. 87.
27. Stanley Cavell, *The Claim of Reason: Wittgenstein, Skepticism, Morality, and Tragedy*, Oxford: OUP, 1979, p. 3.
28. 'Don't take me seriously in a preface. The real philosophical work is what I have just written.' Hegel, cited by Gayatri Chakravorty Spivak in her 'Translator's Preface' to *Of Grammatology*, p. x.
29. Derrida, 'Outwork, prefacing' in *Dissemination*, London: Athlone Press, 1981, p. 7.
30. Derrida, *Of Grammatology*, p. lxxxix.
31. In *Human Nature and History* (Vol. 1, Chicago: Chicago University Press, 1969) Robert Denoon Cumming notes that this obligation has its mythological origin in 'the answer Zeno reportedly received from the Delphic Oracle' which was 'Take on the colour of the dead' and which Zeno interpreted to mean 'Study the ancients' (p. 200).
32. Derrida, *Of Grammatology*, p. 70.
33. Derrida, *Of Grammatology*, p. 70.
34. Derrida 'Différance' in *Margins of Philosophy*, London: Harvester Wheatsheaf, 1982, p. 16.
35. Derrida, *Of Grammatology*, p. 70.
36. Derrida, *Of Grammatology*, p. 70.
37. Derrida, *Of Grammatology*, p. lxxxix.
38. Derrida, *Of Grammatology*, p. lxxxix.
39. Derrida, *Of Grammatology*, p. 3. We might note that the short foreword inserted before the opening chapter of Part II closes by noting that the inclusion of Levi-Strauss's texts in 'an introduction to "the age of Rousseau"' 'will be somewhat more than an exergue' (Derrida, *Of Grammatology*, p. 100).
40. J.L. Austin, 'A Plea for Excuses', in *Philosophical Papers*, Oxford: Clarendon, 1979, p. 186.
41. Derrida, *Limited Inc*, p. 45 and p. 109 fn. 3.
42. Derrida, *Of Grammatology*, p. 3.
43. All the quotations here are from the 'exergue' to Part I of *Of Grammatology*, pp. 3–5.
44. Derrida, *Of Grammatology*, p. 5.
45. Derrida, *Of Grammatology*, p. 5.
46. Derrida, *Of Grammatology*, p. 5.
47. Derrida, *Of Grammatology*, p. 14.
48. Derrida, *Of Grammatology*, p. 13.
49. Derrida, 'Faith and Knowledge', trans. S. Weber, in *Religion*, J. Derrida and G. Vattimo (eds.), Cambridge: Polity Press, 1998, p. 7.
50. Derrida, *Of Grammatology*, p. 6.

Acknowledgements

Most of the essays in this book originated in the series of talks held under the title "For Derrida" at Tate Modern, London, 2005, organised by the Forum for European Philosophy. We are extremely grateful to the contributors to that series for agreeing to develop their work for publication in this book, and to the authors of the specially commissioned essays. We would also like to thank Dominic Willsdon, Curator of Public Events at Tate Modern, for his support and involvement, and the staff of the Tate Archive who allowed us access to the audio recording of the original events. At the Forum for European Philosophy, we would like to thank Alan Montefiore, Catherine Audard, Juliana Cardinale and Catherine Lowe. We are also grateful to our colleagues at the European Institute at the LSE and in the Department of English at Royal Holloway, University of London, for their interest and support. Liz Thompson and Polly Dodson at Routledge have been integral to the book, and we would like to express our gratitude to them here too.

Thanks to the following, for permission to reproduce materials:

An earlier version of Simon Critchley's 'Derrida: The Reader' was published in *Epoché*, 10.2, 2006, pp. 315–326.

Part of Derek Attridge's chapter 'Derrida's Singularity: Literature and Ethics' is also to appear in *Questions: for Jacques Derrida*, edited by Richard Rand, and published by SUNY Press (forthcoming).

A longer version of Christopher Johnson's chapter on 'Derrida and Technology' has been published in *Paragraph*, 28.3, November 2005, pp. 98–116. The illustration in this chapter is from Leroi-Gourhan, *Gesture and Speech*, p. 82 and is reproduced by kind permission of The MIT Press.

Christopher Jonson, 'Derrida and Technology'. A longer version of this essay has been published in *Paragraph*, 28.3, November 2005. Reprinted by kind permission of the Edinburgh University Press.

SG and RE
London 2007

1 Derrida

The reader

Simon Critchley

How did Derrida transform the way in which people like me do philosophy? Let me begin negatively with a couple of caveats and confessions. I was never a structuralist and always found Saussure's linguistics a deeply improbable approach to language, meaning and the relation of language and meaning to the world. Therefore, Derrida's early arguments in this area, particularly the critique of the priority of speech over writing in the hugely influential *Of Grammatology*, always left me rather cold. Talk of 'post-structuralism' left me even colder; almost as cold as rhetorical throat-clearing about 'post-modernism'. So, in assessing Derrida's influence, I would want to set aside a series of notions famously associated with him – like *différance*, trace and archi-writing, what Rodolphe Gasché used to call the 'infrastructures' – in order to get a clearer view of what I think Derrida was about in his work and what we can learn from that work.

I have a similar scepticism about the popular idea of deconstruction as a methodological unpicking of binary oppositions (speech/writing, male/female, inside/outside, reason/madness, etc). In my view, this is a practice which led generations of humanities students into the intellectual *cul-de-sac* of locating binaries in purportedly canonical texts and cultural epiphenomena and then relentlessly deconstructing them in the name of a vaguely political position somehow deemed to be progressive. Insofar as Derrida's name and half-understood anthologised excerpts from some of his texts were marshalled to such a cause, this only led to the reduction of deconstruction to some sort of entirely formalistic method based on an unproven philosophy of language. One of the things that I have always been anxious to show is that although there is a strong tendency towards formalisation in Derrida's work, in particular the formalisation of aporiae, Derrida's work is not a formalism. That is, it is not the sort of philosophical approach that can be criticised as formalism in an analogous way, say, to how Hegel criticised Kantian formalism. Deconstruction is a praxis; deconstructions (Derrida always preferred the plural) are *praxoi*, a praxis of reading.

In my view, Derrida was a supreme reader of texts, particularly but by no means exclusively philosophical texts. Contrary to some Derridophiles, I do not think that he read everything with the same persuasive power: there are better and worse texts by Derrida (how could it be otherwise?): however, there is no doubt that the way in which he read a crucial series of authorships in the philosophical tradition completely transformed our understanding of their work and, by implication, of our own work. In particular, I think of his devastating readings of what the French called '*les trois H*': Hegel, Husserl and Heidegger, who provided the bedrock for French philosophy in the post-war period and the core of Derrida's own philosophical formation in the 1950s. Despite polemics to the contrary, the readings of Husserl are scintillating in their rigour and brilliance, his engagements with Hegel, particularly *Glas,* on which I've worked a lot, are a wonderfully imaginative immanent dismantling of Hegel's system. I think that Derrida was the best and most original philosophical reader of Heidegger, in particular the *Geschlecht* series and *De l'esprit,* but Heidegger informs just about everything Derrida writes, his shadow extends furthest over his work. I will come back to this below.

Far beyond this, Derrida's readings of Plato, of Rousseau and of other eighteenth-century authors like Condillac and his relentlessly sharp engagements with more contemporary philosophers like Foucault, Bataille and Levinas, without mentioning his readings of Blanchot, Genet, Artaud, Ponge (I think the book on Ponge is too little read) and so many others, are simply exemplary. Allow me a word on Derrida's readings of literary texts, which are often different from his approach to philosophically canonical authors. Derrida's readings of philosophical texts, although they often proceed through the identification and articulation of some graphic parapraxis or blind spot (a footnote, a marginal remark, an aside, an elision, a quotation mark), habitually have a systematic approach to the authorship under consideration. Derrida will read texts by Hegel Husserl or Heidegger as elements in the systematic expression of a body of thought and he will play down questions of the developmental shifts in a corpus of work, whether 'young Hegel' against 'older Hegel', or 'Heidegger before 1933' versus 'Heidegger after 1933'. If he reads philosophical authorships as a piece, although not as a unity, then his approach to literature is very often in terms of the *singularity of the literary event,* whether a couple of words by Joyce (the word 'yes', for example) or a single word in Blanchot (*pas*). The name 'literature' becomes the placeholder for the experience of a singularity that cannot be assimilated into any overarching explanatory conceptual schema, but which permanently disrupts the possible unity of such a schema.

We should also mention Derrida's constant attention to psychoanalysis in a series of stunning readings of Freud. As my colleague and distinguished Derrida translator Alan Bass said to me, Derrida had two grandfathers: Heidegger and Freud. Anecdotally, I remember sitting in a launderette at the University of Essex as an undergraduate reading 'Freud and the Scene of Writing' and watching the metapsychology spin before my eyes like the clothes in the dryer. (Incidentally, I first read Derrida in the Essex University Communist Society, where comrades obviously assumed that

Derrida was a Marxist and we tried for several weeks to work out how his work could be reconciled with the weird cocktail of Althusser and Gramsci that we were drinking at the time. Let's just say that although Derrida was not a Marxist in any conventional sense, Marx *survives* in Derrida's work in a decisive manner.)

In my view, what confusedly got named 'deconstruction', a title Derrida always viewed with suspicion, is better approached as *double reading*. That is, a reading that does two things:

1. On the one hand, a double reading gives a patient, rigorous and – although this word might sound odd, I would insist on it – *scholarly* reconstruction of a text. This means reading the text in its original language, knowing the corpus of the author as a whole and being acquainted with its original context and its dominant contexts of reception. If a deconstructive reading is to have any persuasive force, then it must possess a full complement of the tools of commentary and lay down a powerful, primary layer of reading.

2. On the other hand, the second moment of a double reading is closer to what we normally think of as an interpretation (although Derrida's operation of reading is, in his own words, '*en deçà de l'interprétation*', on this side of interpretation, in the space between commentary and interpretation), where the text is levered open through the location of what Derrida sometimes called 'blind spots' (*tâches aveugles*). Here, an authorship is brought into contradiction with what it purports to claim, its intended meaning, what Derrida liked to call the text's *vouloir-dire*. Derrida often located these blind spots in ambiguous concepts in the texts he was reading, such as 'supplément' in Rousseau, 'pharmakon' in Plato, and 'Geist' in Heidegger, where each of these terms possesses a double or multiple range of meaning, a *polysemy*, that simply cannot be contained by the text's intended meaning. Many of his double readings turn around such blind spots in order to explode from within our understanding of that author. The key thing is that the explosion has to come from within and not be imposed from without. It is a question of thinking the unthought within the thought of a specific philosophical text. Derrida often described his practice as parasitism, where the reader must both draw their sustenance from the host text and lay their critical eggs within its flesh. In the three examples of Plato, Rousseau and Heidegger, the crucial thing is that each of these conceptual blind spots is deployed by their authors in a way that simply cannot be controlled by their intentions. In an important sense, the text deconstructs itself rather than being deconstructed (I am also thinking of Paul De Man's early critique of Derrida's reading of Rousseau on this issue).

For me, Derrida's philosophical example consists in the lesson of reading: patient, meticulous, scrupulous, open, questioning, inventive reading that is able, at its best, to unsettle its readers' expectations and completely transform our understanding of the philosopher in question. Because Derrida was such a brilliant reader, he is a difficult example to follow, but in my view one must try. Queer as it may sound, this is what I see as the *pedagogical* imperative deriving from Derrida's work. Deconstruction is pedagogy. Derrida was a teacher, which is something that I think has been too little emphasised in the reception of his work. What one is trying to cultivate with students – in seminars, week in, week out – is a scrupulous practice of reading, being attentive to the text's language, arguments, transitions and movements of thought, but also alive to its hesitations, paradoxes, aporiae, quotation marks, ellipses, footnotes, inconsistencies and conceptual confusions. Thanks to Derrida, we have learnt to see that every major text in the history of philosophy possesses these auto-deconstructive features. Autodeconstruction is arguably the *conditio sine qua non* for a major text – canonicity is deconstructibility.

But there is a wider question at stake here that takes us back to Heidegger's shadow, namely: *why read?* Why should the practice of reading have this extraordinary privilege in Derrida's work? To begin to answer this question we have to understand Derrida's debt to Heidegger, in particular the later Heidegger, and more particularly still the idea of the history of being which found expression in a vast number of Heidegger's writings, but in particular in his *Nietzsche*, published in 1961 and which exerted a powerful influence over Derrida as can be seen in a wide range of early texts, from *Of Grammatology* to *Spurs.* Crudely expressed, the history of being is the claim that the history of metaphysics, from Plato to Nietzsche, is characterised by the growing forgetfulness of being. For Heidegger, the history of metaphysics is a sequence of determinations of the meaning of being, from the concept of *eidos* in Plato through to *causa sui* in medieval scholasticism, and progressing (or, rather, regressing) into modernity with Descartes' notion of the *res cogitans*. In modern philosophy, the engine that is driving the forgetfulness of being, and what Heidegger sees as the distress of the West, is the determination of being as subjectivity that culminates in what Heidegger views as Nietzsche's metaphysics. Nietzsche's word for being is will to power, which completes metaphysics in an inversion of Platonism.

So, roughly and readily, the Heideggerian claim is that between Plato and Nietzsche, between Platonism and its inversion, all of the possible determinations of the meaning of being have been exhausted. It is in this exhaustion of metaphysics, what Heidegger calls 'the completion (*die Vollendung*) of metaphysics' – and, crucially, not the 'end' of metaphysics – that the question of being can be raised anew as a compelling philosophical issue. Now, Derrida submits the Heideggerian history of being to a devastating deconstruction, in particular questioning the valorisation of being as presence, that is a constant feature of Heidegger's work, and the link between being as *logos* to *phone*, to the voice and the primacy of speech over writing and all forms of the graphic, of absence and exteriority. However, what Derrida does adopt in his work is a drastically revised version of Heidegger's historico-metaphysical schema: the history of being becomes the history of writing and metaphysics becomes logocentrism.

My point in underlining this issue is the following: if deconstruction is not, as I have claimed, reducible to some form of textual formalism, then this is because there is a historico-metaphysical specificity to deconstruction. That is, deconstructive reading is not something that takes place *sub specie aeternitatis*, it is rather the consequence of a determinate historico-conceptual situation and gives expression to a specific experience of historicity. This is why I have always tried to place the concept of the 'closure of metaphysics' (*clôture de la métaphysique*) at the core of any consideration of Derrida's work. As Derrida will tirelessly insist, the closure is not the end and he persistently places himself against any and all apocalyptic discourses on the end (whether the end of man, the end of philosophy or the end of history). In my view, allowing for the considerable philosophical differences between Heidegger and Derrida, the closure of metaphysics is a variant of the completion of metaphysics.

This is where we return to this issue of reading. At the time of metaphysics' closure, we cannot and should not hope for any new determination of the meaning of being, for this would be to fall back into metaphysical thinking. On the contrary, within the closure of metaphysics, we read, we open ourselves not to the Heideggerian experience of the thinking of being, but to an experience of reading that dismantles or de-structures the conceptual schemata that have shaped what all too complacently call 'the West' for the past few millennia. As Derrida points out in various places, the word 'deconstruction', a word whose fame he viewed as an unhappy fate rather than something to be celebrated, attempts to translate Heidegger's *Destruktion* and *Abbau*. Although the thesis of the closure of metaphysics drops out of Derrida's later work, and one can see much of his work from the late 1970s as an almost parodic distancing of his concerns from Heidegger's history of being, where the univocity of the Heideggerian sending (*envoi*) of being becomes the playful plurality of the letters, billets-doux and sendings (*envois*) of the long, first part of *La carte postale*, Derrida's work is never a-historical or anti-historicist. Through to the final stage of his work, from *Politics of Friendship* to *Rogues,* one can find a defence of the idea of *heritage*, which renders another Heideggerian theme of *Erbe*. But such an experience of heritage is never the comfort and security of a given and established tradition. Deconstruction is the practice of reading as the *discomfort* of a heritage. The philosophical assumption driving this practice is that if we are to begin to understand who, what and where we are and to begin to change who, what and where we are, then this requires meticulous attention to the heritage that constitutes who, what and where we are. Derrida's practice of reading is at the very antipodes of any alleged bibliophilia.

In the long, fascinating and now rather saddening interview with *Le Monde* from 19 August 2004, republished after his death, Derrida describes his work in terms of an 'ethos of writing'. Derrida cultivated what I would call a *habitus* or a *praxis* of uncompromising philosophical vigilance, a vigilance at war with the governing intellectual common sense and against what he liked to call – in a Socratic spirit, I think – the *doxa* or narcissistic self-image of the age. There was something deeply Socratic about Derrida's gadfly abilities to sting the great fat rump of our traditional philosophical assumptions wherever their posterior was reared into view. And there is perhaps something deeply Platonic about Derrida's predilection for forms of indirect communication, where he wrote not dialogues but what he called 'polylogues' for multiple and multiply gendered voices. Derrida was a ventriloquist.

Now, let me draw breath for a moment, as this is something that I've always wanted to say in public and publish in print. Derrida's treatment by mainstream philosophers in the English-speaking world was shameful, utterly shameful. He was vilified in the most ridiculous manner by professional philosophers who knew better but who acted out of a parochial malice that was a mere patina to their cultural insularity, intellectual complacency, philistinism and simple jealousy of Derrida's fame, charisma and extraordinary book sales, not to mention his good looks and snappy dress sense. There are exceptions to this rule and some mainstream philosophers in the UK and the US took Derrida seriously, for example Richard Rorty, whatever one may think of what he says, and I also think of Samuel Wheeler's work on deconstruction and analytic philosophy.

In my local context, in England, the incident which brought matters to a head was the initial refusal in late Spring 1992 to award Derrida an honorary doctorate at the University of Cambridge, a refusal that found support amongst prominent voices in the Philosophy Faculty, with the notable exception of Tom Baldwin and Susan James, both of whom left Cambridge in the following years. The slightly embarrassing technical problem here was that the philosophers who were offering censure against Derrida had not, of course, read him at all. They just knew it was rubbish. The logic of the situation here is a little like that described by the great Irish satirist Flann O'Brien, in one of his legal cases from the utterly fantastical Cruiskeen Court of Voluntary Jurisdiction. The topic that is being debated in the court is literary immorality or dirty books. I quote,

> After Mr Lax had made several further submissions, his Honour remarked that the punctilio of judicial processes should occasionally be cast aside to afford the bench some small clue as to the nature of the issue it was called upon to determine. 'Gentlemen' he added, 'is this book you have here any good? I mean, is it … very bad? Is it disgusting, I mean?'
> Mr Lax: it is filthy my Lord.

His Honour: Have you read it, Mr Lax?
Mar Lax: Certainly not, my Lord. I would not soil my eyes with such nefarious trash, my Lord.[1]

Flann O'Brien describes the behaviour of certain analytic philosophers with regard to Derrida perfectly. They know it is 'nefarious trash' without having read it.

To return to the Cambridge affair, after finally receiving the honorary doctorate with his usual civility, humour and good grace, a letter was sent to the University of Cambridge from Ruth Barcan Marcus, the then Professor of Philosophy at Yale, and signed by some 20 philosophers, including Quine, who complained that Derrida's work 'does not meet accepted standards of rigor and clarity' – as if we or they knew what they were when they were at home. I would like to take this opportunity to register in public my gratitude to them for the attention they gave to Derrida because it helped sell lots of copies of my first book – *The Ethics of Deconstruction* – that also came out in 1992 and paid for a terrific summer vacation.[2]

One would like to imagine that things have changed or improved since 1992, and in some ways they have, but one still finds tremendous hostility to Derrida that is in direct proportion to the learned philosophers' ignorance of his work. For example, Habermas' hostility (and I was involved in setting up a secret meeting between Derrida and Habermas in Frankfurt during June 2000) lessened when he actually started to read what Derrida wrote and realised that despite their philosophical differences they had surprising common political stances on a broad range of issues.

However to choose two counter-examples, Simon Blackburn, the present professor of philosophy at Cambridge, wrote an obituary on Derrida for the *Times Higher Education Supplement* (12 November 2004), along with a piece by myself and a couple of others. Like some headmaster in a minor private school, Simon wrote that he thought that, 'Derrida had tried hard, but failed philosophically'. Now, despite my respect for Simon, I know he hasn't read Derrida and would question his decision to pass judgement on Derrida's work. I wouldn't dare to do the same in the case of someone like Quine or Davidson. It seems to me that we are confronting a huge institutional blind spot in philosophy, or perhaps a cultural blind spot whose symptom is the name 'Derrida' and which explains some of the embarrassing cultural epiphenomena we have witnessed in the UK and the US over the years, the most recent distressing example being the awful *New York Times* obituary which ran with the headline, 'Jacques Derrida, abstruse theorist, dies at 74'. It seems to me that the entire intellectual and cultural formation of the resistance to Derrida is a phenomenon that requires careful deconstruction.

But I have been saving the best until last. Brian Leiter, professor of law and self-appointed aficionado of graduate programs in philosophy in the

English-speaking world, runs a weblog, *Leiter Reports*. In the days following Derrida's death, there was an extraordinarily ill-informed discussion on his blog about the ruckus caused by the *New York Times* obituary, at the end of which Leiter wrote,

> If he [i.e. Derrida, S.C.] had become a football player as he had apparently hoped, or taken up honest work of some other kind, then we might simply remember him as a 'good man'. But he devoted his professional life to obfuscation and increasing the amount of ignorance in the world: by 'teaching' legions of earnest individuals how to read badly and think carelessly. He may have been a morally decent man, but he led a bad life, and his legacy is one of shame for the humanities.

Such breathtaking moralistic stupidity leaves me speechless and I cannot even begin to bring myself to comment on it. But that is not all. Not only did Derrida lead a bad life and apparently single-handedly undermine the humanities (quite an achievement, all things considered), he was also the efficient cause of Reaganism and *a fortiori* of Bushism. Warming to his theme, Leiter continues, and I assure the reader that I am not making this up,

> Was it entirely accidental that at the same time that deconstruction became the rage in literary studies (namely, the 1980s), American politics went off the rails with the Great Prevaricator, Ronald Reagan? Is it simply coincidental that the total corruption of public discourse and language – which we may only hope has reached its peak at the present moment – coincided with the collapse of careful reading and the responsible use of language in one of the central humanities disciplines? These are important questions, and I wonder whether they have been, or will be addressed.[3]

These are not important questions: they are extremely silly speculations and Leiter should simply be ashamed at himself for equating the interest in deconstruction with the rise of American neo-conservatism. Once again, it might have helped if Leiter had actually taken the trouble to read Derrida's work before offering philosopher king-like judgements on its merits. And to think that a person who has the arrogance to publish such stupidities sits in judgement on the quality of graduate programs in philosophy and considers himself an authority in Continental philosophy. It is painfully laughable.

At the heart of many of the polemics against Derrida was the simply weird idea that deconstruction was a form of nihilistic textual free play that threatened to undermine rationality, morality and all that was absolutely fabulous about life in Western liberal democracy. In my view, on the contrary, what was motivating Derrida's praxis of reading and thinking was an ethical demand. My claim was that this ethical demand was something

that could be traced to the influence of the thought of Emmanuel Levinas
and his idea of ethics being based on a relation of infinite responsibility to
the other person. This is the way I read the famous phrase in the Carzodo
Law School paper, 'deconstruction is justice' where justice is adumbrated
in Levinasian terms, '*le rapport à autrui – c'est à dire la justice*' ('The relation
to the other – that is to say, justice').[4] Furthermore, crucially, if deconstruction is justice, then justice is undeconstructable, that is, there is no way of
relativising or dismantling the demand that underpins Derrida's work. At
the core of Derrida's work, functioning as an *a priori* structure that is not
reducible to a ground or foundation is an experience of justice that is felt
in the other's demand. Against the know-nothing polemics, deconstruction
is, I think, an engaged and deeply ethical praxis of reading of great social
and political relevance. Derrida's work from the 1990s shows this relevance
with extraordinary persistence in a highly original series of engagements
with Marx, with European cultural and political identity, the nature of law
and justice, democracy, sovereignty, cosmopolitanism, forgiveness, the
death penalty, so-called rogue states, the *lex amicitia* about which Peter
Goodrich writes so eloquently above and elsewhere, and finally with what
Derrida liked to call an alternative possible globalisation, an '*altermondialisation*'. To go back to my rather gnomic remark about Marx, I think it is in
connection to the possibility of an *altermondialisation* that Marx survives in
Derrida's work, something that he tries to thematise in the notion of the
New International.

Allow me a word in passing on the important theme of democracy in
Derrida, what he calls 'democracy to come', *la démocratie à venir*, and which
was the theme of one of his last publications, *Voyous (Rogues)*. Derrida
concludes *Politics of Friendship* with the following question,

> 'If one wishes to retranslate this pledge into a hypothesis or a question,
> it would, then, perhaps – by way of a temporary conclusion – take the
> following form: is it possible to think and to implement democracy,
> that which would keep the old name 'democracy', while uprooting
> from it all these figures of friendship (philosophical and religious)
> which prescribe fraternity: the family and the androcentric ethnic
> group? Is it possible, in assuming a certain faithful memory of demo-
> cratic reason and reason *tout court* – I would even say, the
> Enlightenment of a certain *Aufklärung* (thus leaving open the abyss
> which is again opening today under these words) – not to found, where
> it is no longer a matter of *founding*, but to open out to the future, or
> rather, to the 'come', of a certain democracy *(non pas de fonder, là où il
> ne s'agit sans doute plus de **fonder**, mais d'ouvrir à l'avenir, ou plutôt au
> 'viens' d'une certaine démocratie.*')[5]

Of course, these are rhetorical questions in the best French style and the
answer is '*oui*'. As Derrida admits, this is '*Juste une question, mais qui suppose*

une affirmation' ('Just a question, but one that presupposes an affirmation'). The affirmation here is that of *la démocratie à venir*, but the question is: *how* might such a notion of democracy be conceived?

La démocratie à venir is much easier to describe in negative rather than in positive terms. Derrida is particularly anxious to distinguish the idea of democracy to come from any idea of a *future* democracy, where the future would be a modality of presence, namely the not-yet-present. Democracy to come is *not* to be confused with the living present of liberal democracy, lauded as the end of history by Fukuyama, but *neither* is it a regulative idea or an idea in the Kantian sense *nor* is it even a utopia, insofar as all these conceptions understand the future as a modality of presence. It is a question of linking *la démocratie à venir* to the messianic experience of the *here and now* (*l'ici-maintentant*) without which justice would be meaningless. So, the thought here is that the experience of justice as the maintaining-now (*le maintenant*) of the relation to an absolute singularity *is* the *à venir* of democracy. The temporality of democracy is *advent*, it is futural, but it is arrival happening *now*, it happens – thinking of Benjamin – as the now blasting through the continuum of the present.

La démocratie à venir is a difficult notion to get hold of because it has an essentially contradictory structure, that is, it has both the structure of a promise, of something futural 'to come', and it is something that takes place, that happens right *now*. In other words, *La démocratie à venir* has the character of what Derrida tends to call 'the incalculable', an irreducible and undeconstructible remainder that cannot simply become the source of a deduction or the object of a determinate judgement. As such, in my view, *La démocratie à venir* has the character of an ethical demand or injunction, an incalculable experience that takes place now, but which permits the profile of a promisory task to be glimpsed.

Finally, and this is a step that Derrida continually suggests, but does not really take, it would be a question of thinking the ethical imperative of *La démocratie à venir* together with a more concrete form of democratic political action and intervention. In this sense, democracy should not be understood as a fixed political form of society, but rather as a process or, better, processes of *democratisation*. Such processes of democratisation, evidenced in numerous examples (the new social movements, Greenpeace, Amnesty International, *médécins sans frontiers*, indigenous rights groups, alternative globalisation movements, etc.), would work across, above, beneath and within the territory of the democratic state, not in the vain hope of achieving some sort of 'society without the state', but rather as providing constant pressure upon the state, a pressure of emancipatory intent aiming at its infinite amelioration, the endless betterment of actually existing democracy, or should I say what passes for democracy at the present moment.

Derrida's work is possessed of a curious restlessness; one might even say an anxiety. A very famous American philosopher, sympathetic to Derrida, once said to me, 'he never knows when to stop or how to come to an end'.

In the interview with *Le Monde*, he describes himself as being at war with himself, '*je suis en guerre contre moi-même*'. He was always on the move intellectually, always hungry for new objects of analysis, accepting new invitations, confronting new contexts, addressing new audiences, writing new books. His ability in discussion simply to listen and to synthesise new theories, hypotheses and phenomena and produce long, detailed and fascinating analyses in response was breathtaking. Like many others, I saw him do it on many occasions and always with patience, politeness, modesty and civility. Derrida had such critical and synthetic intelligence, a brilliance as Levinas was fond of remarking; '*il est brillant*' Levinas used to say. The whole ethos of his work was at the very antipodes of the inert and stale professional complacency that defines so much philosophy and so many philosophers. He found the Ciceronian wisdom that to philosophise is to learn how to die repellent for its narcissism and insisted that 'I remain uneducatable *(inéducable)* with respect to the wisdom of learning to die'.

To philosophise is not to learn how to die. With regard to death, human beings remain gloriously uneducatable, splendidly inauthentic. To philosophise, on the contrary, is to learn how to live. In the words that begin *Specters of Marx*, Derrida ventriloquises in another voice, as so often in his work, '*Je voudrais apprendre à vivre enfin*' ('I would finally like to learn to live').[6] The dead live, they live with us, they survive, which is, of course, a difficult thing to say. It is here, perhaps, that Derrida's tireless meditations on the spectral, on ghosts and what he called *survivance*, living on, can be turned, finally, towards him and his work. To pick another Ciceronian quotation, this time the epigraph to *Politics of Friendship*, '*et, quod difficilius dictu est, mortui vivunt*' ('And, what is more difficult to say, the dead live').[7] Wherever Derrida is read, he is not dead. If you want to communicate with the dead, then read a book. Here and now, in the present that holds within itself the promise of the future, the dead live. Derrida lives on.

Notes

1. Myles na Gopaleen, *The Best of Myles* (Picador, London and Sydney, 1968), pp. 141–42. I'd like to thank Joe Booker and Peter Goodrich for giving me this reference.
2. See *The Ethics of Deconstruction. Derrida and Levinas* (Blackwell, Oxford, 1992/Second Edition, Edinburgh University Press, 1999).
3. http://leiterreports.typepad.com/blob/2004/10/the_derrida_ind.html
4. Jacques Derrida, 'Force of Law: the "Mystical Foundation of Authority"', *Deconstruction and the Possibility of Justice*, eds. D. Cornell et al (Routledge, London and New York, 1992), p. 22.
5. Derrida, *Politiques de l'amitié* (Galilée, Paris, 1994), p. 339.
6. Derrida, *Spectres de Marx* (Galilée, Paris, 1993), p. 13.
7. Derrida, *Politiques de l'amitié*, p. 9.

2 Derrida's singularity
Literature and ethics

Derek Attridge

I

Faced with what seemed like the impossible task of preparing a short talk on Jacques Derrida's legacy for the Tate Modern series, "Derrida's Legacy", I found myself indulging in the kind of delaying tactic everyone is familiar with: it suddenly seemed extremely important that I should count the books by Derrida on my shelves, both French originals and the English translations which, in many cases, stand next to them. There turned out to be one hundred and twenty-two. A few of the books are made up of interviews, two or three are co-authored and some are very short, but it remains a staggering number for one man to have written – all the more staggering when you consider the range of topics and authors treated. A look at the "By the same author" pages in one of his last Paris-published books tells the same story – around 70 books in French, as well as numerous other contributions to other people's volumes. I can't think of any philosopher or literary critic writing in English today whose life's work is likely to come anywhere near this total.

The sheer quantity of Derrida's work, though it conveys something important about what he left behind, doesn't, of course, say anything about its significance or its uniqueness. But my diversionary exercise led to something else: I found myself looking at the first page of many of the French books, re-reading the words inscribed there in barely decipherable handwriting, running sometimes to several lines. For once we became acquainted in the 1980s, through our work together on a collection of his essays on literary texts he sent me, as he did a number of his friends, a copy of every book when it appeared, and usually added a short note on the half-title – always addressed not just to me but to my wife and to my two young daughters, for whom he played the role of a surrogate grandfather. This happened frequently enough for his inscriptions to be a means of conveying recent news or responding to something I had sent him.

Through the painful sense of loss that the re-reading produced, I was struck by the thought that this combination of public utterance – on a vast scale – and private communication, of the general and the singular, is indicative of an important aspect of Derrida's work, one that's particularly relevant to the field in which I teach and write: literature and literary criticism. Although he always thought of himself first of all as a philosopher, and although that's how he will no doubt always be primarily remembered, his legacy in the field of literary studies is, and will continue to be, a substantial one. And one rather crude way of summing up the importance of literature to him is to say that while philosophy has its eye always on the general, the literary work is inescapably singular.

So while he examined the tradition of Western philosophy for the traces of the various singularities it has never been able to overcome in its reaching for universality, he approached literary works as singular stagings of many of the issues that philosophy has perennially grappled with. And not only philosophy, for these issues are of immediate concern to any thought about how we live our lives – issues of language and signification, translation, hospitality, friendship, ethics and responsibility, lying and telling the truth, giving and forgiving, faith, sacrifice, death and many more. At a time when literary study in some parts of the academy seems be dissolving in a tepid bath of cultural commentary, and when our paymasters are more and more wedded to the enumerable and the assessable, Derrida reminds us of the challenge of the inventive literary work: the pleasurable demands it makes on us to see things differently and to think along new paths.

This is not a call to return to an old valuation of the literary masterpiece – though there remains much of interest in those old valuations – but an argument about singularity itself, which, for Derrida, is inseparable from what he called "iterability". Whatever has meaning – from the simplest sign to the most complex literary text – has to be repeatable, but, as Derrida showed us, should also be opened to change in new contexts – and to infinite change, since the possibility of new contexts is an infinite one. A word, a poem, a novel, if it was not open in this way, would simply die, permanently closed in upon itself. For the reader or critic to do justice to the literary work, therefore, he or she has to do justice to that singularity not by attempting to fix it for all time but by producing an answering singularity – what Derrida called the counter-signature to the work's signature, verifying and affirming it. His readings – themselves open to ever-new contexts, of course – often move in unexpected directions, but always strive to register and respect the singular inventiveness of the work.

Let me mention one example – although "example" is the wrong word, for Derrida's engagements with literary works are so varied that one cannot stand for all the others. (This, as it happens, is one of the issues addressed in the piece I've chosen.) Kafka's fable "Vor dem Gesetz" ("Before the Law"), which is not much more than a page long, tells of a "man from the country" who comes to a doorkeeper standing "before the Law". The man stays there for many years, all the while trying to gain admittance through the open gate. Just before he dies, still outside the gate, he asks the doorkeeper why, in all this time, no one else has begged for access to the

Law, and is told, "No one else could ever be admitted here, since this gate was made only for you". On this, he shuts the gate and the story ends.

Derrida's discussion of this story, in an essay which takes its name from the story itself, is a richly detailed exploration both of textual minutiae – down to the pointed nose of the doorkeeper – and of the large questions that are posed within it.[1] One of these questions is that of the relation of literature to the law: both the determination of literature by the law (the legal status of the title, the institution of copyright and so on) and the not-so-obvious dependence of the law on literature (the narratives that under-lie the law's apparent autonomy and timelessness). Kafka gives us a literary work that is recognised as such because of the laws that govern literature, but which challenges, both in its singularity and in its narrative staging of singularity, those very laws. The law is open to all and yet at the same time inaccessible (what would it mean to be in the presence of the law itself, as distinct from its various doorkeepers?); the law is both wholly general – or it would not be law – and yet meaningful only in so far as it applies to (or refuses access to) singular individuals.

Derrida's essay explores these and other related issues, always returning to Kafka's words to puzzle out what they might mean. Like any good liter-ary critic, his aim is always to do justice to what is unique and surprising in the work. And like any good literary critic, the work he produces is itself unique and surprising: a singular response to a singular text. He has not told us the truth about Kafka's story, since truth is always dependent on the context in which it is framed, but he has conveyed its meaningfulness for him in a particular time and place. The readers of Derrida's essay are implicitly invited in their turn to do justice to the singularity of this extraor-dinary piece of literary and philosophical commentary. We can never artic-ulate its laws, or the laws of literature, in wholly general terms, but each of us can, like the man from the country, find ways of creatively inhabiting the space outside the particular gate that it presents.

Derrida's legacy in the literary field does not, therefore, take the form of the model or paradigm. His essays on literary works cannot be imitated, for the reasons just given: they are unique responses that call not for replication but for an answering inventiveness. An imitation would therefore not really be an imitation at all, as it would lack the inventiveness of the original it was claiming to imitate. He has left us, as I have stressed, a huge amount of writ-ings to explore and respond to (and the work published during his lifetime is only part of his legacy, as will become evident when the archive of his semi-nars is made public). But perhaps even more important is the spirit in which he engaged with texts and ideas, in the face of widespread misunderstand-ing and denigration. The generosity which he showed in inscribing his books to my family and me is not separable, I believe, from the generosity of his thought (a quality which is entirely compatible with scrupulousness and rigour) when he read Plato, Shakespeare or Joyce. My hope is that we will be capable of the same generosity in continuing to read him.

II

Pick up a recent encyclopaedia or companion devoted to ethics and, if it was published in the UK or USA the chances are that you won't find Derrida in the index. Yet this is a philosophical field, and an area of daily life, in which his legacy – along with that of his friend Emmanuel Levinas, also likely to be omitted from such a volume – is potentially as important as it is in the domain of literary study. The two are closely connected, in fact: the concern with singularity I have been stressing in Derrida's approach to literature is also at the heart of his ethical philosophy.

It was the cats that really got me hooked on Derrida's account of ethical obligation. They sprang out of the following sentence from *The Gift of Death*: "How would you ever justify the fact that you sacrifice all the cats in the world to the cat that you feed at home day after day for years, while other cats die of hunger at every instant?"[2] I recall vividly the first time they got their claws into me: it was in the attic lounge of the chateau of Cerisy-la-Salle in 1992, a day or two after Jean-Michel Rabaté had arrived with a trunkful of copies of *L'Éthique du don*, in which Derrida's lengthy essay was first published, hot from the Paris presses. I was playing truant from that morning's sessions of the ten-day conference on Derrida's work in order to read the essay, and I was most unjustly being rewarded for my lack of commitment by the gift of some of his most startling articulations.

Derrida introduces the cats as part of his radical quotidianisation, if I may call it that, of the story of Abraham and Isaac. This short Biblical narrative – 19 verses of Genesis chapter 22 – has, of course, been subject to numerous and varied commentaries and retellings. For the faithful, it often exemplifies the virtue of human submission to the will of the deity, no matter how absurd or monstrous the form in which the latter appears;[3] for the sceptical, it may signify instead the unpalatable authoritarianism of the major monotheisms.

But for Derrida, as for Kierkegaard, the story of Abraham's willingness to kill his son in response to a divine command cannot be reduced to either of these postures; for them it exemplifies a terrifying paradox, the paradox entailed in *responsibility to the other*. Derrida follows, with great fidelity, Kierkegaard's rendition of the story in *Fear and Trembling*[4] (which Kierkegaard presents as Johannes de Silentio's rendition), drawing out clearly the proto-deconstructive force of Kierkegaard/Silentio's analysis. The other is absolute (its name in the story is God), and one's responsibility to the other is absolute. The realm of ethics, however, the realm of general laws of conduct and relationship (such as the law which forbids murder and which enjoins on the father the protection of his children) is, it seems, only relative and can be overridden by the obligation to the other, an obligation which always takes the form of the singular – here the singular command of Jehovah, "Take now thy son, thine only son Isaac, whom thou lovest, and get thee into the land of Moriah; and offer him there for a burnt offering upon one of the mountains which I will tell thee of" (Genesis 22.ii, Authorized Version). A command is addressed to a single individual, enjoining a single act upon another single individual at a single time and place.

For Kierkegaard, Abraham is the prime exemplar of the knight of faith, who, having achieved "infinite resignation", does not rest there, who takes the extraordinary step of believing in what he calls "the absurd"; believing, that is, that in spite of all appearances, in spite of all rational calculations, performing the terrible deed will be for the good, because "for God all things are possible" (46). And of course Abraham turns out to be right. "And the angel of the Lord called unto him out of heaven, and said, Abraham, Abraham: and he said, Here am I. And he said, Lay not thine hand upon the lad, neither do thou anything unto him" (Genesis 22.xi–xii). Abraham's faith is proved, God's blessing is ensured and the future – for this is, of course, a story about the future – is saved.

Kierkegaard's didactic use of the story to clarify his distinction between the knight of resignation and the knight of faith doesn't prevent him from retelling the story several times to heighten its drama and its horror, nor from asserting the continuing difficulty of coming to terms with it:

> Thinking about Abraham...I am shattered. I am constantly aware of the prodigious paradox that is the content of Abraham's life, I am constantly repelled, and, despite all its passion, my thought cannot penetrate it, cannot get ahead by a hairsbreadth. I stretch every muscle to get a perspective, and at the very same instant I become paralyzed. (33)

And later: "Abraham I cannot understand; in a certain sense I can learn nothing from him except to be amazed" (48).

Like Kierkegaard, Derrida is horrified by the story of Abraham and Isaac.

> The story is no doubt monstrous, outrageous, barely conceivable: a father is ready to put to death his beloved son, his irreplaceable loved one, and that because the Other, the great Other asks him or orders him without giving the slightest explanation. An infanticide father who hides what he is going to do from his son and from his family without knowing why: what crime could be more abominable, what mystery could be more appalling (*tremendum*) from the perspective of love, humanity, the family, morality? (67/67–68)

But it is at this point that Derrida makes his swerve from Kierkegaard, and the cats start their stealthy advance. He goes on:

> But isn't this also the most common thing? What the most cursory examination of the concept of responsibility cannot fail to affirm? ... As soon as I enter into a relation with the other, with the look, request,

love, command, or call of the other, I know that I can respond only by sacrificing ethics, that is, by sacrificing that which obliges me also to respond, in the same way, in the same instant, to all the others. ... Day and night, at every instant, on all the Mount Moriahs of this world, I am ... raising my knife over what I love and must love, over those to whom I owe absolute fidelity, incommensurably. (68/68–69)

The difference between Kierkegaard and Derrida here is crucial. For both, Abraham's intended action involves renouncing ethics – Kierkegaard calls it a "teleological suspension of the ethical" – in the name of absolute responsibility to the absolute and singular other. But whereas for Kierkegaard the absolute other speaks only in God's voice, for Derrida it speaks also, although differently, in Isaac's voice.[5] The paradox is thus much tauter than it is for Kierkegaard: Abraham, *whether or not he obeys God's command*, will fail in his binding responsibility to the other. To spare Isaac is to defy God; to kill him is to murder the other, the other other, who is no less divine. It is no longer just a question of overriding the ethical, as some bloodless general code, in the name of singularity and alterity, for Derrida has complicated the distinction between those two orders. Ethics, Derrida states in the paragraph I have just quoted, is "that which obliges me also to respond, in the same way, in the same instant, to all the others", and earlier in the same paragraph he had talked of the "infinite number" of these others, constituting a "general and universal responsibility (what Kierkegaard calls the ethical order)" (68/68). But if ethics is the simultaneous responsibility towards every other, *as singular other*, and if, as Derrida insists, "*tout autre est tout autre*," "every other is wholly other", ethical behaviour is, from the very first moment, from before the very first moment, utterly impossible – it is easier to do the bidding of a singular divinity, however outrageous, than attempt to live by the general norms of ethics.

Now anyone who has read Derrida knows well enough that to term a certain practice "impossible" is not, for him, the same as saying that it can never happen. Some of the most valuable practices we engage in are, he suggests, impossible, such as giving, forgiving, judging or bearing witness. These things happen all the time, in spite of or rather because of the fact that they are impossible. They happen, that is to say, not because someone knows in advance how to truly give, wholly forgive, responsibly judge or fully bear witness – to possess in advance a formula for any of these things is precisely to *prevent* it from happening – but because the realm of possibility (the realm, let us say, of thought, of knowledge, of philosophy, of cause and effect, of presence, of chronology, of calculation) depends on that which it excludes, the impossible. It is because possibility doesn't totally govern the scene that giving, forgiving, judging and witnessing happen (however fleetingly, precariously and imperceptibly).[6]

But the question that has to be asked is whether the impossibility of ethical behaviour, as I have just represented it, is of the same order as these other impossibilities. If ethics enjoins on me equal responsibility to and for every person in the world, living, dead and unborn, and does this at every instant, it is hard to see how *any* act could be called, even fleetingly or imperceptibly, "ethical".[7] But Derrida doesn't leave it there. To make it still harder , he brings in the cats. Here again is the sentence in which they make their appearance: "How would you ever justify the fact that you sacrifice all the cats in the world to the cat that you feed at home day after day for years, while other cats die of hunger at every instant?" (70–71/71). I don't have a cat, but every time I read this sentence I feel momentarily appalled by the pitiful meowing of all those cats out there those, every instant of every day, *I am not feeding.* We are a long way from the terrible encounter with the almighty on Mount Moriah, and Derrida might seem to risk accusations of trivialising the Biblical narrative in translating it into this common domestic scene. But there is no escape from the implacable logic of his analysis. If there is a general law of ethics, how can its generality suffer limitation through a *more* general ethical law that allows it to apply only to humans? By what pre-emptive and violent stroke can the animal world be excluded? Or the plant world? Or the possible inhabitants of other planets? "An *infinite* number", says Derrida, "The *innumerable* generality", and he clearly means it. He even mentions places and languages; in being here, I am not in all the other places I might be in; in favouring English, I am discriminating against all the other languages I might use. Nor are the non-human others less important to the argument than the humans. If anything, they are *more* important; they are, as Derrida says, "even more other others than my fellows" (69/69).

The impossibility of the ethical act appears to offer, then, not the tiniest toehold for possibility to get a grip. The most universally benevolent deed I could ever perform would still be as nothing compared with the goal of complete ethical generality. As if this were not enough, Derrida tightens the noose even further. Although I can never begin to satisfy the demands of ethics, although my every action, indeed my very existence, breathing the air I breathe and occupying the space I occupy, is falling short of the ethical, *there is no way I can justify my failure.* Here again, the cats enforce the point. My preference for the cat I call my "own" over all the other cats in the universe is as inaccessible to the language of explanation and justification as Abraham's preference for God over Isaac (and over his own ethical obligations and paternal feelings). Once I begin to speak, I enter the discursive realm in which only the ethical as a systematic code can be articulated and heard – the realm of law, of calculation, of generality. To comment on the story of Abraham and Isaac at all is to find Abraham guilty of a terrible crime. Only in silence, in secrecy, can one understand – no, that's not the right word, as Kierkegaard knew – take account of, countersign, affirm Abraham's appalling decision.[8] We cannot learn from it, says Johannes whose last name is Silentio.

My responsibility to the singular other, then, the centrepiece of the Levinasian thought that Derrida has absorbed and refashioned in many works, runs counter to ethics as a general system and cannot be justified. Moreover, it runs counter to my responsibility to other singular others. "Je ne peux répondre à l'un (ou à l'Un), c'est-à-dire à l'autre qu'en lui sacrifiant l'autre" (70), writes Derrida. I'll attempt my own paraphrase: "I can respond to the one (or to the One), that is, to the other, only by sacrificing the other—the other other—to it".[9] This is a much more hard-nosed approach to the problem of multiple others than Levinas' invocation of "le tiers", made much of by Simon Critchley in his book on Levinas and Derrida.[10] It brings us back to the question of the impossibility of ethical behaviour. I asked earlier if this was the same order of impossibility as that which we associate, in Derrida's work, with the gift, forgiveness, justice, witness (and, we might add – bearing in mind that these issues are raised by a *story* – literature). We know that justice – justice to the absolute singularity of the other, the person, the case, the text – is impossible, and that it happens. Abraham does justice to the absolute singularity of Jehovah, of the command, the call. We can't say how he does it, he can't say how he does it, but he does it, and without hesitation. But he also decides, and it is the same decision, to do the worst possible *injustice* to his son. And if the act of doing justice is always also the act of doing an injustice, ethical acts – acts which involve no injustice – cannot happen. It might seem then that the impossibility of being ethical belongs to a different order of impossibility from that of doing justice, giving, forgiving, writing or reading the literary, which do, after all, happen.

But what are we left with? Some kind of impulsive subjectivism or decisionism? Pick your favourite other, act responsibly to him, her or it, and let the rest go hang? Feed your own cat, *cultiver votre jardin*, and forget about the state of the world? And don't even bother to justify or even discuss your choice? This would be a terrible misreading of the story of Abraham and Isaac, of Kierkegaard, of Derrida. The ethical, the responsibility towards the generality, and therefore the political (as the construction and implementation of programmes to further the common welfare) remain an absolute and unavoidable demand. We need look no further than the word "sacrifice". You can sacrifice only what you value. Abraham's decision is an act of responsibility towards God *only because Isaac is his beloved son*, born miraculously to him in his old age, the promised beginning of the chosen generations, the embodiment of the future.[11] There is a fierce logic to God's command: of all the things Abraham could be asked to do, sacrificing Isaac, sacrificing ethics, sacrificing the future, is the most difficult; and of all the people who might have been asked to do it, Abraham is the person for whom it is most difficult. In that difficulty, in the horror that Kierkegaard depicts so powerfully, is the acknowledgement that ethics, as responsibility to the multiplicity of others, matters. Without the strongest possible commitment to ethical and political norms, acts of singular justice, of incommunicable responsibility to this or that unique other, cannot happen; there is nothing to sacrifice, no decision beyond the calculable to be made. The slightly ludic, or even ludicrous, nature of Derrida's image of a world teeming with famished cats should not mislead us; it is by no means a *reductio ad absurdum*. I believe that Derrida wants us to confront the situation in all seriousness. Starving cats are not a joke.

Taking the full measure of Derrida's sentence means acknowledging that there is no comfortable position vis-à-vis ethics, politics, responsibility, justice, no avoiding of the issue, no waiting till the storm blows over. It is not a question of weighing one duty against another, which would be to remain within the realm of calculable ethics, but of acting in the knowledge of the aporia implicit in every deed, "the sacrifice of the most imperative duty (that which binds me to the other as a singularity in general) in favour of another absolutely imperative duty binding me to the wholly other [*au tout autre*[12]]" (71/71). Both duties are binding, and they cannot be judged against one another. And the cats are there to impress upon us that this aporetic space is not some rare and distant realm but right here where we live our daily lives.

To those who would resist this account, who would insist that there is no need for any sacrifice of individuals or of ethics in general, that the observance of moral norms is all that is necessary for responsible behaviour, Derrida has another answer. "Civilized society", which would condemn any man who behaved as Abraham did on Mount Moriah (Derrida imagines a father taking his son up to the heights of Montmartre to kill him), and whose claim to civilisation rests on those moral norms, functions smoothly *only because* it sacrifices tens of millions of children (not to mention adults, animals and others) (82/85). This sacrifice is not performed out of responsibility nor is it carried out in agony. (So it is not, properly speaking, if we can speak properly of these things, a sacrifice.) And, on TV screens, in newspapers, in public appearances, it receives endless justification.

So far, we have considered the situation of Abraham as he stretches out his arm. In deciding to kill Isaac, he has answered the call of the absolute other, and betrayed every human obligation, including his obligation to the future. Now observe: in the feline version of the story, not only do I *decide* to feed my cat, but I *do* feed it, and the other cats starve. This is what happens in the world, where no angelic voice stays my feeding hand and offers me an alternative which will save both my cat and all the others. The Bible story, designed to reassure us of the goodness and wisdom of the divine plan, gives us a happy ending, but it is false to everyday experience, an "ideological" resolution, perhaps, of a real and inescapable contradiction. On our daily Mount Moriahs, God is silent.

This would seem to be the logic of Derrida's position, departing from Kierkegaard's argument that faith in the absurd, in God's capacity to achieve the impossible, is what resolves everything – though in doing so he cleaves all the more strongly to the real force of Kierkegaard's text, which lies in its depiction of the unassimilable horror of the story. Actually, in this text, Derrida doesn't overtly draw this conclusion; his major interest in the chapter, following on from his discussion of Jan Patočka's linking of the secret and responsibility, is in Abraham's necessary secrecy. But it is implicit in everything he says: we carry out our daily, unjustifiable sacrifices without any hope that the victims will be spared. Not altogether without hope, though; since acting out of responsibility to, and in affirming, the other is always acting out of responsibility towards, and affirming, the future. It is acting in the spirit of what Derrida elsewhere calls a certain "desert-like messianism (without content and without identifiable messiah)".[13] Abraham's decision to kill Isaac evinces immense trust in the future, a trust which goes contrary to all predictability – for what is predictable is the instantaneous cancellation of the promised future of blessed generations.

We are not yet at the end of the difficulties that beset any attempt at responsible behaviour, however. Answering the call of the singular other in such a way that other others are necessarily sacrificed is not justifiable, not ethically acceptable, not even comprehensible; it can be admired, however, it does bear witness to human worth, it does affirm the future. But what if the call is false or misheard? What if I am hearing a reflection of my own voice? (There is a midrash on Genesis 22 which suggests that this is what happened.) Or the voice of a death-dealing machine? What if Abraham is deluded? This is how Kant reads the story, and the point is made again by Lyotard in *The Differend*:

> Abraham hears: *That Isaac die, that is my law,* and he obeys. The Lord speaks at this moment only to Abraham, and Abraham is answerable only to the Lord. Since the reality, if not of the Lord, then at least of the phrase imputed to Him, cannot be established, how can it be known that Abraham isn't a paranoiac subject to homicidal (infanticidal) urges?[14]

How can God's command to Abraham be distinguished from Nazi commands to kill Jews? A sceptic might say that Abraham's duty was to attend to the demand of a mysterious voice from the sky *last of all*. Perhaps the only way to read the story as a sceptic is to treat it as a fantasy: let us imagine that there was such a thing as an all-powerful God, and that he ordered a man to kill his son – in this case, the genuineness of the call would simply be given of the story. But we cannot escape in this way when we translate the problem to our daily wrestle with responsibility. Given that we cannot make ourselves answerable to every other in the world, how do we choose? Of all the demands made on us by others, which are genuine and which are spurious? (One of those who took this question very seriously was Shakespeare: remember Hamlet's agonising uncertainty about the ghost who summons him to kill a relative.) Clearly there is no answer to that question in the form of rules or calculus; the aporia we face is precisely the

absence of rules. As Lyotard argues, obligation is necessarily and structurally incomprehensible.

John D. Caputo reflects on this dilemma in *Against Ethics*,[15] taking his cue
from Levinas, Blanchot and Lyotard, as well as from Derrida. Reduced to
two words, his response to the problem is "obligation happens". It cannot,
finally, be explained, grounded, justified; but it happens all the time. And
it is always singular: this person, this case, this demand obliges me, here
and now. My cat, and not the millions of other cats in the world. To observe
only this, however, is to risk leaving obligation in the realm of the capri-
cious or the arbitrary, and Caputo has much more to say about it, none of
which I shall attempt to summarise. (It is not primarily a book of arguments.) What is worth stressing, however, is what he draws from Levinas'
emphasis on the other as *destitute* – "the widow, the stranger, the orphan" –
and from Lyotard's discussion of *les juifs*, with a small "j", all the non-
peoples rendered other by Western thought and Western history.[16]
Obligation happens to me most authentically when I am confronted not by
the all-powerful, as Abraham was, but by the powerless.

Responsibility to the other is not just a question of the obligation or
demand that I feel most intensely because it addresses me with the greatest
imperiousness. If this were the case, the existing system of power relations
would determine the exercise of responsibility, and would thereby reproduce itself endlessly. The subordination of female to male, of black to
white, of poor to rich would continue unabated. The future would come
not as the other, but as the same. Responsibility has an *active* dimension; it
is not merely a passive response. I am obligated to *seek out* the other, to *learn*
to hear its voice and see its face. Derrida has always stressed that, while one
cannot make the other come, one can prepare for its coming. (One name
for this activity of preparation is "deconstruction".[17]) When my cat comes
meowing to me in the morning, there is nothing automatic about my
responsibility to feed it; perhaps I have found out that the cat next door is
hungry and sick, obliging me to sacrifice my own cat. That is to say, the
generalised responsibility of ethics that Derrida talks of can become, at any
moment, particularised and imperative – and to act responsibly (though
this is now not clearly distinguishable from acting ethically) is to do the
work necessary to produce such particularisations. The last thing the
Biblical story and its various readings do is to applaud spontaneity:
Abraham has pondered for three days on the deed, and has behind him a
long lifetime of thought and labour. It requires work to acquire knowledge
of the needs that surround one, and of ways in which one might address
them effectively. In a patriarchal society, such as Abraham's or ours, there
is an obligation to labour to hear the voices of women, to attend to Sarah,
who has been excluded, who will be sacrificed on the same altar as Isaac
without achieving any of the glory of her husband. Every other systematic
exclusion and oppression requires similar work. And so the impossibility of
ethics does not, cannot, inhibit action: it is not, finally, different in kind

from the impossibility of doing justice, giving, forgiving, writing or reading the literary. No justice, however, without the work of the law; no responsibility to the infinite other without the labour of ethics and politics – even though law, ethics and politics go into the abyss with every act of justice and singular responsibility.

Notes

1. "Before the Law", in *Acts of Literature*, ed. Derek Attridge (New York: Routledge, 1992), 181–220.
2. "Donner la mort" first appeared as a long essay in *L'Éthique du don: Jacques Derrida et la pensée du don*, edited by Jean-Michel Rabaté and Michael Wenzel (Paris: Métailié-Transition, 1992), 11–108; this sentence occurs on pages 70–71. In English it was published as a book, *The Gift of Death*, trans. David Wills (Chicago: The University of Chicago Press, 1995); this sentence occurs on page 71. Further references will be given in the text, first to the original, then to the translation. I have occasionally made slight alterations to Wills's excellent translation in the belief that alternative translations do greater justice to the untranslatable complexity of the original. A revised translation is promised for 2008. (Subsequently, the essay appeared as the larger part of a book also entitled *Donner la mort* [Paris: Galilée, 1999].)
3. In the Qur'an, the centrality of the idea of submission is such that Isaac is *told* what is about to happen, and accepts it.
4. Søren Kierkegaard, *Fear and Trembling; Repetition*, trans. Howard V. Hong and Edna H. Hong (Princeton: Princeton University Press, 1983).
5. Here we become aware that Derrida's is to some extent a Levinasian reading of Genesis and of Kierkegaard: it is precisely in encountering the face of the other that I encounter God. Derrida's reading is, in a way, more Levinasian than Levinas' own. In *Proper Names*, Levinas proposes that the most telling moment in the drama is the *second* command, the order to spare Isaac; Abraham's ability to hear this command, which returns him to the ethical order vis-à-vis Isaac, is the essential ethical point (Stanford: Stanford University Press, 1996, 74, 77). See also Derrida's note 8 on p. 108/note 6 on p. 78, and his discussion of the problematic distinction between the ethical and the religious in Kierkegaard and Levinas (80–81/83–84). Of course, for Levinas the term "ethics" generally has a rather different significance from what it has for Kierkegaard, Heidegger, and Derrida (at least until his later writing on Levinas). Derrida's discomfort with the term and the systematic philosophy it evokes (a discomfort which partially echoes Heidegger's in the "Letter on Humanism") is concisely stated in *Altérités* (Jacques Derrida and Pierre-Jean Labarrière, *Altérités* [Paris: Editions Osiris, 1986], 70–72). In *Adieu: To Emmanuel Levinas* (Stanford: Stanford University Press, 1999), however, Derrida endorses Levinas' understanding of ethics more fully, though not without a certain rewriting ("Levinas does not say it in exactly this way" [32]) whereby thirdness, and thus the juridico-political, becomes an integral feature of the ethical response to the Other. If it were not for this mediation the ethics of the face-to-face would threaten violence – but at the same time, in an inescapable double-bind, the juridico-political itself violates the purity of the ethical relation. We are back with the cats.
6. One characteristic formulation of Derrida's is the following from *The Other Heading: Reflections on Today's Europe*. "The condition of possibility of this thing called responsibility is a certain *experience and experiment of the possibility of the impossible: the testing of the aporia* from which one may invent the only *possible invention,*

the impossible invention" (Bloomington: Indiana University Press, 1992, 41). I deal with this topic in an essay entitled "The Art of the Impossible?", in *The Politics of Deconstruction: Jacques Derrida and the Other of Philosophy*, ed. Martin McQuillan (London: Pluto Press, 2007), 54–65.

7. There is an intriguing moment in an interview when Levinas appears to come close to Derrida's position; explaining that the sixth commandment is not limited to literal acts of murder, he says "For example, when we sit down at the table in the morning and drink coffee, we kill an Ethiopian who doesn't have any coffee" (*The Provocation of Levinas*, ed. Robert Bernasconi and David Wood [London: Routledge, 1988], 173). This idea is not, as far as I am aware, developed anywhere in his work.

8. Derrida further develops the implications of Abraham's secrecy, and relates it to the (non)category of "literature", in "La littérature au secret: Une filiation impossible", published together with *Donner la mort* in the book of that name (see note 1). A translation by David Wills is forthcoming in the new edition of *The Gift of Death*.

9. Wills shifts the emphasis in his translation: "I can respond only to the one (or to the One), that is, to the other, by sacrificing that one to the other" (70).

10. Simon Critchley, *The Ethics of Deconstruction: Derrida and Levinas* (Oxford: Blackwell, 1992), 225–37. In his more recent work, Critchley has somewhat revised his view that Levinasian ethics provides a grounding for politics absent from Derrida's deconstruction; see *Ethics—Politics—Subjectivity* (London: Verso, 1999). Levinas does not extend the ethical beyond the dual relationship: "Because there are more than two people in the world, we invariably pass from the ethical perspective of alterity to the ontological perspective of totality" ("Ethics of the Infinite", in Richard Kearney, *States of Mind: Dialogues with Contemporary Thinkers* [New York: New York University Press, 1995], 187). Derrida's reworking of Levinas may be seen as an attempt to keep alive the thinking of alterity in the larger sphere.

11. Kierkegaard writes: "Since God claims Isaac, he must, if possible, love him even more, and only then can he *sacrifice* him, for it is indeed this love for Isaac that makes his act a sacrifice by its paradoxical contrast to his love for God" (*Fear and Trembling*, 74). This passage is cited by Derrida, who also stresses that "in order for there to be a sacrifice, the ethical must retain all its value" (66/66).

12. Wills's misreading of this phrase as *à tout autre*, "to every other" (71), which blurs the contrast, is corrected in the new edition, as is his slip in translating *du tout autre* as "for every other" instead of "for the wholly other" (77/79), with the same effect.

13. Jacques Derrida, *Specters of Marx: The State of the Debt, the Work of Mourning, and the New International*, trans. Peggy Kamuf (New York: Routledge, 1994), 28.

14. Jean-François Lyotard, *The Differend: Phrases in Dispute*, trans. Georges Van Den Abbeele (Minneapolis: University of Minnesota Press, 1988), 107. Kant poses a similar question in *The Conflict of the Faculties* (New York: Abaris Books, 1979), 115, *Religion within the Limits of Reason Alone* (New York: Harper & Row, 1960), 175.

15. John D. Caputo, *Against Ethics: Contributions to a Poetics of Obligation with Constant Reference to Deconstruction* (Bloomington: Indiana University Press, 1993).

16. Emmanuel Levinas, *Totality and Infinity: An Essay on Exteriority*, trans. Alphonso Lingis (Pittsburgh: Duquesne University Press, 1969) and Jean-François Lyotard, *Heidegger and "the jews,"* trans. Andreas Michel and Mark Roberts (Minneapolis: University of Minnesota Press, 1990). As Jill Robbins points out, the destitution to which Levinas refers is primarily that of the face, irrespective of the condition of the human individual it belongs to: "The face's destitution is an essential destitution" ("Visage, Figure: Speech and Murder in Levinas's

Totality and Infinity", in Cathy Caruth and Deborah Esch, eds., *Critical Encounters: Reference and Responsibility in Deconstructive Writing* [New Brunswick: Rutgers University Press, 1995], 283). To lay stress on literal destitution, therefore, is to move away from Levinas' more absolute formulations and to stress the contingencies of ethical life, which is what Caputo does.

17. See, for instance, "Psyche: Invention of the Other", in *Acts of Literature*, ed. Derek Attridge (New York: Routledge, 1992), 340–43. Levinas also emphasises the unremitting exertion required by ethics: "I have described ethical responsibility as *insomnia* or *wakefulness* precisely because it is a perpetual duty of vigilance and effort which can never slumber" ("Ethics of the Infinite", 195).

3 In the event

Geoffrey Bennington

I

One way of talking about 'Derrida's event'[1] is to try to understand the event *of* Derrida, the philosophical or perhaps more broadly 'cultural' event that he was. It seems to be no accident that we might be inclined to do this upon the fact or event of Derrida's death, on the basis of his now (and henceforth) 'being' dead, to understand the philosophical or cultural event that he was, in the past, or perhaps more properly that he *will have been,* in a projected future past, a future perfect that is also a perfect future in which things will finally have been what they always were to be. That's certainly one kind of approach one might be inclined to make, and it seems to be invited by the event of Derrida's death: now that Derrida is dead, the thought would go, the time has come to have an at least preliminary stab at *putting him in his place,* assigning him his rightful position and importance in the philosophico-cultural history of, say, Modern French Thought, or maybe Modern European Thought, or even just Modern Thought, or Western Thought, or (why not?) just Thought.

This kind of assessment, which seems to be essentially related to the fact (if not quite the event) of Derrida's death, appears to be fundamentally necrological, and wants, *post-mortem,* to get things straight, ordered and hierarchised, to deal with the estate and the legacy. It's no accident that its most appropriate tense should be the future perfect, the tense of what will have been, what will have turned out to be in some projection or fantasy of a Last Judgement, and one of the favourite adverbs of this type of assessment is indeed 'ultimately'. 'Ultimately, then, Derrida ...'.[2] Nothing was more common in the notices and obituaries immediately provoked by the event (or at least the news) of Derrida's death, even when (perhaps especially when) those pieces had been (or may as well have been) prepared long in advance (it was at least 5 years earlier that the London *Times* had approached me to write such an anticipatory obituary of Derrida; I never replied, I'm afraid).

Let's say that that's one way of approaching Derrida's event. Derrida *will have been* such and such a figure, and the event that he was or will have been is, as it were, rounded off or completed by his death. Thinkers, like other cultural figures, die, and their death provokes a flurry of activity seeking to order, assess, classify and thereby, I'd be tempted to say, to forget and to neutralise. One thing that seems certain to survive the death is just this kind of talk, a sort of discursive machinery that assumes certain ways of processing events and writing them down, writing them up and writing them off into the great, ongoing and ultimately ultimate History of Everything.

II

We might imagine in this vein that sooner or later some form of 'biography' of Derrida might get written, but it would seem difficult in this case to imagine a biography that managed to take into account what the subject of that biography thought and wrote. What would a biography of Jacques Derrida have to look like to be a Derridean biography? I have tried to argue elsewhere that biography is itself a fundamentally philosophical concept, so that a biography of a philosopher is in some senses the most biographical biography imaginable.[3] It is easy to show, on the basis, say, of Plato's *Phaedo*, that the character we call 'the philosopher' is in part defined by leading a life that will have been philosophical enough to warrant a biography, and that life is philosophical enough insofar as it is oriented towards death, a preparation for or pedagogy of death.

This essential relationship between philosophy and death, or the philosophical life and death, is also what calls for biography, rather than autobiography. Autobiography ('the least inadequate name for what I do', as Derrida says somewhere) is a tricky way for a philosopher to deal with death: writing my autobiography, the story of my life, I pretend to be gathering my life up into a totality, rounding it off in preparation for death, but by the very fact of writing the autobiography I am adding a new event to my life (to parody Lyotard in *Le différend*, the synthesis of all the syntheses that make up my life is a further synthesis in my life), a new event which may be the most important event of my life, which by definition the autobiography can never catch up with – by becoming the narrator of my own life, I am enacting a fantasy of immortality, insofar as, structurally speaking, narrators cannot die. But biography, at least in its classical forms, waits for the death of its subject before telling his (usually his) life and gathering it up into a meaningful whole. *Tel qu'en lui-même enfin l'éternité le change.* Biography fulfils the philosophical programme of the philosopher by being predicated on his death: the biography of the philosopher, his written life, is written *from* his death, writing his life out in the future perfect tense that it *will have been*. But only this death confirms that the philosopher really was a philosopher in the philosophical sense of that term: the death of the philosopher allows for his life in the sense of the written account that will consecrate him as a philosopher and thereby consecrate philosophy as philosophy. Real life is always elsewhere, and the philosopher's real life comes after his death. Diogenes Laertius gives us some precious indications about this in the Introduction to his book: the distinction between a sage and a philosopher, due, according to Diogenes, to Pythagoras, is that the latter merely *seeks to attain* wisdom during his life (whereas the sage claims to have achieved it). The written life can then be the account of that search, and, because it is predicated on the idea that the search is not quite fulfilled in life (but only in death), the writing can include all sorts of elements which are *not yet* of the order of wisdom. If the philosopher *is* a philosopher only to the extent that he has *not yet* achieved wisdom, then his biography, teleologically dedicated to charting the path of philosophy towards the wisdom achieved only in death, can allow itself to recount all manner of more or less unedifying anecdotes along the way, and these anecdotes will tend to confirm *a contrario* the ontological status of the philosopher himself. Socrates is still the clearest example of this set-up, if I can use the notion of example here: let's say that Socrates is the *exemplary* philosopher.

What I have called elsewhere the ontologico-biographical supplement, then, is constitutive of the philosophical concept of biography, and indeed the philosophical concept of philosophy. Without it, that is without philosophy's giving rise to philosoph*ers*, philosophy would not quite be philosophy. But this supplement which makes all the difference to philosophy, and which as such, in the case of individual philosophers, is the proper domain of the biographer, *is not itself philosophical* in any obvious sense at all. Biographies of philosophers, even when written by philosophers, are not in principle works of philosophy, or destined solely for philosophical reading. The feature of a philosopher which most saliently makes him into a philosopher is not itself philosophical, but of the order of the anecdote, and it is not clear what philosophy (as opposed to biography) can have to say about it. For philosophical biography (or the biography of philosophers) is not primarily concerned to give a genealogical account of the thought of the philosopher concerned, not simply to document facts about the philosopher's *philosophical* life, but deals with his life as a whole insofar as that life is not philosophy but should bear some relation to philosophy. This means that philosophical biography always teeters on the brink of triviality or the merely anecdotal (if only because it is predicated on the idea that the reader of the biography does not understand the thought of the philosopher concerned), and also that philosophy is constitutively compromised by this more or less unhappy relationship with philosophical biography – for philosophy cannot do without the ontological supplement documented in biography – and therefore cannot do without potential triviality. Any biography that tried to escape its normal teleological form would have, perhaps, to refigure this whole economy.

I think there is something very unsatisfactory about this whole set-up and its generally presupposed culturalist historicism. It's not just that those of us who were more or less close to Derrida, intellectually and personally, experienced his death in a way that makes this type of recuperative bio-philosophical assessment difficult to want to do (and difficult to stomach), leaving us very far from the *ultimatelys* and the *in the last analyses* and the *future-historians-will-tell-us-thats*, and the *Derrida's-main-contribution-will-have-beens*, in a state that makes even an event such as this, 'Derrida's event', a challenge, more of a challenge than previous non-posthumous Derrida events, at any rate, so that it feels harder to know what's going to happen next. But also that Derrida's event, the event of Derrida in the sense of the event as thought about by Jacques Derrida, seems to be more or less radically incompatible with that type of reaction.

For part of the event that Derrida is, and not the least important part, will have been a way of thinking about and writing about the event that makes it, and him, difficult to process in the ways I've been describing.

III

One way of casting this difficulty is in terms of mourning. As those of us who are in mourning try to mourn Derrida's death, maybe it is time to look again at some of the things Derrida said, at least from *Glas* (1974), but more especially in later texts, about death and mourning. Broadly speaking, the problem is this: the so-called 'normal' or 'successful' mourning consists in a process of *getting over it*, of recovering from the loss of the other by withdrawing one's investments or cathexes in that other back into the self, back into the service of the self, the ego. Whether at a personal level or at the level of the kind of reaction I have just been mentioning, this is a teleological process, the outcome of which is to *lose the loss*, to turn the loss into a profit, to come back to oneself, to *show a return*, in spite of the other's definitive departure. However 'healthy' we might want to think this process is, this model of mourning seems extraordinarily self-involved and self-interested (even jubilant in the case of several of the pieces published since Derrida's death), part of a more general take on what we all now call 'the other' that is precisely concerned to neutralise alterity in the interests of identity. (A lot of the recent talk about 'the other', in all its supposedly 'ethical' piety, is in fact a fairly transparent alibi for just this kind of self-interest.) And indeed this whole set-up is part of an age-old philosophical conception about life and death, and about philosophy as a process of 'learning how to die' which is of a piece with the 'biography' conceptuality I was mentioning earlier. It is against just this conception that Derrida protests in a lot of later texts, often reflecting on the death of friends and colleagues, and perhaps most strikingly in the interview given to the French newspaper *Le monde* less than two months before his death.

For example, in *Béliers*, originally written in homage to Hans-Georg Gadamer, after the latter's death, and which opens explicitly on the question of melancholia, Derrida is prepared to say that some *failure* of this structure of 'normal' mourning, something more of the order of what Freud calls, then, 'melancholia' (broadly speaking, the state of one who does not achieve the goal of mourning, but remains attached to the lost other), is in some important, 'ethical', sense *preferable* to mourning 'proper'. In fact, he thinks that only something that looks more like melancholia, as a kind of protest against mourning, a militant melancholia, then, gives any 'ethical' dimension to mourning. For example, as part of a meditation on Celan's enigmatic line 'Die Welt ist fort, ich muss dich tragen' [literally: 'the world is gone, I must carry you']

> According to Freud, mourning consists in carrying the other in oneself. There is no world any more, it is the end of the world for the other when the other dies, and I take into myself this end of the world, I must carry the other and the other's world, the world in me: introjection, interiorization of memory (*Erinnerung*), idealization. Melancholia is supposed to be the failure and pathology of this mourning. But if I *must* (this is ethics itself) carry the other in myself in order to be faithful to that other, to respect its singular alterity, *a certain melancholia must still protest against normal mourning* [my emphasis]. It must never resign itself to idealizing introjection. It must rail against what Freud says about it with such calm certainty, as though to confirm the norm of normality. The 'norm' is nothing other than the good conscience of amnesia. It allows us to *forget* that keeping the other inside oneself, *as oneself*, is already to *forget* the other. Forgetting begins right there. So melancholy *is necessary.*[4]

This is part of a movement of thought whereby the death of the other is always, rather literally, each time singularly, *the end of the world*, as the French title of what was first published in English as *The Work of Mourning* has it, and as Derrida also says much earlier in *Béliers*:

> For each time, and each time singularly, each time irreplaceably, each time infinitely, death is nothing less than an end of *the* world. Not *only one* end among others, the end of someone or something *in the world*, the end of a life or a living being. Death does not put an end to someone in the world, nor to *a* world among others, it marks each time, each time defying arithmetic, the absolute end of the one and only world, of what each opens as a one and only world, the end of the unique world, the end of the totality of what is or can present itself as the origin of the world for such and such a unique living being, human or not. (*Ibid.*, pp. 22–3).

But this 'melancholic' state of half- or semi-mourning (*demi-deuil*, as Derrida also sometimes calls it,[5] trying to capture, as is often the case in deconstruction, a kind of inhibition, arrest or interruption of what might otherwise seem to be a 'normal' teleological process pursuing its course to the end) does not in fact wait for the event of death to kick in. Rather it marks one's relation to the other *from the start*, just because the radically interruptive structure of any relation to any other is a measure of that other's very alterity.[6] My relation to the other is marked from the start by the asymmetry, distance, separation and interruption that makes ethics possible (while making any certainty that I am ever in fact behaving ethically quite impossible) as it respects precisely what makes the other other (and not me). And so one can speak of an 'originary mourning', or rather originary half-mourning or originary melancholia, as Derrida does in that last interview, an originary melancholia that then defines living itself, *vivre*, as a survival, a *survivre*, that would have a conceptual priority over one's usual (metaphysical) notions of life and death.

IV

Once we've complicated the status of the event of death in this way, with all that it entails, what is there left of the event in Derrida? What is an event worth calling an event in Derrida's work? Or, to use an idiom that returns almost obsessively in his later writing, what is an event *worthy of the name?*[7] We call all manner of things events, after all, but maybe something about why we do so can be brought out by trying to isolate the features of an event that's a *real* event, that's really worth calling an event.

One predicate Derrida insists on is this: an event worthy of the name must be radically unpredictable or unforeseeable. An event that arrives on cue, as predicted or programmed, loses its edge as an event just because you saw it coming. A real event (worthy of the name, then) seems to derive its eventhood from some quality of out-of-the-blueness. Events in this sense befall us, surprise us, don't politely announce their arrival and then arrive as announced; rather they land on us, hit us, appear out of nowhere, from above, below, from the side or from behind, rather than from up ahead. Derrida often stresses that events in this strong sense (and thereby the eventhood of events more generally, what makes events events) cannot adequately be thought of in terms of a horizon of expectation – what you see coming against the horizon is not an event (or at least, what in an event you could see coming was not its eventhood). This never-any-certainty-about-an-event means that I am never in control of it, and never sure of it, never sure it will happen. And this leads Derrida to what looks like a modulation in his thinking: from an earlier position where there was a kind of unconditional affirmation of the event in this sense, a kind of call on the event to come and happen in its unpredictability,[8] there seems to be a shift of emphasis at least to a formulation of a kind of transcendental 'perhaps-ness'. No event would not be marked by this 'perhapsness' of its very happening.[9]

Whence too the explicit suggestion in some of Derrida's late work that events are always in some sense *traumatic*. This is probably less a psychological remark than an attempt to borrow something of the thought that in trauma there is a kind of overwhelming of a system caught short in its preparation, something of an inability to process what befalls, advenes or supervenes – and this would be true of the so-called happy events as well as unhappy ones.[10]

Some rather paradoxical consequences flow from this thought of the event (which is also an event of thought, perhaps).

1) How simple is it to think in this perspective of events happening in their place and time? If I don't, and can't see it coming, and if I can't process it in its arrival, then when exactly can it be said to happen? Freud famously used the term *Nachträglichkeit* (in an early text Derrida says that this is Freud's real discovery, though it seems clear that Freud himself did not think so: as a student of mine recently pointed out, *Nachträglichkeit* itself only became an important or even thematised concept after the event, *Nachträglich*[11]). Freud used that term to try to capture something of this structure: ('deferred action' seems a poor translation of this: rather *Nachträglichkeit* seems to suggest a kind of intrinsic after-the-eventness of the event in this sense, i.e. that of an event worthy of the name and thereby in some sense traumatic). If events are traumatic and therefore marked as events by a kind of after-the-eventness, then events in the strong sense Derrida is trying to bring out can be said to be events that don't entirely or simply happen in their happening or at the moment of their happening. In the kind of cases described by Freud, at any rate, it often makes more sense to say that the event happens as an event only in a strange kind of repetition after the event (sometimes long after the event), or at any rate that the eventhood of the event cannot be given a simple date and time, and defies simple insertion into a continuity.

2) Second paradoxical consequence. If an event worthy of the name is marked as radically unpredictable, irruptive and not integrable into any straightforward temporal or causal continuum, then an event worthy of the name must presumably also exceed or interrupt the name and concept of event itself. Just as a singularity, if it is really to be singular, has to resist in some sense being recognised *as* a singularity (as merely an instance of the general concept of singularity), so an event should each time be a challenge to the very concept of event that we've been using more or less confidently. At which point the 'worthy of the name' part becomes complicated too – an event *really* worthy of its name would seem to have to be *so* worthy of its name that its name would no longer be so worthy of *it*. As Derrida puts it in an interview just after and about the event now known as '9/11', an event in the strong sense we have been following entails failure of comprehension and appropriation (so that an event is by definition something I don't quite understand, marked by the fact that I don't understand it), and that really ought to put questions to the concept of event itself (and by extension, perhaps, to philosophy and talk of essences and truths and

concepts more generally), so that, he asks: 'Would an event that still confirmed to an essence, a law or a truth, or even to a concept of the event, be a major event? A major event ought to be unforeseeable and irruptive enough to unsettle even the horizon of the concept or the essence from which one believes one can recognize an event *as such*'.[12]

V

An event so worthy of its name that it would suggest a kind of impossibility (Derrida sometimes defines deconstruction as 'an experience of the impossible') or unthinkability (and so, I'd like to say, always a kind of unworthiness to go with its worthiness) may, in a sense, never quite *happen*. An event so 'pure' as to escape recognition altogether might not even be worth calling an event. In fact, Derrida's work, from the start, stresses an economy of the kind of pure or radical event we've been sketching with all the things that seem determined to deprive it of its eventhood. Events are always also involved in some type of repetition or repeatability, reproducibility or recognisability. A logic of the event as singularity always goes along with what Derrida also recently calls a 'logic of the machine', of mechanical repetition or reproduction.

This is of course why the kind of recuperative cultural-historical reactions to Derrida's event, with which I began, can even get started. The suspicion, however, would be that those reactions are not given sufficient pause by the eventhood of the event that I've been trying to suggest is what Derrida is trying to bring out. Repetition may be compulsive, but there's still repetition and repetition. What Derrida famously calls *iterability*, in one of his earliest explicit discussions of the event,[13] may affect the event from the start, dividing its uniqueness and giving rise to the possibility of different versions and accounts of the 'same' event, but iterability also entails alteration and difference, so that something new, a new event, also takes place in every account of an event. If we take seriously the after-the-eventness structure of *Nachträglichkeit*, then it ought perhaps to be harder than is often thought to carry on in the massively culturalist and historicist mode that is unfortunately still (and perhaps increasingly) the norm in this domain.

I'd like to suggest in conclusion that Derrida's work in general, 'deconstruction', if that's what we want to call the series of events signed with his name, consistently exhibits and performs just the kind of complex after-the-eventness that he also thematises and describes. One way of bringing this out consists in asking the question: 'When is the deconstruction?' of any of Derrida's texts. A spectacular example here is the reading of Plato published in 1972 as 'Plato's Pharmacy', in which Derrida brings out of Plato's texts a way of thinking about writing quite different from the view that Plato most obviously seems to be putting forward. Derrida is certainly not just reporting the received Platonic view and then disagreeing with it or putting forward an alternative theory; rather claiming to read in and out of Plato (perhaps *through* Plato would be a more Derridian way of describing it)[14] another way of construing writing. This 'other view' is at least as much 'in' Plato as it is 'in' Derrida. It does not seem a satisfactory description of this situation to say simply that 'Derrida deconstructs Plato' (in 1972, then) nor that 'Plato deconstructs himself' (in fifth-century BC Athens, then). Rather the event of deconstruction seems to happen disconcertingly across or between these two dates (and in fact across a wide range of intervening dates too, the whole history of the 'reception' of Plato). And this seems to be what Derrida is trying to bring out when he says in a slightly different context that 'Plato's signature is not yet complete', the event 'signed' Plato being ongoingly and more or less unpredictably countersigned by any number of subsequent events that become, after the event, components of the supposedly 'original' Plato event.[15] And it looks as though this situation can be generalised across the whole of Derrida's work, the whole of 'deconstruction' as it carries through and interrupts the 'tradition'. The undeniable event of Derrida's reading of Plato happens, then, but exactly when and where it happens is probably impossible to say, and insofar as we are still here trying to figure that out, it seems also that, like Plato's signature, the event of Derrida's reading is also not complete, but open for reading and re-reading in the future. This structure of reading, which is absolutely fundamental to deconstruction, is something that cultural and historical approaches will never in principle understand.

All of this tends to dissolve or explode 'Derrida's event' into a kind of scattering or dispersion of its eventhood across a range that defies any simple accounting or accountability. The irreducible multiplicity entailed by that thought of scattering also (but that's another story I try to tell elsewhere) defines deconstruction as irreducibly 'political'. To the extent that it still seems important to gather that dispersion or scattering enough to identify a 'Derrida event' at all, we might want to say that Derrida's own work, in its constant reprises and displaced repetitions, its constant re-readings of itself, constantly tries to find ways of thinking together, in the same thought, singularity and repetition, the singular repeating as the same each time differently. Quite a good name for this might still be 'thought'. Derrida's event is an ongoing series of after-the-event reprises and iterations of an event of thought about the event and its constitutive after-the-eventness. And one thing this means is that Derrida's event never quite or entirely happened, or finished happening, and is to that extent still to come, yet to happen, here today in London, for example, and then again elsewhere, tomorrow.

Notes

1. This is an expanded version of an informal talk given in the 'For Derrida' series at the Tate Modern in February 2005, for the session entitled 'Derrida's Event'.
2. I reserve for a future occasion a discussion of the function of the word 'ultimately' in philosophical argument and in cultural criticism.

3. See 'A Life in Philosophy', in my *Other Analyses: Reading Philosophy* (ebook available from bennington.zsoft.co.uk), 405–425, from which I excerpt a couple of pages here.

4. Jacques Derrida, *Béliers: le dialogue interrompu: entre deux infinis, le poème* (Paris: Galilée, 2003), p. 74.

5. For example in 'Circonfession' (in Bennington and Derrida, *Jacques Derrida* (Paris: Seuil, 1991)), especially period 32.

6. See most recently Derrida's clarifications in Mustapha Chérif, *L'Islam et l'Occident: Rencontre avec Jacques Derrida* (Paris/Alger: Odile Jacob/Editions Barzakh, 2006), especially pp. 102–3 (where however 'rapport de nos rapports' on p. 103 is clearly a mis-transcription of 'rapport du sans-rapport'), but already 'En ce moment même dans cet ouvrage me voici' (in *Psyché: inventions de l'autre* (Paris: 1987), pp. 159–202 (especially pp. 176–81)), and the insistent allusions to Blanchot's 'rapport sans rapport'.

7. I first drew Derrida's attention to his frequent use of this idiom at another event involving Simon Glendinning, namely the conference entitled 'Derrida's Arguments', held at Queen Mary, London, in 2001, explicitly following up on the 2000 University of Reading conference 'Arguing with Derrida' that Glendinning had organised. (See my '...you meant', in *Other Analyses: Reading Philosophy* (op. cit.), pp. 83–94 (p. 92)). We subsequently discussed it on a number of occasions, notably at the SUNY Stony Brook *Politics and Filiation* conference (New York, November 2002): in *Voyous* (Paris: Galilée, 2003), p. 28, Derrida says that this is a 'locution dont je me sers si souvent et qui appellera un jour, de ma part, une longue justification [a turn of phrase I use so often and that will one day lead me to provide a long justification]'.

8. Cf. the analyses of an irreducible affirmation preceding any possible question in, for example, *De l'esprit: Heidegger et la question* (Paris: Galilée, 1987); *Ulysse Gramophone: deux mots pour Joyce* (Paris: Galilée, 1987) and, for the 'call' on the event, Jacques Derrida, *D'un ton apocalyptique adopté naguère en philosophie* (Paris: Galilée, 1983).

9. See the analysis of the 'perhaps' in *Politiques de l'amitié* (Paris: Galilée, 1994), p. 58 ff., and the more informal presentation in the discussion with Alexander Garcia Düttman, 'Perhaps or Maybe'. *PLI: Warwick Journal of Philosophy* 6 (1997), 1–18.

10. Cf. Jacques Derrida, *Papier machine: le ruban de machine à écrire et autres réponses* (Paris: Galilée, 2001), p. 114: '... always essentially *traumatic*, even when it is happy: an event is always traumatic, its singularity interrupts an order and tears, like any decision worthy of the name, a normal tissue of temporality or history'.

11. Cf. 'Freud et la scène de l'écriture', in *L'écriture et la différence* (Paris: Seuil, 1967), pp. 303, 314, 317. I am grateful to Susi Schink for pointing out to me the *nachträglich* nature of the concept of *Nachträglichkeit*.

12. *Le 'concept' du 11 septembre: dialogues à New York, Octobre-Décembre 2001, Avec Giovanna Borradori* (Paris: Galilée, 2004), pp. 138–9 [my translation].

13. See 'Signature, evénément, contexte', in *Marges: de la philosophie* (Paris: Minuit, 1972), and more generally Jacques Derrida, *Limited Inc* (Paris: Galilée, 1990).

14. Cf. *La voix et le phénomène* (Paris: PUF, 1967), p. 98: '*Through* [the] text, i.e. in a reading that can be neither simply that of commentary nor that of interpretation'.

15. Cf. Jacques Derrida, Claude Lévesque and Christie McDonald, *L'oreille de l'autre: otobiographies, transferts, traductions: textes et débats avec Jacques Derrida* (Montréal: VLB, 1982).

4   Derrida's event

Nicholas Royle

'Derrida's event': won't that have been the transformation of everything? I feel tense, to the point of trembling. Trembling is already the signal, symptom or experience of a strangeness of 'event', upsetting time, uncertainly concerning something that has already happened or is about to happen or happen again, as we find written in *The Gift of Death*: 'the event that makes one tremble portends and threatens still'.[1] Tension's *tense*: there is something untranslatable about this word which, in English, is haphazardly double, a homophone that refers to being stretched tight, strained or producing strain (from the Latin *tendere*, to 'stretch') as well as the grammatical sense of 'tense' as 'time', a translation or rather a deformation of the French word *temps*. In what tense should we speak of Derrida or of 'Derrida's event'? I have felt myself stretched by this strange *tense* since 9 October 2004 (but doubtless also before this), when I was in the midst of dealing with the proofs of an essay I had written called 'Blind Cinema', due to be published as the introduction to the book of the film *Derrida*, by Kirby Dick and Amy Ziering Kofman. Within a few days of his death I heard from the US publishers that they wanted me to change the tense: I was to go through the essay (an essay which Derrida himself had seen 'in the present tense') and change it to past tense 'as and where appropriate'. One of the unexpected and less intolerable aspects of attempting to respond to this bizarre yet apparently realistic and commonsensical request was finding my revised version of the proofs actually transpired to contain a larger number of instances of the present tense. 'Derrida writes', 'Derrida remarks in an interview', 'Derrida argues', and even 'Derrida thinks'. This convention of the so-called present tense, in the context of philosophical as well as literary writing and (even more perhaps) in the context of film, is at once quite familiar and strange. It tends towards, it portends spectrality. Derrida's work, the 'event' constituted by his œuvre, perhaps calls for a new *ghost tense*.

Let's not be so naïve as to suppose that he cannot speak. Moreover, we have to attempt to answer for the fact that – for Derrida, which is also to say *from* Derrida – a ghostly response is always possible. That much is perhaps already legible in the 'for' of 'For Derrida': it is a 'for', as he himself says in the context of the poetry of Paul Celan, 'whose rich equivocation remains ungraspable ("in the place of", "on behalf of", "destined for")'.[2] Writing of Freud in *Archive Fever* Derrida comments: 'Naturally, by all appearances, we believe we know that *the phantom does not respond.* He will never again respond ... Freud will never again speak'.[3] And what Derrida says here about Freud, we can also say about Derrida. As his text knows – and knows also that things are not so simple. In order to illustrate this, he calls up the example of the telephone answering machine. We know that Freud is dead, and Derrida is dead. Derrida writes:

> Now in spite of these necessities, these obvious facts and these substan- *LM*
> tiated certitudes, in spite of all the reassuring assurances which such a
> knowing or such a believing-to-know dispenses to us, through them,
> the phantom continues to speak. Perhaps he does not respond, but he
> speaks. A phantom speaks. What does this mean? In the first place or
> in a preliminary way, this means that without responding it disposes of
> a response, a bit like the answering machine whose voice outlives its
> moment of recording: you call, the other person is dead, now, whether
> you know it or not, and the voice responds to you, in a very precise
> fashion, sometimes cheerfully, it instructs you, it can even give you
> instructions, make declarations to you, address your requests, prayers,
> promises, injunctions. Supposing, *concesso non dato*, that a living being
> ever responds in an absolutely living and infinitely well-adjusted
> manner, without the least automatism, without ever having an archival
> technique [such as that of the answering machine] overflow the singu-
> larity of an event, we know in any case that a spectral response (thus
> informed by a *techne* and inscribed in an archive) is always possible.
> There would be neither history nor tradition nor culture without that
> possibility. It is this that we are speaking of here. It is this, in truth, that
> we must answer for.[4]

The voice of the dead person, cheerful at the end of the telephone line, is not alone: as Derrida has noted elsewhere (for example, in *Mémoires*), the voice from beyond the grave 'already haunts any said real or present voice'.[5] Derrida stresses the 'substantiated certitudes' but also affirms a 'perhaps', a perhaps that will have haunted these certitudes. The phantom speaks. *Perhaps* the phantom does not respond; but a spectral response is always possible. This possibility is inscribed in the singularity of an event. There would be no history otherwise, no tradition, no culture. Derrida's concern in *Archive Fever* is to explore the fact that 'archivization produces as much as it records the event'.[6] What goes into (and is left out of) an archive, how what goes in, how it is named (or not), ordered (and disor-dered), framed and described (or not), are part of the production of the event. This is what leads Derrida to his remarkable question: 'How can one prove an absence of archive? How can one not, and why not, take into account *unconscious,* and more generally *virtual* archives?'[7] 'There is no meta-archive', he remarks.[8] 'The structure of the archive is *spectral*', he argues.[9] The archive is not something done and dusted, a thing of the past. On the contrary, for Derrida (and for all of us), 'the archive is never closed. It opens out of the future'.[10] This corresponds with his conception of inheritance, as he describes it in an interview entitled 'The Deconstruction of Actuality', specifically in relation to Marx and Shakespeare, and above all in relation to the Ghost in *Hamlet*, 'perhaps the main character of [*Spectres of Marx*]':

> To inherit is not essentially to *receive* something, a *given* which one then *has*. It is an active affirmation, a response to an injunction, but it also presupposes initiative, the endorsement or counter-signing of a critical choice. To inherit is to select, to sift, to harness, to reclaim, to reactivate.[11]

To inherit is thus also indissociably bound up with a sense of the secret, the logic of 'an undecidable reserve'.[12]

An event is never over and done with. And the happening of an event is never pure or absolutely assured: 'An event cannot be reduced to the fact of something happening ... it is what may always fail to come to pass'.[13] '*Never quite* taking place' is part of the alleged 'success' of 'an event'.[14] Everywhere in Derrida's writing there is the implicit, sometimes explicit injunction to submit the concept of event to 'systematic questioning'.[15] Attentive as always to the etymology and history of a word, Derrida's 'event' (itself of course already a translation of the French '*événement*' and there-fore already a quite other kind of 'event') tenses, if I may put it like this; it *tenses* with the force of a 'come': 'event', like '*événement*', comes from the Latin *evenire*, to come out (from), to happen. To reckon with the 'event' in Derrida it is necessary to engage with the question and experience of the 'come', the coming in and of the event and indeed the 'to come', the open-ing of the future ['*l'avenir*']. As he asks in the essay 'Psyche: Inventions of the Other', apropos the 'unique structure of an event' and invention: 'What does it mean, *to come*?'[16] The 'come' does not come after the event: it is the condition of an event. Thus he remarks in 'The Deconstruction of Actuality':

> The event must be considered in terms of the 'come', not conversely. 'Come' ['*viens*', implying the intimate form '*tu*': 'come', 'come hither'] is said to another, to others who are not yet defined as persons, as subjects, as equals (at least in the sense of any measurable equality). Without this 'come' there could be no experience of what is to come, of the event, of what will happen and therefore of what, since it comes from the other, lies beyond anticipation ... There would be no event, no history, unless a 'come' opened out and addressed itself to someone, to someone else whom I cannot and must not define in advance – not as subject, self, consciousness, not even as animal, God, person, man or woman, living or dead. (It must be possible to *summon* a spectre, to appeal

to it for example, and I don't think this is an arbitrary example: there may be something of the revenant, of the 'come again' ['*reviens*'], at the origin or conclusion of every 'come'.)[17]

The evocation of a ghost tense, once again: the differential tensing of a spectre at the origin and conclusion of every 'come'.

In an interview in April 1989, four years before delivering the lectures that became *Spectres of Marx*, Derrida speaks of Shakespeare: 'I would very much like to read and write in the space or heritage of Shakespeare, in relation to whom I have infinite admiration and gratitude; I would like to become (alas, it's pretty late) a "Shakespeare expert"; I know that everything is in Shakespeare; everything and the rest, so everything or nearly'.[18] The rest is silence, the secrecy of inheritance, the desire to affirm and to countersign. How does one go about trying to become a 'Shakespeare expert'? (Who would ever dare to describe themselves as a 'Shakespeare expert' or indeed as a 'Derrida expert'? Derrida's phrase 'Shakespeare expert' appears between the tweezers of quotation marks, suggesting a characteristic sense of irony and comedy, but also as if to draw attention to the connotations of trying, testing and experimentation that belongs with the word 'expert', the sense of 'trying thoroughly'. Derrida, like Shakespeare, is so trying.) How does one go about trying to countersign Shakespeare, to countersign the event called *Hamlet*, for example, or even some minuscule aspect of such an event?

By way of conclusion I would like to offer a few brief remarks about the word 'event' (or 'events') in Shakespeare, in particular in the context of *Hamlet*. The first thing to say is that its appearances are consistently associated with a sense of strangeness. To conjure with the name of 'event' in Shakespeare is to conjure with strangeness. So, for example, we find the 'event' as 'wondrous strange' (in *3 Henry VI*, 2.1.32), 'that obscene and most preposterous event' (in fact a provoking reference to the act of writing itself, in *Love's Labour's Lost*: 1.1.245), the 'event' as that which is not 'customed' (in *King John*: 3.4.155), 'strange events' (in *As You Like It*: 5.4.133), 'strange event' (in *Timon of Athens*: 3.4.17), 'strange and terrible events' (in *Antony and Cleopatra*: 4.15.3), 'events' that are 'not natural' and increase '[f]rom strange to stranger' (in *The Tempest*: 5.1.230–1), and life itself described in *As You Like It* (by Jacques, no less, or Jaques) as 'this strange eventful history' (2.7.164).[19] (This last case, by the way, is uniquely eventful, the only occasion in Shakespeare writings where the word 'eventful' appears and the earliest recorded appearance of the word 'eventful' in English: yes, strange history, to invent the eventful.)

As I remarked a moment ago, 'event' comes from the Latin, it has to do with what comes from or comes out. In English the word 'event' is indeed used to signify 'outcome'. In *Hamlet*, for example, when Hamlet speaks in the soliloquy at the end of Act 4 of 'thinking too precisely on th'event' (4.4.41), the word 'event' is generally understood to have the primary meaning of 'outcome', 'result', 'consequence'.[20] (This might lead us away into a dreamy, impassioned and interminable digression on Derrida's 'outcome' or 'outcomes', above all the 'learning outcomes' of reading Derrida.) But in the same soliloquy, within 10 lines, Hamlet is also contemptuously invoking that 'delicate and tender prince,/Whose spirit, with divine ambition puff'd,/Makes mouths at the invisible event' (4.4.48–50). Here is the sense of outcome again, but it is at the same time emphatically a question of what is 'invisible', unforeseeable. Too precise, too trying or not, Hamlet's thinking thus corresponds with Derrida's stress on the event as necessarily bound up with the unforeseeable, the unpredictable and unprogrammable. As he declares near the start of his compellingly hazardous essay on chance (an essay that is in part about Shakespeare and in particular the strange workings of 'nature' in *King Lear*), 'My Chances': 'Unexpectability conditions the very structure of an event'.[21]

Among the innumerable things to which Derrida seems drawn in his various readings of and remarks on *Hamlet*, we might think most immediately of the time being out of joint, anachronicity, inheritance and spectrality. Here are five lines from *Hamlet*. They come in the opening scene. Derrida, so far as I am aware, does not cite them anywhere. Indeed they have received relatively little attention from critics, in part no doubt because they tend to be excluded from many editions of the play and from most stage performances. They are lines that appear in the Second Quarto (1604) but are absent from the First Folio (1623). They are of interest here, however, first because they contain the only other instance in the play (beside the two from the soliloquy in Act 4 scene 4 that I have just mentioned) of the word 'event' (or 'events'); and second, on account of the fact that they immediately precede or precurse the second appearance of the Ghost. Let us then listen in to Horatio, the first one in the play who seeks a response from the Ghost, demanding that the Ghost speak. Horatio has just been evoking the time preceding the death of Caesar when 'The graves stood tenantless and the sheeted dead/Did squeak and gibber in the Roman streets' (1.1.115–6). He then goes on:

> And even the like precurse of feared events,
> As harbingers preceding still the fates
> And prologue to the omen coming on,
> Have heaven and earth together demonstrated
> Unto our climatures and countrymen.
>
> *Enter* GHOST
>
> But soft, behold, lo where it comes again! (1.1.121–6)

This sentence preceding the entry of the Ghost (which is already a coming back, the second entry of the Ghost in this opening scene) is strange, as if the scholar Horatio is rambling, still or already again a bit distracted; we can't be sure finally whether or not he has finished his sentence when the Ghost appears. There is a sense that he perhaps has more to add, additional material regarding what is 'demonstrated' ('Have heaven and earth together demonstrated/Unto our climatures and countrymen ...'). For this sentence, effectively ushering in the Ghost, the tense is out of joint.

Along with the syntax, the language likewise is complex and peculiar, above all in so far as it affects a sort of anacolouthon of 'event' or 'events'. If Horatio's statement constitutes a completed grammatical sentence (in the absence of an archived manuscript, and relying on the mixed evidence of the Second Quarto and First Folio, many critics suppose that Shakespeare wanted these lines deleted, and even that he had given up – in other words that we are dealing here with a 'composition-cut', not a 'theatre-cut' – before finishing the sentence), if Horatio's lines are to make sense as they stand, it would be in the form of a formidably convoluted, multiply chias-matic inversion: what 'heaven and earth [have] together demonstrated' to Horatio and his fellow 'countrymen' would be 'the like precurse of feared events, / As harbingers preceding still the fates/And prologue to the omen coming on'. 'Feared events' are events anticipated with fear, yet 'precurse' in the sense of 'advance warning' (literally something 'running ahead', a word that occurs or recurs nowhere else in Shakespeare) seems to anticipate what is anticipated, running ahead of what is nevertheless already 'feared'. 'Harbingers' are likewise forerunners, those telling of something or some-one that is coming: 'harbingers preceding still [always going before] the fates'. Correspondingly contorted, 'fates' means bizarrely both 'events that are fated to happen' and 'the Fates that ordain them'. We cannot tell how this syntax is 'coming on': 'As harbingers preceding still the fates/And prologue to the omen coming on ...' The 'and' invites us to construe 'prologue' as conjoined with 'fates', at the same time as dividing and strangely repeating this image or figure of something coming before coming, a 'prologue to the omen coming on'. Shakespeare does not use the word 'omen' anywhere else and here, in this singular instance, its sense is antithetical, strangely double. 'Omen' is, in the words of the Arden editor Harold Jenkins, 'strictly, that which foreshadows an event, but here the event foretold'.[22] Strictly undone: tense and tension dissolved.

What to make of this extraordinary sentence (if it is one) about the 'coming on' of the event, that marks the coming again of the Ghost ('But soft, behold, lo where it comes again!')? If we can speak here of a kind of ghost tense in Shakespeare, a spectralisation of the 'coming' or 'coming on', conjoined and disjointed in the coming again of the Ghost, it would perhaps serve to evoke that strangeness of the event that Derrida calls 'liter-ary'. As he describes it in an interview:

> The literary event is perhaps more of an event (because less natural) than any other, but by the same token it becomes very 'improbable',

hard to verify. No *internal* criterion can guarantee the essential 'literari-ness' of a text. There is no assured essence or existence of literature. If you proceed to analyse all the elements of a literary work, you will never come across literature itself, only some traits which it shares or borrows, which you can find elsewhere too, in other texts, be it a matter of the language, the meanings or the referents ('subjective' or 'objective').[23]

Derrida's interest when reading a text is in trying to respond to a ghostly 'come'. He is concerned to countersign, to produce writing events of his own. As he puts it in an essay on James Joyce's *Ulysses*: 'we must write, we must sign, we must bring about new events with untranslatable marks'.[24] There is here what he calls 'distress', 'the distress of a signature that is asking for a *yes* from the other, the pleading injunction for a countersignature'.[25] As the divided syntax suggests, the distress is on both sides. Thus he concludes: 'Only another event can sign, can countersign to bring it about that an event has already happened. This event, that we naively call the first event, can only affirm itself in the confirmation of the other: a completely other event'.[26]

Postscript

Distress, yes, I would add, but also desire. For let's remember that Derrida's work, these writing events that still await us, is also about what he calls 'the greatest possible pleasure'.[27] The connotations of the 'come' and 'coming' in his writings consistently include the sexual. Perhaps his most intensive account of the operations of signing and countersigning would be *Signsponge*, his little book on the poetry of Francis Ponge. His engagement with Ponge turns, in part, around something dared or ventured: 'What I am risking here ought to be an event', he says near the beginning.[28] At one moment in the book Derrida seeks to describe the double and radically fictive or poematic figure of a 'single countersigned signature': it would be an 'event [that is] idiomatic every single time', 'the momentary singularity of a certain coitus of signatures'.[29] Intrigued by this sexual reference I once asked him if he would say a little more. In a word-processed letter dated 13 July 1991, below the 'Jacques' with which he signs himself, there is a postscript in which he writes: '"Coitus", which can have the sense you know, signifies first of all the experi-ence that consists in going (*ire*) towards the other, to the other, with the other. A coitus of signature signifies all that, in other words the crossing of this event crossed with the sense you know'. In a short handwritten stroke, he underlines the 'with' ('towards the other, to the other, <u>with</u> the other').[30]

Notes

1. Jacques Derrida, *The Gift of Death*, trans. David Wills (Chicago: Chicago University Press, 1995), p.54.

2. Jacques Derrida, *Demeure: Fiction and Testimony* (with Maurice Blanchot's *The Instant of My Death*), trans. Elizabeth Rottenberg (Stanford: Stanford University Press, 2000), p.31.

3. Jacques Derrida, *Archive Fever: A Freudian Impression*, trans. Eric Prenowitz (Chicago: Chicago University Press, 1996), p.62.

4. *Archive Fever*, pp.62–3.

5. Jacques Derrida, *Mémoires: for Paul de Man*, trans. Cecile Lindsay, Jonathan Culler and Eduardo Cadava (New York: Columbia University Press, 1986), p.26.

6. *Archive Fever*, p.17.

7. *Archive Fever*, p.64.

8. *Archive Fever*, p.67.

9. *Archive Fever*, p.84.

10. *Archive Fever*, p.68.

11. 'The Deconstruction of Actuality: An Interview with Jacques Derrida', trans. Jonathan Rée, in Martin McQuillan, ed., *Deconstruction: A Reader* (Edinburgh: Edinburgh University Press, 2000), p.548.

12. 'The Deconstruction of Actuality', p.548.

13. 'The Deconstruction of Actuality', p.536.

14. See Jacques Derrida, 'Limited Inc a, b, c...', trans. Samuel Weber and Jeffrey Mehlman, in *Limited Inc* (Evanston, Illinois: Northwestern University Press, 1988), p.90.

15. 'Limited Inc', p.58.

16. Jacques Derrida, 'Psyche: Inventions of the Other', trans. Catherine Porter, in *Reading de Man Reading*, eds. Lindsay Waters and Wlad Godzich (Minneapolis: University of Minnesota Press, 1989), p.29.

17. 'The Deconstruction of Actuality', p.535, trans. mod. (The original French version of this passage can be found in Jacques Derrida and Bernard Steigler, *Échographies de la télévision: Entretiens filmés* (Paris: Galilée-INA, 1996), pp.19–20.)

18. Jacques Derrida, 'This Strange Institution Called Literature' (interview with Derek Attridge), trans. Geoffrey Bennington and Rachel Bowlby, in *Acts of Literature*, ed. Derek Attridge (London and New York: Routledge, 1992), p.67. In the original French version of this interview, Derrida glides into English, 'un "Shakespeare expert".'

19. All Shakespeare quotations and references (apart from *Hamlet*) are here based on *The Norton Shakespeare*, ed. Stephen Greenblatt, Walter Cohen, Jean E. Howard and Katherine Eisaman Maus (New York: Norton, 1997).

20. *Hamlet* quotations and references are based on the updated edition of the New Cambridge Shakespeare text, ed. Philip Edwards (Cambridge: Cambridge University Press, 2003).

21. Jacques Derrida, 'My Chances/*Mes Chances*: A Rendezvous with Some Epicurean Stereophonies', trans. Irene Harvey and Avital Ronell, in *Taking Chances: Derrida, Psychoanalysis, and Literature*, ed. Joseph H. Smith and William Kerrigan (Baltimore and London: Johns Hopkins University Press, 1984), p.6.

22. See Harold Jenkins, ed., *Hamlet* (London: Methuen, 1982), p.174.

23. 'This Strange Institution Called Literature', p.73.

24. Jacques Derrida, 'Ulysses Gramophone: Hear Say Yes in Joyce', trans. Tina Kendall and Shari Benstock, in *Acts of Literature*, ed. Derek Attridge (London and New York: Routledge, 1992), p.282.

25. 'Ulysses Gramophone', p.283.

26. 'Ulysses Gramophone', p.309.

27. 'This Strange Institution Called Literature', p.56.

28. Jacques Derrida, *Signéponge/Signsponge*, trans. Richard Rand (New York: Columbia University Press, 1984), p.18.

29. *Signéponge/Signsponge*, pp.48–50.

30. The original French of Derrida's letter runs as follows: '"Coït", qui peut avoir le sens que vous savez, signifie d'abord l'expérience qui consiste à aller (*ire*) vers l'autre, à l'autre, <u>avec</u> l'autre. Un coït de signature signifie tout cela, c'est-à-dire le croisement de cet événement croisé avec le sens que vous savez'.

5   Metaphor and Derrida's philosophy of language

David E. Cooper

Metaphor is a good topic. For one thing, it gathers around it a large number of issues from several fields of enquiry: linguistics, philosophy of language, metaphysics, history and philosophy of science, literary criticism, aesthetics and so on. For another thing, metaphor is a tail that sometimes wags the dog. Linguists and philosophers of language have tended to regard metaphor as a rather marginal and annoying phenomenon which, nevertheless, they feel reluctantly compelled to cater for – in an Appendix, if not the main body of a work. But one sometimes suspects that how they cater for it is not only a key to understanding their wider treatment of language, but may actually be driving that treatment. How metaphorical meaning is accommodated may shape how literal meaning is understood, not vice-versa.

For both these reasons, I was attracted 20 years ago, when writing a book on metaphor (Cooper 1986), to Jacques Derrida's discussion of the topic, especially in his paper, 'White Mythology' (in Derrida 1982). In that paper, he develops, in an inspiring and detailed way, the old idea – left vague by such champions of it as Vico, Shelley and Anatole France – that metaphor has always played an essential, if generally unrecognized, part in philosophical discourse. And I dimly discerned, as well – without making much of it in the short section of my book devoted to Derrida – that his account of metaphor might be central to what I took, not entirely accurately, to be his general view of language. In this paper, two decades on, I hope to replace that dim discernment by a more lucid one.

Considering how much Derrida wrote about metaphor, surprisingly little has been written on what he wrote. But I want to suggest in this paper that some of what he wrote is not only pivotal to his wider conception of language, but also serves to crystallize a problem that he needs to address if that wider conception is to be defended against a predictable line of criticism.

Derrida writes about metaphor in many contexts – in his several discussions of poetry, especially Mallarmé's; in his examination of Rousseau's claim that language was originally figurative in character; in two essays where he assesses the contentions, by Paul Valéry and Anatole France, respectively, that the language of metaphysics in particular derives from, and is still influenced by, a number of metaphors, and, of greater relevance to present concerns, he also writes in the essay on France, 'White Mythology', about the notion of metaphor as one which is itself metaphysical. 'Metaphor remains, in all its essential characteristics, a classical philosopheme, a metaphysical concept' (1982: 219). This is, he argues, because metaphor is classically or traditionally defined in terms of those metaphysical oppositions *par excellence*, 'sensual/spiritual' and 'sensible/intelligible'.

Such remarks might, and indeed do, tempt people to think that Derrida is either denying the existence of metaphors or erasing all distinction between the metaphorical and the literal. But the temptation should be resisted. Unlike Heidegger who, likewise convinced that the idea of 'the metaphorical exists only within metaphysics' (Heidegger 1978: 89), refuses to apply the term 'metaphor', Derrida is happy to recognize that there are 'metaphorical relations', even if the expression is indulged in too readily by linguists and literary critics (see, e.g., 1992: 125). And while he may speak of 'explod[ing] the reassuring opposition of the metaphoric and the proper', his more considered view is that there should be a 'check' on this opposition and that what is called for is not its erasure, but a 'new articulation' of it (1982: 263, 270). As this remark suggests, it is not Derrida's purpose, either, to replace the 'opposition' of literal and metaphorical by 'a simple empiricism of difference in degree', but to develop a 'discourse' in terms of which this genuine opposition may be 'reinscribed' (1988: 117).

More attractive is the thought that Derrida is 'privileging' the metaphorical over the literal. This thought is wrong, however, if taken to mean that, for Derrida, metaphorical talk is either temporally or logically prior to literal talk – a view he explicitly rejects in his criticism of Rousseau's postulate of an 'originary' figurative language (1974: 270ff). However, the thought is correct, I suggest, if taken to mean that metaphor is 'privileged' in something like the sense in which, it is sometimes said, writing is 'privileged' by Derrida over speech. As Simon Glendinning points out, there are, for Derrida, structures and aspects of language – for example, 'iterability' – which are 'most perspicuous' and 'most evident' in the case of writing, so that there is a *raison d'être* to the 'strategic generalization' of the term 'writing' to language at large (Glendinning 2004: 11f). Speech, it turns out, is more similar to writing than it is to speech as traditionally conceived. Likewise, ordinary, literal talk turns out to be more similar to metaphorical talk, properly construed, than to literal talk as traditionally conceived. We can indeed distinguish between written and spoken language, and between metaphorical and literal talk: but in each case, a focus on the first member of the pair enables a better understanding of the second, since crucial aspects of the latter are at their most salient in the former.

Let me begin by rehearsing some of the related claims about metaphor, familiar in the traditions of rhetoric and philosophy he discusses, that Derrida thinks we should reject. To begin with, he rejects that conception of metaphor according to which, as he rather dramatically puts it, 'metaphor ... always carries its death within itself' – of a kind of utterance, that is, which, while 'provisionally' departing from literal usage, always allows for a 'reappropriation of literal, proper meaning' (1982: 270f). He rejects, in other words, the claim that a metaphorical utterance always expresses a proposition that may be stated in perfectly literal terms. As Geoffrey Bennington remarks, for Derrida, a metaphor looks 'more and more like a metaphor' when it does not die a 'death in the concept', is not 'effaced' by ending in a literal proposition (Bennington 2001: 46). Second, Derrida denies that metaphors – 'fresh', non-conventional ones, at least – are to be treated as cases of polysemy or multiplicity of meaning. Discussing a poem by Mallarmé, he writes that the 'undecidability' of certain expressions in the poem is not due to their being polysemous: the reader's task is not that of deciding which among several meanings possessed by an expression in the poem is the relevant one. The expression, as it occurs in the poem, is a 'huge reservoir of meaning', rather than one with a 'determinate meaning' (1992: 115).

Third, Derrida rejects the idea that 'the metaphorical effect is to be studied in the field of consciousness', that a metaphor's interpretation is determined by what a speaker or author *thought* when producing it (1982: 225). This, I take it, is tantamount to denying that a metaphor's meaning is some proposition that its maker intends to communicate. Finally, and more generally, he rejects the attempt to understand the phenomenon of metaphor in terms of *meanings* at all – where a meaning is conceived of as an 'atemporal or nonspatial' entity, a 'content', such as, perhaps, a set of truth-conditions or a Fregean propositional sense (1982: 228).

In effect, Derrida is not only rejecting the 'classical' notion of metaphor – as a word or sequence of words with a special meaning distinct from its ordinary, literal one – but rejecting, too, the more recent (and, these days, more popular) 'pragmatic' or 'speech act' account, according to which its meaning is not a sense or proposition expressed by the word(s) *per se*, but one intended by the speaker. (For this account, see Searle 1979.)

Having rehearsed some claims about metaphor that Derrida rejects, let me now draw attention to some related features of metaphorical talk to which, more positively, he wants to draw particular attention. To begin with, he emphasizes that metaphorical utterances are typically, perhaps always, only indeterminately (or 'undecidably', as Derrida prefers) interpretable. Interpretation of a metaphor 'can be pursued ... infinitely ... No reference properly being named in [the] metaphor, the figure is carried off into the adventure of a long ... narrative which nothing assures us will lead us back to the proper name' (1982: 243). Second – and one reason for this undecidability – metaphors, like those of Mallarmé, can have many and incalculable effects, ones due, moreover, to a variety of factors: not just to the familiar use of a word, but to its syntax, sound, written form, its placing on a page and so on. All of these and more, Derrida suggests, are in play in the occurrences of the word '*blanc*' in a Mallarmé poem, thereby prompting associations with, among much else, snow, marble, pages and virginity (1992: 115f). Finally – and another reason for metaphor's undecidability – metaphors are themselves caught up with one another in a vast web, the use of any one of which reverberates, as it were, through the whole. Derrida quotes, with some sympathy, Gaston Bachelard's remark that 'metaphors summon one another and are more coordinated than sensations', objecting only to Bachelard's further claim that there must be a 'systematic logic of metaphoric productions' (1982: 265). The web is much too loosely structured, its boundaries far too indefinite, for there to be a serious prospect for such a 'logic', for a set of 'rules' for determining the relations of metaphors to one another.

My rehearsal of the points, negative and positive, that Derrida makes about metaphor will, of course, be ringing a bell in many readers' ears. For those points are strikingly akin to ones that he is standardly taken to be making about discourse at large. There is no need to spell this out in detail, but a few indications of kinship will be useful. Corresponding to his denial that a metaphor is an ambiguous utterance, whose relevant sense might be determined by, say, context, Derrida criticizes J.L. Austin for holding that context or convention may fully determine, with 'no remainder', identification of a performative utterance – and for thereby holding that there is 'no "dissemination" escaping the horizon of the unity of meaning' (1982: 322. See also 1988). Corresponding to his denial that a metaphor means what its speaker intends by it is Derrida's more general rejection of the idea that something 'present' to consciousness, like an intention, determines interpretation. Due to 'iterability', no speaker is 'master' of how his words should be taken (1981: 28). Corresponding to his claim that a metaphor, once uttered, is on an 'adventure' without any assurance of arriving at a decidable literal meaning are Derrida's remarks, a propos all written or spoken signs that, once produced, these are 'cut off' from their conditions of production, 'orphaned' and condemned, as it were, to 'essential drifting' (1982: 316). And corresponding, finally, to the emphasis on metaphors forming a web of interanimating expressions, albeit one lacking a 'systematic logic', is his vision of language at large as an unbounded, unregulated complex of *différance*.

Derrida provides little way by way of argument for the claims he makes about metaphor. I think he thinks that these points are really rather obvious, and he is then inviting us to recognize something that is much less obvious – that very similar points apply to discourse in general. The phenomena of dissemination, unsurveyable effects, drift, absence of decidable interpretation and so on, which are salient in the case of metaphorical utterances are much less salient, but nevertheless present, in the case of what we regard as literal ones. (Compare Derrida's strategy in drawing attention to aspects of language at large, such as 'iterability', by initially focusing on writing, where those aspects are worn on the sleeve, so to speak.)

Well, maybe it's not Derrida inviting us to recognize this, but I inviting you to read Derrida as if this is what he is doing. And I invite you to do this since it seems to me to be helpful to view his conception of language as being, to recall Glendinning's phrase, a 'strategic generalization' of his conception of metaphor.

One reason it is helpful is that it helps to crystallize a problem that Derrida's conception of language confronts. Let me approach the issue indirectly by first listening to another bell that must already have been ringing with some readers. People familiar with Donald Davidson's paper, 'What Metaphors Mean', must surely be struck by the affinity between the two philosophers' views on metaphor. 'A metaphor', writes Davidson, 'doesn't say anything beyond its literal meaning (nor does its maker say anything ... beyond the literal...)' (Davidson 1984: 246). Metaphors, *qua* metaphors, do not have meanings; neither they, nor their speakers, are expressing propositions, and they do not have truth-conditions or 'cognitive content'. Metaphorical utterances do their work in quite different ways from that of making statements: they 'provoke' thoughts, 'intimate', 'hint at', prompt imagery and so on. Indeed, 'there is no limit to what a metaphor calls to our attention' (Davidson 1984: 263) to its 'effects'. Like Derrida, Davidson is rejecting both classical and 'pragmatic' theories of metaphor.

But there seems to be one striking difference between the two men. 'As much of metaphor as can be explained in terms of meaning', says Davidson, 'may, and indeed must, be explained by appeal to the literal meaning of words' (Davidson 1984: 257). It is because we can identify the literal meanings of words that we are able to recognize that, on occasions, the words are being used non-literally, and so are prepared to interpret their use – to respond to them – in the ways appropriate to figurative discourse. Now, if what I said about Derrida's position is well-taken, this is not a position to which, it seems, he can subscribe. For Davidson, there seems to be a sharp divide between the identification of (literal) meanings – the systematic calculation, in effect, of the truth-conditions of sentences – and the practice of interpreting and receiving metaphors. But for Derrida, as I construed him, attributions of what we regard as literal or 'proper' meaning are an extension of, and continuous with, the practice of interpreting metaphors. If so, it is hard to see how he can, as Davidson appears to do, treat the interpretation of metaphors as parasitic upon a quite different, and prior, processing of word- and sentence-meanings.

Derrida, it seems, is faced with a problem that Davidson isn't. How, unless we can appeal to a process of establishing what words literally mean, can we even recognize when they are being used metaphorically, let alone embark on interpretation of metaphors? More bluntly, how can Derrida avoid a complete collapse of the distinction between metaphorical and non-metaphorical talk – a collapse that would not only be counter-intuitive or even incoherent, but is one that, as I earlier remarked, Derrida wants to resist? (Unless it is to result in a 'fantastic ideology of truth', Derrida remarks on Nietzsche's pronouncement that all truths are metaphors, it should be taken, not as genuinely erasing the distinction between literal and metaphorical, but as 'provoking' a 'new articulation' of the distinction (1982: 263).)

Now this problem, I suggest, is equivalent to a familiar problem that critics detect in Derrida's conception of language at large. Is not his emphasis on dissemination, undecidability of meaning, the 'essential drift' of words, and so on, hyperbolic, and incompatible with the undeniable fact that we do, much of the time, succeed in communicating with one another through language? For this to be possible, critics argue that language must be markedly more systematic and rule-governed than Derrida's rhetoric can allow for. Focusing on metaphorical talk cannot gainsay this point since, as Davidson apparently argues, such talk and its interpretation are parasitic on talk that is systematic and regular. The questions, then, of whether language at large can be as Derrida's rhetoric suggests it is, and of whether it permits of a viable distinction between the literal and the metaphorical, are of a piece.

It follows that if Derrida is able to provide a 'new articulation' of the literal/metaphorical distinction – one compatible with his emphases on dissemination, undecidability and the like – he may also be able to respond to the familiar criticism of his larger conception of language. How might he do so? The answer, ironically, is by following, some of the way at least, a crucial proposal of Davidson's, whose position in some of his later essays (notably 'A Nice Derangement of Epitaphs' (1986)) is a good deal more subtle than my rehearsal of it might have conveyed. (Hence my use of caveats like 'apparently', 'seems', etc. when rehearsing Davidson's views.)

According to Davidson's mature position, communication and understanding do *not* presuppose the existence of a shared systematic, rule-governed language. Indeed, he is now wary of referring to language, in the singular, at all. Rather, there are simply the languages – ever shifting, ever adjusted, from occasion to occasion – of particular speakers, relatively stable, but nonetheless unfixed, dispositions to use words in certain ways. For me to understand your words, it is not required that you and I share a single language; all that is needed is a tolerable fit between your speech dispositions and my 'passing theory' of how you use your words. And that is all, for Davidson, that is required to enable a distinction between literal and metaphorical talk. Roughly, I take you to be speaking metaphorically when you use some words in a way that, on the surface, contradicts my 'passing theory' of your language, but when, as well, I am loath to revise that theory to accommodate this unexpected use. Instead of saying to myself, 'Ah, I got it wrong. In his idiolect, that sentence can't, as I predicted, mean X', I say 'Since that sentence *does* mean X in his idiolect, but since he's clearly not wanting to state that X, he must be speaking figuratively'. The identification and interpretation of metaphors remains parasitic on an attribution of literal meanings, but this latter practice is no longer grounded in a rule-governed semantic system that transcends the 'passing theories' – always subject to revision and adjustment – that different speakers deploy in order to make sense of their interlocutors.

With some of this, it seems to me that Derrida need take no issue. He himself cheerfully concedes that there are relatively 'stable' 'norms of minimal intelligibility' that enable our understanding of one another, that serve as 'guardrails' against misunderstanding (1988: 147). And if that concession is not to jar with his rhetoric of dissemination, undecidability and drift, it is difficult to see how he can avoid following Davidson in relativizing these norms and this stability to individual speakers and their interpreters, rather than locating them in a system – language – which is taken to ground the dispositions of these speakers and hearers.

Where Derrida would not follow Davidson is in conceiving of these norms as being located in anything as regimented and systematic as the expression 'passing theories' is apt to conjure up. For him, it would be wrong to assimilate the adjustments an interpreter makes, when his expectations of what a speaker's words mean are confounded, to the adjustments a scientist makes to a theory when it encounters recalcitrant data. (One might, to be sure, allow for 'special cases' – like deciphering the symbols of a dead language – where the interpreter's position is more comparable to the scientist's.) When, in particular, I interpret a speaker's utterance metaphorically, I do so not to preserve my theory of his idiolect, but simply to minimize the offence the utterance gives to my expectations of him. Derrida would surely regard Davidson as having substituted for one big system – language – a number of individual, albeit overlapping systems, when what is really needed is to eschew this talk of system. Talk of applying 'passing theories' to utterances needs loosening up in favour of talk of the 'guardrails' that guide interpretation, or of expectations and dispositions 'conforming to an iterable model' (1988: 18).

It is true, of course, that if people's 'guardrails', 'expectations', 'models', or 'passing theories', are not to pass one another by – if, that is, there is to be a tolerable degree of fit between them and the utterances they help to interpret – then there must also be a degree of uniformity among the speech dispositions of interlocutors. Indeed, remarks Derrida, implicit in the making of any utterance is the understanding that the utterance is, in principle, communicable to 'every possible user in general' (1988: 8). It is therefore incumbent on Derrida, as upon Davidson, to gesture at an explanation of this actual or potential uniformity.

Derrida makes this gesture when he refers to the dependence of 'norms of minimal intelligibility' on 'socio-historical conditions' and 'relations of power' within speech communities (1988: 147). This gesture has an interesting implication, one that becomes more obvious with Derrida's insistence that there are only 'unstable stabilities', and that 'the norms of minimal intelligibility are not absolute or ahistorical, but merely more stable than others' (1988: 147). Stabilities are the lucky outcome of whole constellations of contingencies: stabilization is 'the momentary result of a whole history of ... relations of force, of tensions, ... of wars' and so on (1988: 145). The interesting implication of all this is that we can at least imagine conditions in which, while linguistic communication is still possible, there is much less stability than we in fact find. Our 'whole history' might not have produced the 'momentary result' of stabilization, and presumably there was a time, before history had done its work, when no such result had yet emerged. To imagine such conditions, however, is not to imagine human life without language: people could still have produced utterances and these would have had their 'effects' on hearers. Words and other communicative tools would still have 'performed'.

I suggest that to hold that we can at least imagine these conditions of instability is equivalent to holding that we can also imagine people speaking languages that do not allow for the distinction between literal and metaphorical talk to be drawn. For where there is not even 'unstable stability', there cannot be those relatively established 'guardrails' and expectations which constrain, *inter alia*, whether we take people's words literally or metaphorically. Now, whether we *can* in fact imagine the situation where the resources for making the distinction between literal and metaphorical are missing is an interesting issue, and one that has been addressed by various thinkers, including Gadamer (see the discussion of his and others' views on this issue in Cooper 1986). It is also, I think, a fairly precise and tractable one – hence an issue on which it might be rewarding to focus when assessing the viability or otherwise of Derrida's explanation of our current 'norms of minimal intelligibility'. So that would be one more reason for recommending, as I have been, that Derrida's discussion of language be viewed through the prism of his remarks on metaphor.

References

Bennington, G. (2001) For the sake of argument, in S. Glendinning (ed.), *Arguing With Derrida*, Oxford: Blackwell, 34–51.

Cooper, D.E. (1986) *Metaphor*, Oxford: Blackwell.

Davidson, D. (1984) *Inquiries into Truth and Interpretation*, Oxford: Clarendon Press.

Davidson, D. (1986) A nice derangement of epitaphs, in E. LePore (ed.), *Truth and Interpretation: Perspectives on the Philosophy of Donald Davidson*, Oxford: Blackwell, 433–446.

Derrida, J. (1974) *Of Grammatology*, tr. G. Spivak, Baltimore: Johns Hopkins University Press.

Derrida, J. (1981) *Positions*, tr. A. Bass, Chicago: University of Chicago Press.

Derrida, J. (1982) *Margins of Philosophy*, tr. A. Bass, Chicago: University of Chicago Press.

Derrida, J. (1988) *Limited Inc.*, tr. S. Weber, Evanston: Northwestern University Press.

Derrida, J. (1992) *Acts of Literature*, tr. D. Attridge, London: Routledge.

Glendinning, S. (2004) Language, in J. Reynolds and J. Roffe (eds.), *Understanding Derrida*, New York: Continuum, 5–13.

Heidegger, M. (1978) *Der Satz vom Grund*, Pfullingen: Neske.

Searle, J. (1979) Metaphor, in A. Ortony (ed.), *Metaphor and Thought*, Cambridge: Cambridge University Press.

6   Derrida and technology[1]

Christopher Johnson

It could be said that the question of technology is one of the determining questions of our so-called 'modernity', but if one were faithful to the spirit of Derrida's thought, then one would immediately qualify this kind of declaration by saying that technology has always been in different ways the determining question of humanity, of the human, of becoming-human or 'hominization'. What Derrida has given to us are critical and conceptual tools, or perhaps more accurately, *ways* of thinking, which can help us to think about technology. In the very first chapter of *Grammatology*, for example, we are warned that writing in the everyday sense of the term cannot be viewed as simply a kind of technical auxiliary to spoken language – 'technics in the service of language' – and that 'A certain sort of question about the meaning and origin of writing precedes, or at least merges with, a certain type of question about the meaning and origin of technics'.[2] In *Of Grammatology*, Derrida is therefore questioning the reflex of thinking that would place the technological *after* the human, writing after speech – for a whole tradition of philosophical thought, speech is the defining and distinguishing feature of the human, the human being is by essence the *speaking* animal. The question concerning technology would, according to Derrida's way of thinking, always have to exceed the 'human' in the narrow sense of the term, to include the animal, the animate, or, to anticipate, the *articulated*.

It was this kind of thinking which influenced my own thinking about technology a few years ago when taking part in a research group set up to explore relationships between science, technology and culture.[3] Technology being at the centre of our interests, one of the first questions we asked ourselves, when beginning our programme of reading and discussion, was: what are we looking at? What is the object we are studying? What, for example, is technology? My own immediate response, prompted by the spirit of Derrida's thinking, was that the question concerning technology was not a question of essence – what *is* technology? – but rather of context or, to use Gregory Bateson's term, punctuation of context, in other words, of where we decide to establish the boundary, the margin, the line of demarcation between what is and is not technology. My immediate instinct, guided by Derrida, and paraphrasing what he says about writing in *Of Grammatology*, was to ask the question: what is the field of technology? Where does technology begin and where does it end? And my response to this was that *everything* is or can be considered to be technology.

To think of technology as more than something that simply comes after the human is therefore to follow the line of thought already articulated in *Of Grammatology*, where Derrida questions the kind of everyday, non-reflexive thinking which takes the act of writing, for example, to be more 'mechanical', more 'technical' and less natural than the act of speaking, again a simple 'technics in the service of language'. Our thinking, our language, our collective representations encourage us to separate and distinguish between the living and the dead, the biological and the technical, the essential and the artificial, and in each case to subordinate the second term to the first. If we adjust and rethink this context, or how we have habitually framed or divided up this context – at least one definition of deconstruction might be that it involves a rethinking and readjustment of context – then writing is just as 'natural' as speech, which in its turn is just as 'artificial' as writing. Derrida therefore encourages us to think the *complication* or *co-implication* of the 'natural' and 'artificial', where it is impossible to determine an integrally natural and unified origin. According to the logic of the supplement, as Derrida calls it, the very possibility of supplementation – here that of speech by writing – exposes the essential lack at the heart of the 'natural', the structural possibility of its technical extension or 'spacing'. From the point of view of time, this logic of the supplement is also inseparable from what Derrida calls the *movement* of supplementarity, that is, any complex system open to its environment ('life', language, technology) is always in a dynamic process of integration with that environment, in other words, there is always *evolution*.

It is useful to remember that the discipline Norbert Wiener named cybernetics was already an important point of reference for Derrida's definition of the problematic of writing and the project of grammatology in *Of Grammatology*. Rereading the first few pages of this book, what is striking is the extent to which Derrida attributes the possibility of 'deconstruction', the visibility of the limiting field of force (*clôture*, closure, enclosure) that is logocentrism to a certain state of the contemporary scientific-technological landscape. Whilst retaining a certain critical distance from the language of cybernetics, nevertheless Derrida recognizes the strategic role of this discipline in the decentering of traditional forms of humanism.[4] However, what is so interesting about *Of Grammatology* is that the 'cybernetic' component of Derrida's thinking is not directed towards the contemporary *habitus* of control and communication technologies, nor to what is referred to today, somewhat problematically, as our 'posthuman' future, but to the deep past of the human species, its so-called 'natural' history, as described in the work of the ethnologist and prehistorian André Leroi-Gourhan.

Derrida's reading of Leroi-Gourhan in *Of Grammatology* centres on the latter's now classic book *Gesture and Speech*,[5] which deals with the prehistory of human intelligence and the determining role of technology in its emergence. The originality of Leroi-Gourhan is that he starts from the specifics of human anatomy which make the human-technological complex possible in the first place. The morphological changes in the human body plan involved in the transition to bipedalism permit the liberation of the hands and the face for tasks other than the narrowly defined activities of, for example, eating and locomotion. Leroi-Gourhan's argument in *Gesture and Speech* is that it is impossible to explain the evolutionary emergence of language and of human intelligence without reference to the circuit of positive feedback between the human brain and the technosphere, the most complex interventions of the human animal in the environment being mediated through the *hand*. Over the long duration of human evolution there is therefore an irreducible link between the development of the higher cognitive faculties such as language – in a process Leroi-Gourhan describes as the 'liberation' of the cortex – and the hand, due to the close interaction between hand and face in finely coordinated tasks such as tool-making. Leroi-Gourhan does not look simply at the external anatomical features that define the human as the tool-making animal; he also looks at the neurological infrastructure that – in the cybernetic sense – 'controls' the manual and the verbal, gesture and speech. In the third chapter of *Gesture and Speech*, the author turns his attention to the hominid brain, and in particular to the pre-motor cortex, the part of the brain devoted to the fine coordination of different parts of the body. He emphasizes in particular the fact that the control of body parts is not distributed equally across the pre-motor cortex, but that it is massively biased – in a proportion of approximately 80% – towards the head and the upper part of the body, with at least 50% of motor coordination devoted to the hands and the organs of speech articulation.[6] To illustrate this differential distribution of neurological control, Leroi-Gourhan uses a diagram in which the human body plan is flipped over (in order to reflect its spatially reversed representation in the cortex) and its different parts drawn to scale in relation to the amount of neural activity dedicated to them. The result is the somewhat striking image reproduced in Figure 6.1.[7]

The science on which Leroi-Gourhan's analysis of the relationship between speech and gesture is based is now some 40 or 50 years old, but the general principles of that science have not, in fact, changed significantly since that time.[8] What is interesting here is the extent to which Leroi-Gourhan's work seems to provide the scientific foundation, as it were, of Derrida's grammatology. What we have come to accept as one of the central ideas of the *Grammatology* – that is, the idea of the structural *continuity* between speech and writing, as opposed to writing as simply a technological supplement separable from and subordinate to speech – is argued in Leroi-Gourhan's text with reference to the neurological substratum of human body articulation, more

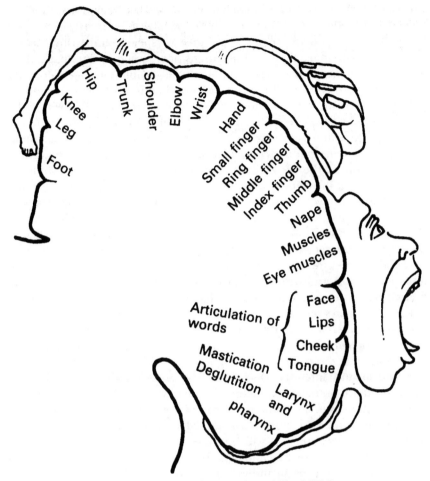

Figure 6.1 Image reproduced by kind permission of The MIT Press.

precisely, the *contiguity* within the motor cortex of the neural circuits governing the movements of the face and the hand:

> Another interesting fact is the contiguity of the respective zones of the
> face and the hand in area 4 [the primary motor cortex] and their
> common topographical position. Hand actions are closely coordinated
> with those of the anterior organs of the face. In the monkey this link is
> primarily related to feeding [and the same is roughly true for humans],
> but in the latter case coordination between the face and the hand is
> equally pronounced in the exercise of [language]. This coordination,
> which is reflected in the use of gesture as a commentary to speech,
> reappears in writing as the transcription of vocally emitted sounds.[9]

Of course, Leroi-Gourhan is not a philosopher: his analysis does not rise to the level of abstraction one finds in *Of Grammatology*, where Derrida will generalize the properly linguistic instance of speech and writing as we commonly experience them with his thesis of an arche-writing that is their structural condition of possibility. What Leroi-Gourhan does do, and compellingly so, indicates the *material* conditions of human cognition, providing as it were a bottom-up description of the articulations of the human body, from the feet that support bipedal locomotion through to the exquisite articulations of the hand.[10] What he shows is that the human mind is an open system, that the complexification of the structure of the brain, the 'liberation' of the cortex, is not simply a fact of 'biological' evolution, but the result of the co-determination – again what Derrida would term the *co-implication* or *invagination* – of 'inside' and 'outside', of the biological and the technological. In a circuit of positive feedback, the complexification of the human animal's modifications of its environment – in particular through the fine coordination of the hand applied to tool-making – retroactively determines the complexification of the neurological and anatomical apparatus that permits such articulations, and lays the foundations of the mental architecture on which human language is built.[11]

Leroi-Gourhan's excavation of the technological *habitus* of prehistoric humanity is therefore also an investigation into the *pre*-human, or more precisely, the *becoming*-human of humanity, its *hominization*, in which technics precedes and is the condition of language, and this is why Leroi-Gourhan's work is of so much interest to Derrida in *Of Grammatology*. His profoundly materialist insistence on the co-evolution of humanity and technology forces us to rethink and reframe the traditional forms of humanism based on the idea of the vital integrity of the bio-anthropological, of a kind of degree zero of the human – the *naked* human – which is prior to the advent of technology and indeed, historically, *invents* technology. This kind of questioning of the punctuation of context that distinguishes between on the one hand, that which is 'human', and on the other hand, that which is non-human, unhuman, *in*human, is one of the most enduring aspects of Derrida's thought.

There is evidently much more to say, and much more which has been said,[12] about the relationship between Derrida and Leroi-Gourhan, a relationship which would certainly merit further consideration. However, for the rest of this discussion I would like to look at the lines of reflection, or perhaps even, obsession, that Leroi-Gourhan's work seems to set in train in Derrida's subsequent writing, following its initial appearance in *Of Grammatology*. To return, briefly, to the diagram above, to Leroi-Gourhan's graphic illustration of the 'real' dimensions of human body parts from the point of view of their neurological representation in the motor cortex, it could be said that the primary intention and effect of this illustration is a didactic one, to the extent that it helps us to conceptualize the possibly counter-intuitive notion of the uneven distribution of neurological control of the human body within the topography of the brain. But it could also be said that another, and perhaps not entirely separate, feature of this illustration is its rhetorical effect. Because the dimensional morphing of the human body that the image so graphically illustrates also suggests the somewhat disproportionate and hypertrophic development of the hand. One could speculate here on what effect this image might have had on Derrida, reading Leroi-Gourhan's book in the mid-1960s, in view of what might be interpreted as the uncanniness of this single hand, the strange familiarity of its unfamiliar distortion. One could speculate further that Derrida would have been interested by this distortion, this disproportion, this monstrosity of the hand. And this would lead, in turn – given the importance of the figure and concept of articulation in Derrida's earlier texts – to the following formulation: *The hand is a monster of articulation*, or, to generalize this statement still further: *The hand is a monster of evolution*.

Although Derrida does not return directly to Leroi-Gourhan in his subsequent work, the theme or problem of the hand does return, episodically, in a number of texts following *Of Grammatology*.[13] The text I would like to focus on for the final part of this discussion is 'Heidegger's Hand', an essay which, in its extended meditation on the motif of the hand in Heidegger, seems to be dealing precisely with *cybernetic* questions about the human, the animal and the machine.[14] The framing question of 'Heidegger's Hand', as Derrida sets it up in the opening pages of the essay, is indeed the question of monstrosity: 'We are going to speak then of Heidegger./We are also going to speak of monstrosity' (161; 416). Inevitably, this question relates to the question of the human and what defines the human: 'For here the question is nothing less, I venture to say, than the problem of man, of man's humanity, and of humanism' (163; 418). The text which provides the main focus for Derrida's analysis is Heidegger's 1954 essay 'What is Called Thinking?'. In this text, the humanity of the human, that which sets it apart from the rest of the so-called 'nature' – its monstrosity – is seen by Heidegger to reside in the human hand: the human animal is a signing animal, an animal capable of pointing, of indication. Derrida himself indicates the etymological link, via the Latin roots of his native language, French, between the verb to show, to indicate, to point to (*montrer*) and the term for monster (*monstre*). In his turn, Derrida's translator attempts to respect and retain the ramifications of the French in a literal distortion of the word 'monstrosity':

> The hand is monstrasity [*monstrosité*], the proper of man as the being of monstration. This distinguishes him from every other *Geschlecht* [species], and above all from the ape.
> The hand cannot be spoken about without speaking of technics. (169; 424).

These three, telegraphic phrases condense within them some of the main points of preoccupation of 'Heidegger's Hand': the monstrosity of the human as the signing animal; the distinction between species, and the exemplary case of the distinction between the human and the ape; the essential link between the manual and the technological. Heidegger's understanding of thinking in 'What is Called Thinking?' is that it is an essentially *embodied* phenomenon – 'Thinking is not cerebral or disincarnate' – but also and more precisely that it involves the hand: 'To think is a handiwork, says Heidegger, explicitly' (171; 426). This last remark follows an extended analysis of one of the analogies Heidegger uses for thinking, his comparison between thinking and the noble art of the joiner or cabinetmaker – the person who works with his (*sic*) hands. Linguistically, this analysis revolves around the German term *Handwerk*, but the metaphor of the craftsman is also more than a metaphor, to the extent that it says something essential about the relationship between the hand and thinking, manipulation and intellection, the manual and the cognitive: 'The hand thinks before being thought; it is thought, a thought, thinking' (171; 427).

Derrida does not seem to disagree with Heidegger on the question of the embodied nature of human thinking, and especially its relationship with that most complex articulation of the human body, the hand. He seems to follow Heidegger this far, and inevitably one senses, in the background of the text and in the back of Derrida's mind, the lessons of Leroi-Gourhan's *Gesture and Speech*. Where Derrida parts company with Heidegger is where the latter begins to distinguish between the human and the animal, when he declares that the ape, *for example*, does not have a hand, only prehensile organs, which seize and grab; only the human, only *man* (*sic*) is in possession of a hand, and is therefore capable of thought, of speech and of the gift. Derrida questions this punctuation of context, typical of that tradition of philosophical thought which establishes an absolute distinction, according to this or that defining feature, between the human and the animal. He is disappointed that a thinker whose thinking is elsewhere so demanding and so rigorous lapses here into the most 'dogmatic' assertions and 'common representations', which risk compromising the integrity of that thinking. If Heidegger's version of humanism seeks in general to set itself apart from traditional metaphysical humanism, in this particular instance it remains squarely within it (173–4; 428–9). Derrida's criticism of Heidegger is particularly severe concerning the latter's attitude towards scientific knowledge. Heidegger's unthinking assertion about the ape's hand fails, for example, to take any account of the contribution of zoological science, which 'accumulates, is differentiated, and becomes more refined concerning what is brought together under this so general and confused word animality' (173; 428). Not only does Heidegger not take account of this kind of knowledge, he is fundamentally *uninterested* in what it has to say (174; 429). The result is that the so-called 'animal' world is presented as a homogenous continuum on the other side of the human, and this punctuation of context is used to define, via the privative assigned to the ape's hand, the meaning and the value of the human hand.

There is thus an 'abyss' of being, according to Heidegger, between the hand of the ape and the human hand. This abyss, comments Derrida, resides in speech and thought. Quoting Heidegger: 'Only a being who can speak, that is, think, can have the hand and be handy (*in der Handhabung*) in achieving [*accomplir dans le maniement*] works of handicraft' (174; 430). So for Heidegger the hand does not stand alone as a determining feature of human thought, it is in fact linked with thought via the intermediary instance of language; there is a sequencing of what Heidegger presents as the distinguishing features of the human, as opposed to, *for example*, the animal. Derrida:

> Man's hand is thought ever since [*depuis*, from the standpoint of] thought, but thought is thought ever since [from the standpoint of] language. That is the order Heidegger opposes to metaphysics: 'Only when man speaks, does he think—not the other way around, as metaphysics still believes'. (174; 430)

The trajectory of Derrida's analysis following this quotation is towards the problematic of the gift. He refers to the double 'vocation' of the hand in Heidegger, on the one hand as the bodily articulation that points or makes signs, and on the other hand as the organ of donation: the hand gives, or reflexively, gives itself. In this respect, Derrida's reading of Heidegger's text is a highly overdetermined reading, to the extent that it gestures towards a number of thematic complexes characteristic of his later work. What I would like to dwell on here, briefly, is the complication, or again, more precisely, the *co-implication* of hand, thought and language in Heidegger's thinking about thinking, as Derrida presents it. On the one hand, Heidegger opposes the traditional metaphysical subordination of language to thought, and reverses that subordination: we (can) only think insofar as we (can) speak. On the other hand, his triangulation of hand-thought-language does not necessarily give equal status to all three faculties, as it were. As Derrida's reading suggests, there is an order to Heidegger's thinking about thought – the sequencing of hand-thought-language is not indifferent: the hand is thought from the point of view of thought and thought is thought from the point of view of language. It could be said that in the cybernetic circuit that links together hand, thought, and language, the hand is, in a sense, left out of circuit. The reason for this may have to do with the residual logocentrism of Heidegger's thought, which Derrida mentions here and which, of course, he has extensively tracked elsewhere. Whereas Heidegger attempts to extricate the hand from its naturalistic determinations (the hand as an organ of prehension, of gripping, taking or seizing) in order to emphasize its human and intersubjective dimensions (the sign, language, the gift), it could be said that his existential-synchronic analyses of the role of the hand in thought and language are haunted by the natural-historical fact of their reciprocal emergence. To extrapolate here from Derrida's earlier reading of Leroi-Gourhan: thought and language are not in any simple way the defining feature of the human, as a certain (logocentric) version of humanism would have it; rather, they emerge from the material conditions of the human body plan, the complication of its anatomical and neurological structures, and in particular the complex articulations of the hand in its transactions with the material world. While Heidegger's thinking about the hand recognizes its implication in human thought and language, this recognition is subject to the restricting condition that the human hand is separate, set apart from the animal 'world', and therefore also in a certain way distinct from its natural-historical past: it only achieves its humanness as a hand through language and through thought, and in that, specific, order.

'The hand cannot be spoken about without speaking of technics' (169; 424). This sentence, quoted earlier, brings together many of the different strands of Derrida's reading of Heidegger, as we have followed it so far, and it leads us, inevitably, to the question of writing. If Heidegger encourages us to think the hand from the point of view of language – speech or the word – this link, or determination, is revealed most graphically, so to speak, in the act of writing. Turning to Heidegger's 1942–3 seminar on Parmenidies, which, he notes, predates 'What is Called Thinking?' and anticipates some of its motifs, Derrida writes:

> If man's hand is what it is since [*depuis*] speech or the word (*das Wort*), the most immediate, the most primordial manifestation [*manifestation originaire*] of this origin will be the hand's gesture for making the word manifest, to wit, handwriting [*l'écriture manuelle*, literally: manual writing], manuscripture (*Handschrift*) that shows [*montre*] and inscribes the word for the gaze. (178; 434)

As we saw above, Leroi-Gourhan's analysis of the relationship between face and hand used the example of writing to illustrate the emergence of speech from gesture, whereas here Heidegger appears to be doing exactly the opposite. The paradox, as Derrida notes, is that while in other contexts Heidegger's thinking about writing is classically logocentric, considering writing in general to be responsible for the alienation and degradation of the spoken word, in this particular context the essentially *manual* activity of handwriting is valorized and given a certain authenticity. In fact, placed in the context of the (then) contemporary state of technology, this defense of the hand that writes, of the *manu*script, has its own, peculiar, coherence. As Derrida reminds us, Heidegger is fundamentally unhappy with the current state of technology, which is responsible for the increasing alienation of the hand: 'The hand is in danger' (171; 426). Artisanal, that is, manual modes of production are being devalued as they are superseded by the automatized (mechanical) processes of industrial production (172; 427). In the specific case of language and writing, the threat comes from what Heidegger sees as the regrettable degradation of manuscript through the use of one, specific, technological development – the typewriter:

> Typographic mechanization destroys this unity of the word, this integral identity, this proper integrity of the spoken word that writing manuscripts, at once because it appears closer to the voice or body proper and because it ties the letters, conserves and gathers together. (...) The typewriter [*machine à écrire*] tends to destroy the word: the typewriter 'tears (*entreisst*) writing from the essential domain of the hand, that is, of the word, of speech'. (...) The machine 'degrades' (*degradiert*) the word or the speech it reduces to a simple means of transport (*Verkehrsmittel*), to the instrument of commerce and communication. Furthermore, the machine offers the advantage, for those who wish for this degradation, of dissimulating manuscripted writing and 'character'. 'In typewriting, all men resemble each other', concludes Heidegger. (178–9; 434–5)

In one way, Heidegger's resistance to the typewriter can be taken as being paradigmatic of the resistance to 'technology' in general, a resistance which is doubtless a structural constant of all human relations to the artefact, the artificial, the supplement. The emergence of 'new' technologies is always a contested field, and the drama or dialectic of emergence, reaction and assimilation is, it seems, re-enacted with each new 'generation' of artefacts. What I would like to do in the conclusion to this discussion, riding on the back, as it were, of Derrida's reading of Heidegger, is to explore a little further the technological complex which is being described here – that is, the supercession of the manuscript by the machine – and the accompanying erasure, as Heidegger sees it, of human 'character'. Because just as, on the one side of the human, Derrida insists on the infinite differentiation of the animal 'world', perhaps one should also insist on the infinite differentiation, on the other side of the human, of the field of technology, as indeed Derrida himself does in another context.[15] In this particular instance, it seems that Heidegger's unhappiness with the typewriter has to do not only with its homogenizing effect, its alleged uniformization of human communication, but also with how the new technology of the typewriter might modify the relationship between the human subject and the technological object. Because if Heidegger seems to accept the fact or necessity of a certain supplementation of the human, then this acceptance of supplementation would probably take as its preferred limit the proximate manipulation of the *tool*. As we saw earlier, the idealized figure of the joiner or cabinet-maker illustrated the synergy of hand and thought: the worker's handiwork brings out the essence of the wood he (*sic*) works on (170; 425). But this worker does not work with his bare hands: hand and thought are mediated by the tool, that which is 'ready-to-hand' and which in its familiarized, everyday use, becomes almost a natural extension of the hand.

However, the tool is different from the machine, or there is a continuous differentiation between the tool and the machine as modes of supplementation. In the case of writing, it could be said that the pen, for example, is an *obvious* extension of the hand: as a tool or instrument, it extends the gesture of tracing or marking into a single point of inscription. As a machine (*machine à écrire, Schreibmaschine*), as a coordinated assemblage of parts that decomposes and separates the act of writing into input (keyboard) and output (typeface), the typewriter bears no proximate resemblance (is not in proportion) to the human – for Heidegger, it is a monster, since it transforms (distorts) the relationship of the hand(s) to writing. As Derrida observes, Heidegger's discourse on the hand singularizes the hand: the distinction of the human is to possess *the* hand, whereas hands in the plural belong to the domain of the animal:

> No, *the* hand of man, this signifies that we are no longer dealing with prehensile organs or instrumentalizable members that *some* hands are [*que sont* des *mains*—rather: that are hands *in the plural*]. Apes have prehensile organs that resemble hands, the man of the typewriter and of technics in general uses two hands. (182; 438).

At its most simple and empirical level, the transition within writing technology from the pen to the typewriter quite obviously does not mean the loss of the hand, as Heidegger might say: as Derrida points out, in its mode of operation the typewriter is still a manual writing (178; 434). Rather, with the writing machine the one-sided, predominantly right-sided manipulation of the pen is bilateralized, replaced with the combined articulation of *both* hands. Thinking back to Leroi-Gourhan's essentially technological definition of hominization, there would be much to say here about how the human body and the human brain might adapt to such shifts in manual technology, and in this context one might refer to what Derrida says elsewhere about the relationship between 'technicity' and 'plasticity'.[16] But to conclude, it is perhaps necessary to remember that the intellectual resistance to emergent technologies, as illustrated in the example of Martin Heidegger, is also, inseparably, an affective one. The anxiety of loss, the anxiety of obsolescence expressed by Heidegger has, as we have suggested, first to do with distance, that is, the alienation of the hand and the human from its proximate, 'authentic' dealings with the world. But perhaps it has also to do with time, and speed, to the extent that the automatic writing of the machine seems to *accelerate* the process of writing, distending in time as well as in space the relationship between thought, language, the hand and the artefact. The example which comes to mind here is of the science-fiction writer Philip K. Dick, of a generation different to that of Martin Heidegger, who could type at the phenomenal rate of 120 words per minute, and who commented to his third wife, Jane, that 'The words come out of my hands, not my brain, I write with my hands'.[17] The anxiety of a certain humanism, faced with the automatism that the machine seems to impose on the human, and the apparent loss of conscious control that this entails, would be that machine civilization represents not the progression but the regression of humanity, regression to a state of homogeneity and oblivion that is closer to the so-called animality.

Notes

1. A longer version of this essay has been published in *Paragraph*, 28.3, November 2005, 98–116.
2. *Of Grammatology*, trans. Gayatri Chakravorty Spivak, Baltimore: The Johns Hopkins University Press, 1976, p. 8; *De la grammatologie*, Paris: Minuit, 1967, p. 18.
3. See website at http://www.nottingham.ac.uk/french/research/ScienceTechnology Culture_Research_group
4. Derrida, *Of Grammatology*, p. 9.
5. André Leroi-Gourhan, *Gesture and Speech*, trans. Anna Bostok Berger, Cambridge, Massachusetts and London: MIT Press, 1993; *Le Geste et la parole. Technique et langage*, 2 vols, Paris: Albin Michel, 1964–5.
6. Leroi-Gourhan, *Gesture and Speech*, p. 84; *Le Geste et la parole*, vol. 1, p. 119.
7. Leroi-Gourhan, *Gesture and Speech*, p. 82; *Le Geste et la parole*, vol. 1, p. 120.
8. See, for example, Susan Greenfield, *The Human Brain. A Guided Tour*, London: Phoenix, 2000, pp. 44–8.
9. Leroi-Gourhan, *Gesture and Speech*, p. 85; *Le Geste et la parole*, vol. 1, pp. 121–2.
10. A similar genealogy is delineated in Friedrich Engels' *Dialectics of Nature*, in a passage reproduced in Robert C. Scharff and Val Dusek (eds), *Philosophy of Technology. The Technological Condition*, Oxford: Blackwell, 2003, pp. 71–7.
11. The centrality of the hand in human cognition and the importance of the cybernetic process of retroaction are leitmotifs of Raymond Tallis's essential book *The Hand. A Philosophical Inquiry into Human Being*, Edinburgh: Edinburgh University Press, 2003.
12. Notably by Bernard Stiegler, in *Technics and Time 1. The Fault of Epimetheus*, trans. Richard Beardsworth and George Collins, Stanford: Stanford University Press, 1998, pp. 134–79; *La technique et le temps 1. La faute d'Épiméthée*, Paris: Galilée, 1993, pp. 145–87. On Stiegler and Leroi-Gourhan, see Richard Beardsworth, 'From a Genealogy of Matter to a Politics of Memory: Stiegler's Thinking of Technics', *Tekhnema. Journal of Philosophy and Technology*, 2, 1995, 85–115 (97–100).
13. *On Touching—Jean-Luc Nancy*, trans. Christine Irizarry, Stanford: Stanford University Press, 2005, p. 344, note 19; *Le toucher, Jean-Luc Nancy*, Paris: Galilée, 2000, p. 172, note 1. A few pages later, Derrida also refers back to his reading of Leroi-Gourhan in *Of Grammatology*, and Stiegler's subsequent development of it (345, note 26; 177, note 2).
14. '*Geschlechte* II: Heidegger's Hand', trans. John P. Leavey, Jr., in John Sallis (ed.), *Deconstruction and Philosophy*, Chicago and London: University of Chicago Press, 1987, pp. 161–96; 'La main de Heidegger (Geschlechte II)', in *Psyché. Inventions de l'autre*, Paris: Galilée, 1987, pp. 415–51. References to this essay will henceforth be given in the main body of the text, with page numbers of the original French text following those of the English translation.
15. Derrida, *On Touching*, pp. 286–7; *Le toucher*, pp. 322–3.
16. Derrida, *On Touching*, pp. 219–25; *Le toucher*, pp. 248–53.
17. Quoted in Lawrence Sutin, *Divine Invasions: A Life of Philip K. Dick*, London: Harper Collins, 1994, p. 107.

7 Derrida and the legacies of the Holocaust

Robert Eaglestone

This is an essay about two legacies, the legacy of Derrida's thought and the legacy of the Holocaust. These two are interwoven and, I suggest, throw each other into relief. There are many ways in which the events of 1933–45 are passed down to the present. Indeed, the memory of the Holocaust has gone deeper than can easily be traced. Philipe Lacoue-Labarthe writes that it 'never ceases to haunt modern consciousness as a sort of endlessly latent "potentiality", both stored away and yet constantly at hand within our societies'.[1] Its legacy is present in the lives of the dwindling numbers of survivors and their families. It is there in forms of historical cultural production including archives, works by historians, museums and memorial days. It is present in the written or filmed testimonies of survivors, texts that we are still learning how to read, which 'make us encounter … strangeness' and that show us that 'we do not even know what testimony is and that, in any case, it is not simply what we thought we knew it was'.[2] It also has a presence in the wider public sphere, in global juridical traditions, in the United Nations definition of genocide, and in the tradition of international courts of human rights and of war crimes. More than this, debates over 'ethnic cleansing', human rights and the treatment of refugees and asylum-seekers are all shaped by the memory of the Holocaust. Becoming more diffuse still, debates over genetics, too, and much of the interpretation of Darwin's legacy take place under the shadow of the Holocaust. Indeed, all the discourses that already presuppose ideas of who we take ourselves to be, questions of representation and of ethics, are interwoven with the Holocaust. This legacy has become very wide indeed.

It is clear, too, that the Holocaust, as both a specific event and as an example of the enormity of human suffering, is present in Derrida's work. As Gideon Ofrat points out, 'the refugees who seek hospitality in his various books … the ghosts that frequent his thoughts' are emblematic of this.[3] Indeed, Derrida writes that the thought of the incineration of the holocaust, of cinders, runs through all my texts. What is the thought of the trace, in fact, without which there would be no deconstruction? The thought of the trace is a thought about cinders and the advent of an event, a date, a memory. But I have no wish to demonstrate this here, the more so, since, in effect, 'Auschwitz' has obsessed everything that I have ever been able to think, a fact that is not especially original. Least of all does it prove I have ever had anything original or certain to say about it.[4]

The central figures for this 'obsession' in Derrida's thought are the trace and the cinder. The former term he takes from Levinas, and the latter marks the way in which he develops that idea.[5] However, this essay explores not the development of this thought, but its legacies.

The legacies of Derrida's thought, which is more than his published writing, seems to have two modes. The first is, in a way, trivial and sociological. It concerns the 'application' and wider more diffuse legacy of his thought in the contested tradition of deconstruction. The second is more complex and, I will suggest, has a deeper effect.

While the question of 'applying' deconstruction is technically a complex one, despite the endless lectures to undergraduates on this subject, Derrida's work has had a huge 'applied' impact across a wide range of discourses. In relation to the Holocaust, his work has had an impact on how the events have been approached and memorialised. Daniel Libeskind's Jewish Museum in Berlin (technically, the 'Extension to the Berlin Museum with the Jewish Museum Department') is clearly influenced by deconstructive thought. One can read books that deconstruct 'the Holocaust', that is books which aim to 'deconstruct' how the 'Holocaust' as an event in history is represented, understood, exhibited and so on. But perhaps this is cultural critique, carefully describing and judging, implicitly or explicitly, how this most terrible event is presented and remembered. There have also been strange, ill-informed attacks on Derrida's work in this context, seeing it incorrectly as aiding Holocaust denial.[6] In the wake of the de Man affair, some critics oddly saw Derrida's work as fascistic.[7] These are still part of this legacy.

In addition to these engagements, both positive and negative, there are examples of interesting 'parallel thinking' in the study of the Holocaust, a result of the diffusion of Derrida's work, complex analogues or productive meetings. The work of the Holocaust historian Saul Friedländer is a case in point. Friedländer is a Holocaust survivor, a Jew from Czechoslovakia who was hidden in a monastery school as a boy. His early work as a historian is of the classic empirical type: a study of Pius XII, of US and Reich foreign relations, of Kurt Gerstein (the 'Counterfeit Nazi'). However, his own memoir, *Quand Vient le Souvenir ...*, from 1978 marks a turning point. A source for W. G. Sebald's *Austerlitz*, it tells the story of his survival during the Holocaust and the effects that this survival had on his later life. But these reflections then disrupt (or, better, deconstruct) his empirical historical work. His next book *Reflets du Nazism* (1982) argued that 'any analysis of Nazism based only on political, economic and social interpretation will not suffice' and that there was a need to 'trace the latent discourse ruled by a profound logic of the images used by the Nazis and those who write or make films about that period'.[8] This, in turn, led to his extremely influential edited collection, *Probing the limits of representation* (1992). In many ways, this volume marks the first serious engagement between the discipline of history and deconstruction in the US, raising issues about ethics, representation and truth. This led Friedländer to argue that Holocaust history needed a new way of writing, a 'new voice', and he began to develop this. He turned to areas outside the normal range of historical scholarship – the dreams of victims, the idea of trauma itself, wider philosophical considerations – and he also sought to locate reflexively the voice of the commentator in his historical writing. These ideas, these applications of a diffuse deconstruction, have been taken up by other historians in different ways. In *No Common Place*, the testimony of Alina Bacall-Zwirin with Jared Stark, the text is made up of direct transcriptions of the conversations between Bacall-Zwirin and Stark with notes of the time and the place of the conversations and metatextual citations which serve to foreground both the testimony and the techniques of its construction. Mark Roseman's *The Past in Hiding* offers a parallel approach, telling the story of the survivor Marianne Ellenbogen neé Strauss and unweaving this by telling the story of this story's construction at the same time.

Friedländer is keen not to suggest that his work is deconstructive as this would, he argues, 'demand a primacy of the rhetorical dimension in the analysis of the historical text'.[9] This is a very 'American literary critical' reading of Derrida's work, and it seems to me that the intellectual trajectory of Friedländer's career takes him closer to Derridian deconstruction than he suggests. If deconstruction concerns the relationship between what can be discussed, the text and the 'exorbitant' which lies outside the text but forms its context, then in Friedländer's work, this exorbitant is the 'Final Solution' and the binding memory of it: the Holocaust's haunting presence. This is not to suggest that Friedländer, or any of the other historians who follow the logic of his thought, is a 'deconstructor', but it is to suggest that the legacy of deconstruction, even as an American event, even as a series of questions, is interwoven with opening a space which disrupts disciplinary boundaries and guidelines to make them more responsive. This is part of the diffusion of Derrida's legacy.

These interrelationships between Derrida's legacy and the developing memory of the Holocaust are, in part, about the uses of deconstruction. More important is perhaps the sense of how Derrida's work itself is an engagement with the Holocaust. Derrida's work is not a way of viewing the Holocaust, as a microscope views a strange plant. Rather, as Derrida himself suggests, it grows itself from these cinders.

Many people have hypothesised that there is a link between the Holocaust, along with other massive events of human suffering, and the tradition of Western thought. This link is invoked in such ready irony as the leading Holocaust historian Raul Hilberg's comment on development of mass killing at Auschwitz: 'Simple as this system was it took years to work out in the constant application of administrative techniques. It took

millennia in the development of Western culture'.[10] It is summed up by the
Nobel laureate and Holocaust survivor Imre Kertesz when he writes that
'Auschwitz must have been hanging in the air for a long, long time,
centuries, perhaps like a dark fruit slowly ripening in the sparkling rays of
innumerable ignominious deeds, waiting to finally drop on one's head'.[11]
It is part of the analysis of the Holocaust by Adorno and Zygmunt Bauman,
in which they find modernity itself culpable. While Hannah Arendt warns
us that there 'is an abyss between men of brilliant and facile conception
and men of brutal deeds and active bestiality which no intellectual explanation is able to bridge', her great work of historical philosophy *The Origins
of Totalitarianism* is also an attempt to bridge this abyss.[12] And, though in
Manifesto for Philosophy, Alain Badiou ridicules the guilt of post-War philosophers for the role of philosophy in the Holocaust, he does not deny that
culture itself is part of the explanation.

It is in this context of the 'dark fruit' of Auschwitz that Derrida's work
stands most clearly and its legacy is most valuable. He outlines what seems
to me to be the central issue towards the end of one of his clearest engagements with the Holocaust, a book of 'ghost, of flame, and of ashes',
Of Spirit.[13] Derrida writes

> And as, since the beginning of this lecture, we have been speaking of
> nothing but the "translation" of these thoughts and discourses into
> what are commonly called the "events" of "history" and of "politics"
> (I put quotation marks around all these obscure words), it would also be
> necessary to "translate" what such an exchange of places can imply in
> its most radical possibility. This "translation" appears to be both indis-
> pensable and for the moment impossible. It therefore calls for quite
> other protocols, those in view of which I have proposed this reading.
> What I am aiming at here is, obviously enough, anything but abstract.
> We are talking about past, present and future events, a composition of
> forces and discourses which seem to have been waging merciless war
> on each other (for example from 1933 to our time) .... Nazism was not
> born in the desert. We all know this, but it has to be constantly recalled.
> And even if, far from the desert, it had grown like a mushroom in the
> silence of a European forest, it would have done so in the shadow of
> big trees, in the shelter of their silence or their indifference but in the
> same soil. I will not list these trees which in Europe people an immense
> black forest, I will not count the species. For essential reasons, the pres-
> entation of them defies tabular layout. In their busy taxonomy, they
> would bear the names of religions, philosophies, political regimes,
> economic structures, religious or academic institutions. In short, what
> is just as confusedly called culture, or the world of spirit.[14]

Derrida's work, then, is an act of 'translation' from one discourse –
philosophy – to another – the political or historical. This seems both vital,

because without this an understanding of the past and in turn the present is elusive, and impossible, not least because 'men of brutal deeds and active bestiality' did not read Heidegger. But Derrida's work implies two things. First, that the 'other protocols' he has been employing in this book and elsewhere are striving to do this, and second, that the space that philosophy opens up is not simply external to the ground on which we all live, but is that ground. It is thought of this sort, which can analyse Heidegger's avoidance and occasional use of Geist, the focus of *Of Spirit*, which allows these moves to be made. It is this patient thought that explores the trees of the forest in which Nazism grew, and which illuminates how they still grow around us.[15]

I want to suggest that it is this sort of programme of 'translation' which, while it does not offer any axioms about preventing genocides or 'never again' sloganeering, does make a number of specific interventions that are relevant to the legacy of the Holocaust, to the growing field of genocide studies, to philosophical thought and to the wider political sphere. I highlight three here.

The first comes directly from *Of Spirit* and concerns what Derrida calls a 'metaphysics of race'.[16] Heidegger is often defended by arguing that his work, especially in the 30s, distances itself from the crude, pseudo-scientific race biologism of the Nazis. However, in his careful analysis of Heidegger's work on Nietzsche and his Rectoral address, Derrida asks a more complex question. He argues that Heidegger interprets the 'thought of race' metaphysically and not biologically; by thus inverting the direction of determination, is Heidegger alleviating or aggravating this 'thought of race'? Is a metaphysics of race more or less serious than a naturalism or a biologism of race?[17]

Derrida here opens up a series of complex debates with profound contemporary ramifications. Much of the study of the Third Reich and the Holocaust by historians have focused on the pseudoscientific processes of the Nazis in relation to race, ideas that are now, rightly, dismissed. However, Derrida is pointing out that Nazi pseudoscience itself drew on a wider and more profound metaphysics of race that is only now in the process of being excavated. In his intervention into contemporary politics, *After Empire*, Paul Gilroy develops exactly this insight and calls the metaphysical forms of appropriation of identity that dominate the West 'raceiological':

> I do not mean physical variations or differences commonsensically coded in, on or around the body. For me, 'race' refers primarily to an impersonal, discursive arrangement, the brutal result of the raceiological ordering of the world, not its cause.[18]

The metaphysics of race is deeply encoded, with political, juridical and social ramifications. Gilroy traces it in one of its most powerful contemporary guises, what he calls 'civilisationism'. He argues that

Samuel Huntingdon's thesis of the 'clash of civilisations', for example, is in fact a modern-day version of nineteenth-century race-thinking. Significantly, 'race' is an almost totally absent category in *The Clash of Civilisations*. In the light of the analysis of 'spirit' given by Derrida, with a focus on the metaphysics of race in Gilroy's larger sense, race can be seen as a metaphysical or cultural concept recoded into versions of national, religious or 'civilisational' identity by Huntingdon. Indeed, Huntingdon's book looks very open to exactly the same protocols of reading that Derrida applies to Heidegger, especially in its avoidance of the use of the word 'spirit', while assuming just such a concept, in its totalising identity politics of 'cultures' and in terms like 'cultural values'.

A second legacy of the Holocaust and of Derrida's thought lies in thinking about how we might be able to approach the Holocaust intellectually. In the 'Post-scriptum' to 'Force of Law', Derrida ventures to describe how Walter Benjamin might have responded to the Final solution. There are two different versions. The first, Derrida suggests, corresponds to what might be a commentary on Nazism, on its use of language (evil is a possibility in all language), on its totalitarian 'logic' of the state and corruption of democratic institutions, and on its total, 'mythical', violence. But, Derrida suggests that this is to think the Final Solution from the point of view of Nazism and so to follow through Nazism's thought.

Derrida also suggests a counter-commentary, based on what the Nazis aimed to exclude: a commentary aiming to analyse the Final Solution from the point of view of Nazism's other, 'that which haunted it at once from without and within'.[19] This view is to be thought from the possibility of singularity, from the view of the victims of the Final Solution and also a more universal demand for justice. For Derrida, the 'Final Solution' must be thought of as a 'project of destruction of the name', meaning the destruction of each singular individual as a singularity and the destruction of the more general naming that which binds and creates communities. ('Name' is not just a metaphor: on 'August 17 another decree prepared by Hans Globke, announced that from January 1, 1939, Jews who did not bare the first names indicated on an appended list were to add the first names Israel or Sara to their names'.)[20] 'From this point of view' he writes,

> Benjamin would have judged vain and without pertinence ... any juridical trial of Nazism ... any judgmental apparatus, any historiography still homogenous with the space in which Nazism developed ... any interpretation drawing on philosophical, moral, sociological, psychological or psychoanalytic concepts.[21]

That is, any analysis that involved concepts that developed in the same forest as Nazism would be 'vain and without pertinence'. The implication is that only that which is truly outside Nazism and the Final Solution could judge it or measure its significance. But, at this point, Derrida bridles, finding something 'intolerable' in this interpretation. If the Final Solution can only be measured by what is outside all these concepts, then this means that one might say that 'only a God can explain this': the Holocaust is 'an uninterpretable manifestation of divine violence'.[22] Derrida writes that one 'is terrified at the idea of an interpretation that would make of the Holocaust an expiation and an indecipherable signature of the just and violent anger of God': the thought makes him 'shudder'.[23] Derrida is not alone in this, or in seeing how a path might be followed to this conclusion. It was in response to both Christians and Jews suggesting this that led to Richard Rubenstein's response in *After Auschwitz* (at least in the first edition in 1966). This is one of the terrible ideas, terrible in its proper sense, that Elie Wiesel wrestles with, too. It is here that Derrida finds Benjamin, and these alternatives, 'too Heideggerian, too messianico-marxist or too archeo-eschatological for me'.[24]

Neither of these paths, then, is enough response in the present to the past, or can 'take the measure of the event'.[25] One is too complicit, describing the Holocaust through the logic of Nazism (nothing *post*-Holocaust about that, just the Holocaust written); the other, dismissing the first, is too much the opposite, in which no 'anthropology, no humanism, no discourse of man on man, even on human rights' could 'be proportionate' (the Holocaust has consumed everything: *nothing* post-Holocaust here, either).[26] Neither is an opening and both correspond in a way to Nazism, to its false logic and science, and to its appeals to myth beyond reason. For Derrida this leaves us again with the task of thinking about the complicity of the discourses we still have, of rights, of ethics, of identity or race, with the Holocaust.

This task of thinking about the complicity of thought with the Holocaust, and of Derrida's thinking the Holocaust in its singularity takes me to a third part of this legacy, a concern for justice. This concerns, again, both issues in Holocaust studies and wider philosophical debates. Derrida, whenever he discusses the Holocaust directly, is keen to stress both its singularity, as exemplified in Auschwitz, and a wider sense of human suffering, 'everything for which Auschwitz remains both the proper name and the metonomy'.[27] Thus the singularity of the Holocaust comes with a question about this very singularity ('why this name rather than those of all the other camps and mass exterminations?' Derrida asks in an interview).[28] In the study of the Holocaust, there has been a long debate over the 'uniqueness' of the Holocaust. This debate has now died down, in part as a result of various studies of the politics of historiography and in part through the creation of various compromise formations (which do not resolve this debate), such as the suggestion that the Holocaust was 'unprecedented'. However, apart from the issues it raises over the politics of history, this debate and Derrida's use of 'Auschwitz and ...' beg profound questions that are central to Derrida's work and legacy. These can be summed up by a line from *The Instant of my Death/Demeure* – the issue of the 'Singular in general'.[29]

For Derrida, the Holocaust is both a universal injustice and a singular injustice. This is hard to think through philosophically; indeed, Derrida says that as 'paradoxical as it may seem, respect is due equally to all singularities'.[30] Western thought cannot but cover the 'singularity' of events up by turning them into examples of an abstract category or general cases. (Indeed, after Kant, the ability to do this is what guarantees identity over time.) Indeed, this philosophical tendency belongs to the very logic of language. For while we may be keen to see each event as particular and unique, our conceptual system, the working of language itself cannot but turn it into an instance of a concept, an example of something. The continued insistence of the uniqueness of the Holocaust, taken out of any political significance, is really a complaint about the ways in which our very way of thinking makes it impossible to discuss as particulars as particulars. This underlies, it seems to me, Derrida's attempts to think singularity. It is the theme of Derrida's essay on Paul Celan: what his poems, and the poem in general

> marks, what enters and incises languages in the form of a date, is that there is a partaking of the shibboleth, a partaking that is at once open and closed. The date (signature, moment, place, gathering of singular marks) always functions as a shibboleth. It shows there is something not shown, that there is ciphered singularity: irreducible to any concept, to any knowledge, even to history or tradition ... A ciphered singularity which gathers a multiplicity *in eins*, and through whose grid a poem remains readable ... the poem speaks, even should none of its references be intelligible.[31]

Indeed, this attempts to think that the singular has been seen, perhaps, as central to Derrida's thought. Recent work by Tim Clark and Derek Atttridge on literature reflect this. More can be done, perhaps, to bring this from the aesthetic into a wider political and historical discussion.

In conversation, Derrida said that 'I do not find in *any* discourse *whatsoever* anything illuminating enough for this period [the twentieth century]'.[32] None of the parts of the legacy of the Holocaust and of the legacy of Derrida's thought discussed above are meant to be illuminating 'enough'. While the diffusion of his ideas into the academy has been a cause of creativity, controversy and wilful misunderstanding, it has also been a source for new ways of responding to the problems that are involved in coming to understand the Holocaust. Turning to his own work, I have suggested that it both reflects on and stems from the Holocaust. It represents a patient, aporetic 'translation' from thought to history, and in this I have highlighted three areas among many. Derrida finds in Heidegger not an escape from biologism but rather, perhaps, its apotheosis in metaphysics: this, I suggested, is still with us today ('undeconstructed') in the discourses of thinkers like Huntingdon, who, while seeming to eschew 'race' and 'spirit' let these terms return implicitly in their texts. Derrida also finds the perspectives that one might take on the Holocaust problematic: either they re-enact the logic that led to the suffering or they push the events into a transcendental realm. Finally, Derrida aims to show how the very nature of the singularity of the Holocaust and other singularities to which we owe respect are always a difficulty for thought which must subsume particulars under concepts: yet it is only through this iterability of the mark that we can bear witness to their singularity. This essay, then, has aimed to show how these two legacies are interwoven and, in their complex knots, draw us to careful and patient thought.

Notes

1. Philippe Lacoue-Labarthe, *Heidegger, Art and Politics: the Fiction of the Political*, trans. Chris Turner (Oxford: Blackwell, 1990), p. 77
2. Shoshona Felman and Dori Laub, *Testimony: Crises of Witnessing in Literature, Psychoanalysis, and History* (London: Routledge, 1992), p. 7.
3. Gideon Ofrat, *The Jewish Derrida*, trans. Peretz Kidron (Syracuse: Syracuse University Press, 2001), p. 152
4. 'Canons and Metonymies: An Interview with Jacques Derrida' *in Logomachia: The Contest of the Faculties*, ed. Richard Rand (London: University of Nebraska Press, 1992), 195–218, pp. 211–12.
5. See Robert Eaglestone, *The Holocaust and the Postmodern* (Oxford: Oxford University Press, 2004).
6. See: Deborah Lipstadt, *Denying the Holocaust: The Growing Assault on Truth and Memory* (London: Penguin, 1994); Michael Shermer and Alex Grobman, *Denying History* (London: University of California Press, 2002). For a response to these sorts of claims, see Robert Eaglestone, *Postmodernism and Holocaust Denial* (Cambridge: Icon, 2001).
7. See, *intra alia*, David H. Hirsch, *The Deconstruction of Literature: Criticism after Auschwitz* (London: Brown University Press, 1991). Derrida's essay 'History of the lie: prolegomena' is in part about a rebuttal of views attributed incorrectly to him about Vichy, in Richard Rand ed., *Futures of Jacques Derrida* (Stanford: Stanford University Press, 2001), pp. 65–98.
8. Saul Friedländer, *Reflections on Nazism: an Essay on Kitsch and Death*, trans. Thomas Weyr (Bloomington: Indiana University Press, revised ed. 1993), p. 13, p. 15.
9. Saul Friedländer, 'Trauma, Transference and 'Working through' in writing the history of the Shoah', *History and Memory* 4 (1992), 39–59, p. 52.
10. Raul Hilberg, *The Destruction of the European Jews* (London: Holmes and Meier, 1985), p. 251
11. Imre Kertész, *Kaddish for a Child not Born*, trans. Christopher C. Wilson and Katharina M. Wilson (Evanston, Northwestern University Press, 1997), p. 28.
12. Hannah Arendt, *The Origins of Totalitarianism* (London: Harcourt Brace, 1973), p. 183.
13. Jacques Derrida, *Of Spirit: Heidegger and the Question*, trans. Geoffrey Bennington and Rachel Bowlby (London: University of Chicago Press, 1987), p. 1.
14. Derrida, *Of Spirit*, pp. 109–10.
15. In conversation, at about the time he was preparing *Of Sprit*, Derrida expands on this:

    I don't agree with you when you say that he [Heidegger] never said anything relevant to German political history, even during the thirties. I think, that if we had time, we could show that he – indirectly, and in his own manner, and so on - perhaps put the good questions. Perhaps. Are we sure today that we can understand what Nazism was, without asking all the questions, the historical questions, Heidegger asks?... I am not sure that we have really understood what Nazism was. And if we have to think and think about that, I believe that we will have to go through, not to stop, at Heidegger's questions, go through Heidegger's trajectory and his project. We cannot understand what Europe is and has been during this century, what Nazism has been and so on, without integrating what made Heidegger's discourse possible...all the questions he was dealing with had to do with Nazism, with the history of Western culture, with Marxism, with capitalism, with technology (178–179) 'On Reading Heidegger: An outline of remarks to the Essex Colloquium', *Research in Phenomenology* 17 (1987) 171–185, pp. 178–9.

16. Derrida, *Of Spirit*, p. 74.
17. Derrida, *Of Spirit*, p. 74.
18. Paul Gilroy, After Empire (London: Routledge, 1994) p. 42.
19. Jacques Derrida, 'Force of Law: The "Mystical Foundation of Authority"', trans. Mary Quaintance, in *Deconstruction and the Possibility of Justice*, eds., Drucilla Cornell, Michael Rosenfeld, David Gray Carlson, pp. 3–67, p. 60.
20. Saul Friedländer, *Nazi Germany and the Jews* (London: Phoenix Giant, 1998), p. 254.
21. Derrida, 'Force...' p. 60.
22. Derrida, 'Force...' p. 61.
23. Derrida, 'Force...' p. 62.
24. Derrida, 'Force...' p. 62.
25. Derrida, 'Force...' p. 59.
26. Derrida, 'Force...' p. 61.
27. Jacques Derrida, *Acts of Religion*, ed. Gil Anidjar (London: Routledge, 2002), p. 382.
28 Derrida, 'Canons and Metonymies', p. 112.
29. Maurice Blanchot/Jacques Derrida, *The Instant of my Death/Demeure*, trans. Elizabeth Rottenberg (Stanford: Stanford University Press, 2000), p. 91.
30. 'Canons and metonymies', p. 212.
31. Jacques Derrida, 'Shibboleth: for Paul Celan', trans. Joshua Wilner, in *Wordtraces: Reading of Paul Celan*, ed. Aris Fioretos (London: Johns Hopkins University Press, 1994), 3–72, p. 35.
32. Derrida, 'On Reading Heidegger', p. 179.

8   Derrida one day

Rachel Bowlby

One morning in January 2005, I was listening to the beginning of *Woman's Hour*,[1] it was the lead-in to the opening feature. There were a few teasing sentences about long-gone pop stars, teenage mooning and bedroom walls. 'Who was yours?' asked Jenni Murray, and added alluringly: 'Mine was Elvis'. We can all relate to this, she seemed to be saying, and there were a few more suggestions for faces that might have been stuck above the bed by erstwhile girls of post-Elvis generations – the Beatles, David Cassidy, and possibly Donny Osmond. Then finally, end of build up, out it came: 'Let's deconstruct the pin-up!' The word was articulated with such bravura and such relish that you couldn't but want to follow her. Any deconstructing that sultry voice was about to speak was good enough for me. Ears pinned, I forgot my usual academic twitchiness about the word coming to be used as a simple alternative to ordinary ones like 'analyse' or 'think about'. Here was a happy showcasing of a bold, strong, glamorous word: *deconstruct* as pure phonic pleasure, all voice, all signifier, without any special historical or technical meaning.

Did Jenni Murray's 'deconstruct' have anything to do with Derrida? Not by name. But Derrida was not, as we remember, averse to some of the more spectacular and seemingly outrageous appropriations of deconstruction in popular culture. Deconstruction was itself a pin-up and a label – a real record label and a cutting-edge item in the contemporary vocabulary of fashion. Derrida's own head and shoulders photographed pretty well too, and he even starred in an arthouse movie about himself. He might well have been flattered as well as amused by the *Woman's Hour* allusion. Deconstruct the pin-up – why not? Pin it down, take it apart, pin it back up with a new look – and move on to the next item.

I thought no more about deconstructing the pin-up. Frustratingly, I couldn't even stay to listen to the feature and find out what, if anything, underpinned the mid-morning deconstruction. But later the same day I was in a bookshop, one big enough to have a separate philosophy section, and there my eye was caught by a solid row of identical books on an upper shelf, their thick spines prominently showing the title *From Plato to Derrida*. This was a big American textbook, the Prentice-Hall *Philosophic Classics*, fourth edition, 2003.[2] A million miles it seemed – in fact it was 50 miles and a few hours – from the deconstructive moment on Radio 4 with its manifest ephemerality, its lively sound, its flaunted superficiality: the poster the temporary surface *par excellence.* Here, at the opposite extreme, at the end of the day, was the solidity and endurance of a permanent object. Derrida was granted the ultimate endorsement of a consecrated fraternity with the greatest philosophers of all time. The book seemed to embody a kind of immortality. What could be more of a vindication of deconstruction and of Derrida?

And yet the sight of the book depressed me. Was it because it was such a heavy tome, and a pedagogical text, in contrast to the light tone and the playfulness of the voice on the radio? That was part of it, perhaps. The text of Derrida's included in the book – no prizes for guessing – is 'Signature, Event, Context'. Like 'Structure, Sign, and Play', this text has been endlessly anthologised, in a way that has come to seem predictable, and to offer an easy-read, 'already-read' Derrida. Yet this is ironic, in that the essay itself argues for nothing other than the unpredictability and necessary variability each time any work is read, which would include it being reread itself, over and over again, whether in institutional contexts or any others. 'Signature, Event, Context' may have become tied for the present to certain pedagogical functions, but nothing guarantees the stability even of such relatively controlled reading 'contexts', and in the longer term it will inevitably – like any text that continues to be read, continues to have a life – keep changing for its readers, as well as providing matter for thought about the fixings and movements that occur as a text is differently presented and consumed. Despite its static position within the covers of the classical volume, nothing ensures or predetermines its future uses or effects.

So the problem was not, as such, the choice of text. I think the real reason for my negative reaction was because the book's very permanence and air of finality – here is the canon, from beginning to end – seemed to point to Derrida's own death. It was a concrete instance of that double structure of survival that he had so often analysed in relation to writers and their words, whereby the 'survival' of the author's work is necessarily through a life apart from their own, and one that they cannot control; it is a life that goes on, if it does, independently of and indifferent to the continuation or end of theirs. The work's survival therefore in one sense marks the author's own mortality as much as it grants a perpetuation or extension of their name. Last of all, perhaps, Derrida described this structure in the interview he gave in 2004 to the French newspaper *Le Monde,* shortly before his death:

> At the point at which I leave my book, or leave or let go of it for publication (no one makes me do this), I become, appearing-vanishing, like that ineducable ghost that never did learn how to live. The trace I leave signifies to me both my death, whether it is yet to come or has already taken place, and also the hope that it may survive me.[3]

Later in the interview, Derrida spoke directly and personally about his thoughts on the survival of his own work:

> At my age, I'm open to the most contradictory hypotheses on this subject. At one and the same time—please do believe me—I have the *twofold feeling* that, on the one hand—and I say this with a smile and a lack of modesty—I have not yet begun to be read, and while there are certainly plenty of very good readers (40 or 50 in the world, perhaps), basically, it's later on that there's a chance of all that appearing; but also just as much that, on the other hand, a fortnight or a month after my death, *there will be nothing left any more.* Except what is kept for library copyright purposes. I swear to you, I believe sincerely and at one and the same time in these two hypotheses.[4]

Derrida situates these extreme reflections in the context of a new kind of unpredictability about survival, owing to both the rapid expansion of technologies of storage or archiving and, on the other hand, the increasing deterioration or destruction of media (which would include, for instance, the paper on which the interview is printed). But in this passage it's hard to believe he believes what he twice asks us to believe he believes: that his name and his writing might be dead as soon as he was. Hard to believe because the hypothesis is so utterly implausible and practically impossible (and now, of course, disproved by what's happened). Twenty or 25 years, however, would have indicated a more realistic possibility: the time it might actually take for a writer to fade away from the visibility of publications, citations or coursework reading lists. There is no reason to think that this will be Derrida's fate; but it is not impossible.

In just a few tens of years, 40 or 50, say, Derrida will have more or less disappeared from what we call living memory. He will, probably – presumably – still be being read, perhaps read more and read as he would have liked, in the first of his two hypotheses about his survival. Deconstruction, the word, may long have ceased to have the edge and cut of a sharp new word; the time may have come and gone for a minor feature on a minor or major channel of some future verbal network in which punters are invited to remember the intellectual passions or fashions of their youth. Or else, or also, with or without its names, Derrida's thinking may have helped to bring about undreamt-of, impossible things. But for the time being, the time of mourning, we are still left with the present memory of Derrida; of the living Derrida who always had more to say and write. Whence, I think, the sadness, at the moment, at seeing Derrida's work put in its place, however exalted; put there, as writing must be, in his place.

Notes

1. *Woman's Hour*, for those unacquainted with the fixtures of British national radio, is broadcast every weekday morning on BBC Radio 4; the programme has been in daily existence for more than 50 years. Jenni Murray is its chief presenter.
2. The book is subtitled *From Plato to Derrida* and compiled by Forrest E. Baird; it has 1217 pages. A fifth edition (1248 pages), still with the same subtitle (no superseding of Derrida – or Plato – yet) is scheduled for 2008.
3. Derrida, 'Je suis en guerre contre moi-même' ('I am at war with myself'), interview with Jean Birnbaum, March 2004, *Le Monde*, 19 August 2004; rpt. (also in *Le Monde*) 12 October 2004, special supplement, 'Jacques Derrida', p. vi.
4. Derrida, 'I am at war', p. vii. The '40 or 50' 'very good readers' are literally 'a few tens', '*quelques dizaines*'. This could mean anything, I suppose, from '30 or 40' up to perhaps '70 or 80'; it would be interesting to know if Derrida had a precise figure in mind for the size of this group.

9   Jacques Derrida
and the new international

Alex Callinicos

I must confess that I felt a degree of ambivalence when I was invited to take part in the discussion of Derrida's legacies at the Tate Modern in which this book originated. This ambivalence originates in my attitude to Derrida's philosophical interventions since the appearance of *Grammatology* and *Writing and Difference* in the late 1960s. For what it's worth, some of the philosophical themes with which Derrida was identified seem to me beyond dispute.[1]

To take two examples, there is the thesis – which more than anything else made Derrida's initial reputation – of the impossibility of a 'transcendental signified': in other words, Derrida challenged the idea, constitutive of what he called the 'metaphysics of presence' foundational of Western thought, that we can gain direct access to the real, unmediated by discourse. There is also the idea – prominent in his later writings and discussed further below – that justice cannot consist in the mechanical application of a rule, but requires a decision, a creative leap that goes beyond the rule. But if I agree with Derrida in accepting some version of both these ideas, they don't seem to me to be insights only available in his work. On the contrary, they belong to the general heritage of post-Kantian philosophy. The latter point is indeed made by Kant himself in the introduction to the *Critique of Judgement*; the former, as Tom Baldwin so effectively brings out, was very powerfully stated by Peirce as early as 1868.[2] My reasons for nonetheless seeking to engage with Derrida, especially in some of his later texts, should become clear in what follows.

Pinning Derrida down

Let me, however, first address a problem with the kind of response to Derrida that I have just given. As Marian Hobson pointed out in our original discussion at the Tate Modern, it reduces the significance of a philosopher to a set of doctrines that can unproblematically be extracted from his or her work and integrated in some synoptic History of Philosophy. This problem is especially severe in the case of the reception of twentieth-century French philosophy in the Anglophone academy: thus Derrida and other ''68 thinkers' such as Deleuze and Foucault have been packaged and marketed as 'poststructuralists', 'postmodernists', or what have you, their pre-masticated 'ideas' shoved down students' throats in dozens of virtually identical textbooks. This kind of commodification is likely to do particular injustice to Derrida because what is 'doctrinal' in his philosophy serves to justify a distinctive style of thinking and writing that is central to any claim that can be made for his originality.

Trying to pin down just what is distinctive about this philosophical style is itself difficult; because of the nature of the case it eludes explicit propositional statement. Two admittedly very hostile commentators, Luc Ferry and Alain Renault, were nevertheless on to something when they ascribed to Derrida a '*negative ontology*': in his writings something beyond the categories of the Western metaphysics of presence is constantly alluded to, but can never discursively be articulated, precisely because these categories are at once inescapable and inherently limiting.[3] Judith Butler in her obituary of Derrida illustrates the pitfalls of trying to situate this project with respect to the larger philosophical tradition when she tries to gloss the idea of justice as 'a concept that was yet to come' by saying that, 'as an ideal, it is that towards which we strive, without end'.[4]

Justice for Derrida, in other words, is a Kantian Regulative Idea – an ideal that is constantly approximated but never attained, nevertheless acting as a goal to orient our actions. As Kant puts it,

> transcendental ideas ... have an excellent, and indeed indispensably necessary, regulative employment, namely, that of directing the understanding towards a certain goal upon which the routes marked out by all, as upon their point of intersection. This goal is indeed a mere idea, a *focus imaginarius*, from which, since it lies quite outside the bounds of possible experience, the concepts of the understanding do not in reality proceed; nonetheless it serves to give these concepts the greatest [possible] unity, combined with the greatest [possible] extension.[5]

Now there are formulations that might seem to support reading Derrida's treatment of justice in this way. For example, writing about the closely related concept of democracy (which, like justice, he claims is intrinsically connected to, if not identical with, deconstruction), Derrida says:

> democracy remains to come; this is its essence insofar as it remains: not only will it remain indefinitely perfectible, hence always insufficient and future, belonging to the time of the promise, it will always remain, in each of its future times, to come: even when there is democracy, it never exists, it is never present, it remains the theme of a non-presentable concept.[6]

But Derrida also in *Force de loi*, the very text cited by Butler, explicitly distances himself from the kind of reading she gives: 'I would hesitate to assimilate this "idea of justice" too quickly to a Regulative Idea in the Kantian sense'.[7] Elsewhere he elaborates on his reservations about current usage of the Kantian concept, where 'the Regulative Idea remains of the order of the *possible*, an ideal possible no doubt that is referred to infinity': apart from its intrication with the entire Kantian programme of locating the limits of possible experience in the transcendental subject, it reduces deciding or acting to following a rule and is necessarily in opposition to 'all the figures of what I place under the title of the *im-possible*'.[8] One of these figures is that of justice, which necessarily exceeds the normalizing categories – ultimately dependent on the metaphysics of presence – that serve to organize the institutions and practices of the law: 'It is possible as an experience of the impossible, there where, even if it doesn't exist, even if it isn't *present*, not yet or ever, *there is* justice'.[9]

Justice therefore isn't something ahead of us, guiding our conduct. It is there, as an *experience* of the gap between itself and law:

> Law [*droit*] isn't justice. Law is the element of calculation, and it is right [*juste*] that there be law, but justice is incalculable, it requires one to calculate with the incalculable, and aporetic experiences are the experiences, as improbable as they are necessary, of justice, that is to say of the moments when the *decision* between the just and the unjust isn't assured by a rule.[10]

Here we see more clearly why justice can't be a Regulative Idea: it lacks the generality that we normally attribute to ideals. Moreover, law and justice are necessarily mutually imbricated: 'law claims to operate in the name of justice and justice requires itself to be installed in a law which must be put to work (constituted and applied) – "*enforced*" by force'. There is justice in the singularity of a decision – a judgement – that seeks to give justice, not by applying a rule, but by addressing the demands of what is unique to a specific situation and therefore cannot be captured in any generality. The impossibility of justice therefore derives not from it being a principle or ideal that is only ever partially approximated to, but from the way in which it both depends on and interrupts the apparatus of the legal system and the state:

> To be just, the decision of a judge, for example, must not only follow a legal rule or a general law but it must assume, approve it, confirm its value, by an act of restorative interpretation, as if the limit of the law did not exist in the first place, as if the judge invented it himself case by case. Each exercise of justice as law can only be just if this is a '*fresh judgement*' ['*jugement à nouveaux frais*'].[11]

Even this very brief presentation should offer some hints of the suggestive nature of Derrida's discussion of justice. The central idea of the tension between but mutual implication of law and justice connects with debates among philosophers and constitutional lawyers in the common law tradition about the extent of judicial discretion in the interpretation of positive law.[12] But Derrida's emphasis on justice as something that is found in a decision also points towards his dialogue with Carl Schmitt, and in particular to his effort to extract the related concepts of decision and event from any philosophy of the subject.[13] This duality captures what is distinctive about Derrida's philosophical interventions, certainly in his later years; they seek to engage often illuminatingly with issues of great philosophical and political importance without falling captive to the at once inescapable but hopelessly compromised categories of Western metaphysics.

To put it another way, what Derrida seeks to do is to pursue a philosophical project that is recognizably post-Kantian in the kinds of problems and themes that it addresses but that is resolutely non-Kantian in how it approaches them. It is a matter of fine judgement how feasible such an enterprise is. The slippage from Derrida's concept of justice to its assimilation to a Kantian Regulative Idea is easy enough to make, as is suggested both by Butler's example and by Derrida's own avowed unwillingness, despite his 'reticences', to give up entirely on the idea of a Regulative Idea.[14] Kant seems to me the hardest philosopher from whose influence to escape. In any case, one can admire and learn from Derrida's attempt to pursue this strategy without necessarily finding it either mandatory or even terribly helpful. Personally I feel much more at home philosophically with the methodologically very sophisticated naturalisms of Quine and Davidson, and with the critical realism associated particularly with the work of Roy Bhaskar, all of which can be seen as also grappling with how to be post-Kantian without being Kantian.[15] Among recent French philosophers, I have found engagement with Badiou and Deleuze more fruitful, in large part because neither is afraid of pursuing metaphysical reflection of a more traditional kind.[16]

Derrida, Marxism, and altermondialisme

For all that, I write here in solidarity with what one might call 'a certain spirit' of Derrida. His later, so-called 'ethico-political' writings (he repudiated the appellation) make it clear that he is best compared with Edward Said.[17] Both saw themselves as intruders from the Arab world into the metropolitan academy, who challenged the Western tradition for its exclusion of the 'other' – women, Blacks, the colonized, the refugee, but who didn't simply reject this tradition, but sought to mine it for resources that could be of use to the marginalized and the excluded: 'Nothing seems to me less outdated than the classic emancipatory ideal', Derrida writes.[18] This is an entirely honourable, and indeed necessary intellectual venture, and one important topic in discussion of his legacy concerns the best way of continuing it.

But my desire to express solidarity with Derrida has also, of course, to do with *Spectres of Marx*. It is partly a matter of simple gratitude on the part of a committed Marxist. To proclaim 'no future without Marx' in 1993, at a historical moment when the Fukuyamas and the Brzezinskis were confident of having consigned Marxism to oblivion, was gratuitous in the best sense – a work of grace, unforced, but offering support when it was most needed. This seems to be much more important than the many disputable points in Derrida's actual reading of Marx and Marxism that Aijhaz Ahmad, Terry Eagleton, and many others were quick to point out.[19]

But the significance of *Spectres of Marx* cannot be reduced to its being Derrida's most direct engagement with Marx and Marxism or even to what it tells us about the broader development of his thought.[20] The book is also a political intervention directed fair and square against what he calls the '*dominant* discourse', the neo-liberal ideology unanimously embraced by elites around the world in the wake of the collapse of the Soviet Union, which

> often has the manic, jubilatory, and incantatory form that Freud assigned to the so-called triumphant phase of mourning work ... To the rhythm of a cadenced march, it proclaims: Marx is dead, communism is dead, very dead, along with it its hopes, its discourse, its theories, and its practices. It says: Long live capitalism, long live the market, here's to the survival of economic and political liberalism![21]

The prime instance of this dominant discourse targeted by Derrida is Fukuyama's *The End of History and the Last Man*. His scathing treatment of this book contrasts with its excessively respectful reception even by some Marxists.[22] Devastatingly describing Fukuyama's text as, 'in the tradition of Leo Strauss relayed by Alan Bloom, the grammar school exercise of a young, industrious, but come-lately reader of Kojève (and a few others)', Derrida homes in on the conceptual oscillation in its treatment of the event: on the one hand, the triumph of liberal capitalism is portrayed as having actually occurred, but,

> *on the other hand*, actual history and so many other realities that have an empirical appearance contradict this advent of the perfect liberal democracy, one must at the same time pose this perfection as simply a regulating and trans-historical ideal. Depending on how much it works to his advantage and serves his thesis, Fukuyama defines liberal democracy here as an actual reality and there as a simple ideal. The event is now the realization, now the heralding of the realization ... A thinking of the event is no doubt what is most lacking from such a discourse.[23]

Clearly at issue here is Derrida's own conception of the event, according to which 'one thinks at the same time the impossibility of predicting an event necessarily without horizon, [and] the singular coming of the other'.[24]

The event thus conceived cannot be reduced to the realization, whether approximate or complete, of an ideal. But the conceptual oscillation that he diagnoses in Fukuyama can also be seen at work in much more important and consequent thinkers. John Rawls's last book, *The Law of Peoples*, is a depressing example, as Rawls seeks to bend and adapt his theory of justice in order to fit the world as it currently exists according to the categories of Western foreign policy, complete with 'outlaw states'.[25] This compares unfavourably with one of Derrida's last books, *Voyous*, published on the eve of the invasion of Iraq in March 2003. In the first of the two essays composing this book, he offers a fascinating deconstructive reading of the word '*voyou*', employed in the French translation of that key legitimating expression of contemporary statecraft 'rogue state' (*Etat voyou*), from which it emerges that the *voyou* is the plebeian other of democracies that define themselves as identitarian communities, and that, because '[t]he abuse of power is constitutive of sovereignty itself', '*a priori*, the states that have undertaken to make war on *rogue States* are themselves, in their fully legitimate sovereignty, *rogue States* abusing their power'.[26]

This conclusion, and the premise on which it relies that democracy – including the democracy-to-come that opens itself to all the excluded – and sovereignty 'are, at the same time, but also successively indissociable and in contradiction with one another' (which seems like a variant of the relationship that Derrida holds exists between justice and law), raise all sorts of questions. Nevertheless, the political judgement – in which Derrida associates himself with Chomsky – that 'the most *rogue* of *rogue States* are those who put into circulation and into operation a concept like that of *rogue State*' – goes a long way to vindicate his claim to be engaging in 'a militant and interminable political critique'.[27] This critique of the existing relations of domination is a recurrent feature of Derrida's later writings. Thus, in a key chapter of *Spectres of Marx*, 'Wears and tears (tableau of an ageless world)', Derrida offers a list of contemporary evils – unemployment, social exclusion, international economic competition, protectionism, foreign debt, the arms trade, nuclear proliferation, inter-ethnic wars, the international crime cartels, the problematic status of international institutions.

In large part, this bill of indictment of neo-liberal capitalism anticipates that delivered by the *altermondialiste* movement that became globally visible in the protests at Seattle and Genoa at the turn of the millennium. And isn't the 'New International' evoked by Derrida, that 'denounces the limits of a discourse of human rights that will remain inadequate, sometimes hypocritical, and in any case formalistic and inconsistent with itself as long as the law of the market, the "foreign debt", the inequality of techno-scientific, military, and economic development maintain an effective inequality as monstrous as that which prevails today, to a greater extent than ever in the history of humanity' – isn't this international, 'a link of affinity, suffering, and hope', 'a kind of counter-conjuration' directed against these evils – itself a remarkable anticipation of this movement?[28]

Indeed many of the distinctive features of the *altermondialiste* movement strongly resonate with themes in Derrida's own thought – the insistence on organizing on a transversal basis, the respect for the diversity and auton- omy of the various networks that it embraces, the refusal to adopt a comprehensive programme postulating a unitary goal for the movement. These striking homologies seem to suggest how 'timely' Derrida's philoso- phy had become – not, of course, in the sense of reflecting the received wisdom of the day (*Spectres of Marx* shows how far he was from that) – but in articulating, and indeed in this case anticipating the preoccupations of new movements of resistance to neo-liberalism and imperialism. (I was personally able to witness the extent of Derrida's engagement with these issues when we both participated in a conference around the theme Returns to Marx organized by the Forum for European Philosophy in Paris in February 2003, during that strange interval between the vast global anti- war protests of 15 February and the invasion of Iraq on 20 March.)

Of course, to register the resonances between a highly complex philo- sophical project pursued over decades and a much more recent political movement driven by its own preoccupations and liable to all sorts of contingencies is in many ways simply to identify a new set of problems. The *altermondialiste* movement is sufficiently long in the tooth now to require more than the mere celebration of its existence; its development has indeed exposed limitations many of which flow precisely from its attempt to escape the styles of thinking and organizing characteristics of the classi- cal left and in particular to avoid direct intervention in the political field.[29] How much help Derrida's philosophical enterprise can be in addressing these questions is doubtful. This is partly because it isn't concerned with directly addressing problems of political analysis and strategy, and it would be quite unreasonable to reproach Derrida for this. But it is also because the very nature of this project itself – the endless complex play with the categories of the Western philosophical tradition, which cannot be tran- scended but must constantly be interrogated – forces him constantly onto the terrain of meta-theoretical commentary.

Thus, in *Spectres of Marx*, before Derrida can confront Fukuyama as the prime instance of the neo-liberal 'dominant discourse', he feels obliged to warn us in a (blessedly short) excursus about 'the problematic character' of his appeal to the concept of the 'dominant discourse' because we should be suspicious of its source in 'the Marxist code' – and more specifically of 'the simple opposition of *dominant* and *dominated*', of the very idea of social class, and, of the base/superstructure distinction, etc., etc., etc.[30] Of course, these are real enough issues, but Derrida's inability to stay very long at the level of the object language does set limits to the value of his writing as 'militant ... political critique'. Sometimes a cigar is just a cigar, and some- times there just is a dominant discourse; if ever the latter proposition were true, it is today with respect to neo-liberalism, as Bourdieu and Chomsky have in their different ways sought to show us.

But I wish to conclude this essay on a note, not of criticism, but of self-criticism. In the late 1980s I wrote a book called *Against Postmodernism*. In it, while acknowledging the philosophical importance of the writings of Deleuze, Derrida and Foucault, and distinguishing them from their packaging and marketing as 'postmodernists', I developed a set of criticisms that in certain respects paralleled those made somewhat earlier by Jürgen Habermas and Peter Dews.[31] In Derrida's case I developed a much more philosophically elaborated version of the objection made in the preceding paragraph, and dismissed the defence of deconstruction as a form of *Ideologiekritik* offered by Christopher Norris.[32] Now, while I stand by the philosophical critique, it is clear that the dismissal was wrong and that Norris was right. Derrida did provide means for challenging the 'dominant discourse' (even if he jibbed at using this concept) – the examples I have given of his critique of Fukuyama and of neo-liberalism in *Spectres of Marx* and of the concept of rogue states in *Voyous* show this very clearly, as do his more general reflections on democracy and justice. Derrida's philosophical heritage is an important conceptual resource for any contemporary left that seeks to challenge neo-liberal imperialism.

This conclusion prompts a philosophical moral. It is important to avoid a certain kind of rationalist error, which moves from the identification of certain serious, one might even think fatal flaws in a particular theoretical discourse to the judgement that this problematic can produce no work of substantive value. When stated in such general terms, this statement seems close to a banal truism. Discourse, even of the most rarefied philosophical kind, is highly complex and governed by more than the law of non-contradiction; part of the point of the kind of close critical attention to theoretical texts of which deconstruction is a variant is to identify the tensions, anomalies, and paradoxes that subvert them but may also allow them to express thoughts of real value. But recognition of this truth can co-exist with a rationalism, even dogmatism, for which this identification justifies dismissing the entire problematic at issue.

Maybe Marxists are particularly prone to this kind of error; certainly the heyday of Althusserian Marxism provided plenty of instances of it (even though Althusser himself was just as much an exponent of the close critical reading of texts as Derrida).[33] But we have ourselves been victims often enough of similar dismissals – for determinism, evolutionism, and so on – that we should have become aware of its perils. One of the merits of the philosophical style that I have been criticizing in Derrida was its willingness to carry on working with specific concepts and discourses despite, or often because of their problematic features. Acknowledging this to be a virtue of deconstruction doesn't require one to give up the critical interrogation of theoretical traditions other than one's own. But it does suggest one should pursue it in a spirit of dialogue and in the recognition that one can reach the right conclusion – politically as well as philosophically – via a variety of theoretical perspectives. Obvious though all this may seem to others, I am grateful to Jacques Derrida for helping me to get there.

Notes

1. Given the volume and diversity of Derrida's writings, any discussion of them, and particularly one as brief as this essay, is necessarily highly selective. I am grateful to my fellow participants in the very lively panel on Derrida's Legacies organized by the Forum for European Philosophy at the Tate Modern on 2 February 2005 and to Sebastian Budgen for a helpful discussion particularly of the issues broached towards the end of this essay.
2. I. Kant, *The Critique of Judgement* (Oxford: Clarendon, 1973), p. 5; C.S. Peirce, 'Some Consequences of Four Incapacities', in N. Houser and C. Kloesel, eds., *The Essential Peirce*, I (Bloomington: Indiana University Press, 1992).
3. L. Ferry and A. Renault, *La Pensée 68* (Paris: Gallimard, 1985), p. 174.
4. J. Butler, 'Jacques Derrida', *London Review of Books*, 4 November 2004, www.lrb.co.uk (online edition). I'm not sure, incidentally, that it is the *concept* of justice that Derrida thinks is to come.
5. I. Kant, *Critique of Pure Reason* (N. Kemp Smith, ed.; London: Macmillan, 1970), A644/B672, p. 533.
6. J. Derrida, *Politics of Friendship* (London: Verso, 1997), p. 306. Also compare the following slogan from the same book – 'no deconstruction without democracy, no democracy without deconstruction' (ibid., p. 105) – with the even balder assertion: '*Deconstruction is justice,*' id., *Force de loi* (Paris: Galilée, 1994), p. 35.
7. Id., *Force de loi*, p. 56. See also id., *Spectres of Marx* (New York, 1994), pp. 64–5, where Derrida denies that the 'democracy to *come*' is 'a regulating idea, in the Kantian sense', and a similar statement in *Voyous* (Paris: Galilée, 2003), p. 62.
8. Id., *Voyous*, pp. 122, 123.
9. Id., *Force de loi*, p. 35.
10. Ibid., p. 38. Derrida here exploits the ambiguity of the term '*droit*', which, like '*Recht*' or '*Diretto*', but unlike 'law', covers both positive law and natural rights.
11. Ibid., pp. 49–50, 50–1 (italicized words in English in the original). Derrida acknowledges his debt for the expression 'fresh judgement' to Stanley Fish: see *Doing What Comes Naturally* (Durham NC: Duke University Press, 1990).
12. To my mind the most satisfying discussion of these issues is offered by Ronald Dworkin: see especially *Law's Empire* (London: Fontana, 1984).
13. See, for example, Derrida, *Politics of Friendship*, pp. 67ff.
14. Id., *Voyous*, pp. 122–5.
15. It is one of the great merits of John McDowell's *Mind and World* (expanded edn., Cambridge MA: Harvard University Press, 1996) that it challenges contemporary analytical philosophy to clarify its relationship to Kant.
16. See, for an attempt to display the fruitfulness of such an approach, A. Callinicos, *The Resources of Critique* (Cambridge: Polity, 2006).
17. For example: 'there never was, in the 1980s or 1990s, as people sometimes claim, a *political turn* or an *ethical turn* of "deconstruction", at least as I experienced it', *Voyous*, p. 64 (italicized phrases in English in the original).
18. Derrida, *Force de loi*, p. 62.
19. For the debate between Derrida and his Marxist critics, see M. Sprinker, ed., *Ghostly Demarcations* (London: Verso, 1999). Daniel Bensaïd offers the prime example of a positive Marxist engagement with *Spectres of Marx*: for example, 'Spectres de Derrida', in *La Discordance des temps* (Paris: Editions de la Passion, 1995) and *Resistances* (Paris: Fayard, 2001), Part II, ch. 3. My own response can be found in 'Messianic Ruminations: Derrida, Stirner, and Marx', *Radical Philosophy*, 75 (1996).
20. With respect to both these topics, *Spectres of Marx* needs to be set alongside Derrida's lengthy and fascinating interview with Mike Sprinker about Louis Althusser, 'Politics and Friendship', in E.A. Kaplan and M. Sprinker, eds.,

The Althusserian Legacy (London: Verso, 1993). One interesting feature of this text is that it contained Derrida's explanation of why he remained in what he describes as 'a tormented silence' about Marxism when the Althusserian project was at the height of its influence in France during the 1960s and early 1970s, at a time when he and Althusser were colleagues at the Ecole Normale Supérieure; he feared that the reservations that he had about Althusser's 'theoreticism' could be used to support the Communist Party leadership's attempt to maintain philosophical orthodoxy and also experienced 'a sort of theoretical intimidation' at the dogmatism that Althusser and his followers themselves displayed: 'Politics of Friendship', p. 188. This interview is worth comparing with Derrida's much more evasive response to probing about his relationship to Marxism in the main interview in *Positions* (Paris: Minuit, 1972).

21. Derrida, *Spectres of Marx*, pp. 51–2.

22. For example, P. Anderson, 'The Ends of History', in id., *A Zone of Engagement* (London: Verso, 1992). For my own assessment of Fukuyama and his reception by Marxists see A. Callinicos, *Theories and Narratives* (Cambridge: Polity, 1995), ch. 1. Despite the philosophical naivety that Derrida remorselessly exposes in *The End of History and the Last Man*, Fukuyama has had a lasting influence on the Anglo-American foreign policy elite: see, for example, R. Kagan, *Paradise & Power* (London: Atlantic Books, 2003) and R. Cooper, *The Breaking of Nations* (London: Atlantic Books, 2003).

23. Derrida, *Spectres of Marx*, pp. 56, 62–3.

24. Id., *Voyous*, p. 13.

25. J. Rawls, *The Law of Peoples* (Cambridge MA: Harvard University Press, 1999). See the crushing critique of this text (along with others by Norberto Bobbio and Jürgen Habermas also supportive of contemporary 'humanitarian' imperialism) by Perry Anderson: 'Arms and Rights', *New Left Review*, (II) 31 (2005). Anderson's careful reading nevertheless uncovers moments where the gulf between ideal and reality bursts into Rawls's writing: ibid., pp. 37–9.

26. Derrida, *Voyous*, p. 145. Both here and in the quotations in the following paragraph the italicized phrase '*rogue State*' is in English in the original. See Derrida's detailed discussion of the term '*voyou*' in ibid., ch. 6.

27. Ibid., pp. 143, 138, 126. The reason why the critique is interminable is because, as we saw above, democracy is always already to come. The idea of democracy is subjected to lengthy interrogation throughout the first of the two essays that make up *Voyous*: J. Derrida, 'La Raison du plus fort (Y-a-t-il Etats voyous?)', ibid., pp. 17–161.

28. Derrida, *Spectres of Marx*, pp. 85, 86.

29. For discussion of these issues see, for example, A. Callinicos, *An Anti-Capitalist Manifesto* (Cambridge: Polity, 2003) and 'The Future of the Anti-Capitalist Movement', in H. Dee, ed., *Anti-Capitalism: Where Now?* (London: Bookmarks, 2004).

30. Derrida, *Spectres of Marx*, p. 55.

31. A. Callinicos, *Against Postmodernism* (Cambridge: Polity, 1990), esp. ch. 3. See also J. Habermas, *The Philosophical Discourse of Modernity* (Cambridge: Polity, 1987) and P. Dews, *Logics of Disintegration* (London: Verso, 1987). Derrida's rather bad-tempered and defensive response to Habermas's critique does not show him at his best: 'Afterword: Toward an Ethic of Discussion', in *Limited Inc* (Evanston IL: Northwestern University Press, 1988), pp. 156–8.

32. Callinicos, *Against Postmodernism*, pp. 73–80. Norris offers this defence of deconstruction in, for example, *The Contest of Faculties* (London: Methuen, 1985) and *Derrida* (London: Fontana, 1987).

33. See Althusser's masterly opening essay, 'From *Capital* to Marx's Philosophy', in L. Althusser and E. Balibar, *Reading Capital* (London: NLB, 1970).

10 Derrida's irony?

Or, in order that Homeland security do not come too early to the case

Marian Hobson

Provisos

It is unlikely that there is only one legacy, to pick up the title of the Tate series that gave rise to the present volume. Equally, it's a bit early to say what the legacies are, quite apart from the problem of naming the legatees, for which it is definitely premature. Likewise, at a greater distance in time, someone will be able to discuss in detail the concerns Jacques Derrida himself obviously had about his legacies. While alive he made himself open to discussion with many others, of very different philosophical traditions and persuasions (Reading 1999, London 2000, Frankfurt 2001, to name only three). But he also operated with a quite small circle of close friends and collaborators, to whom he could open, with whom he could relax, on whom he could rely. And one can imagine that he envisaged his after-life in others' minds and books, and the possibility that the most originally faithful might come from somewhere not foreseeable, not even plausible from today. I shall return to this kind of presaging of the unanticipatable at the end of this essay.

Globalisation and language

Alex Callinicos's comments at the series are an example *post-mortem* of that openness. And my exchange with him was less a quarrel over an inheritance than a disagreement over a "will", as it is called in English, for it centred round the relation of deeds and words. At the end of the exchange, Dominic Willsdon had summed up Callinicos's position, and his own, as that of "Derrida's putting us in a kind of holding pattern", and as never quite getting "to the point of actually doing the politics". The present currency of the latter phrase is not negligible: a late-rising friend of mine is said "not to do mornings". The verb "not to do" Dominic used implies less deeds than social positioning and advertises the speaker's tolerance of another's recognizable lifestyle, political or not. What the verb doesn't mean is "not taking action". If it did, it would be radically untrue. Both Willsdon and Callinicos needed reminding – or perhaps they didn't know – that

Derrida had gone to meet philosophers in difficulty in pre-1990 Czechoslovakia, and had as a consequence been arrested on his way back; that he had written about Mandela in a France that was still doing business in South Africa, and at a time when *apartheid* was more or less ignored by most public movements there.

Derrida *had* then taken action on some political questions. What Alex wanted was a will, in the form of deeded security in a homeland position, on recognizable lines, Marxist lines. And he hadn't quite got that in Derrida's *Specters of Marx* (1993) though he had received:

> a very powerful piece of political critique [...] I think it is wrong to call it a 'deconstruction' because that implies a degree of respect for the work deconstructed, but rather a demolition of Francis Fukuyama's proclamation of the end of history. [...] The new international invoked by Derrida, denounces the limits of a discourse on human rights that will remain inadequate [...] and inconsistent with itself as long as the law of the market, foreign debt, the inequality of techno-scientific, military and economic development maintain an effective inequality as monstrous as that which prevails today.

So the wilfulness of Derrida's way of writing ("[its] arcane and often apparently self-referential character") is compensated for by the content of this chapter at least. After that, Alex also acknowledged:

> In thinking our way through the many controversies about the future of this movement, [the new international forum formed at Porto Alegre in Brazil] Jacques Derrida's distinctive philosophical style, which allowed him to anticipate [the] emergence [of the new international], maybe to conjure it into existence or help to do so, may prove to be of more help than my initial scepticism about the particular philosophical framework into which he put his main claims.

Alex has then left aside the usual "content" of a philosophical position, or to use the current, rather strange piece of philosophers' English, its "claims": these are "main", are made within a "particular philosophical framework" and Derrida's is one about which he, Alex, is initially sceptical. But he handsomely admits that it is the "distinctive philosophical style" that may bring us, readers of Jacques Derrida, where he, Alex Callinicos, wants us to be, in a particular kind of homeland, in which language both matters and doesn't. Yet Alex does not examine this further, so that the remarks are left, as if "on account", to imply: that style and content are usually unrelated in any meaningful way that could be pointed to; that nevertheless, Derrida's style can have effects which are tangible, indeed, we are led to believe, effects which produce "a kind of counter-conjuration" against "these evils", that is, "the law of the market, foreign debt, the inequality of techno-scientific, military and economic development" which produce "an effective inequality as monstrous as that which prevails today, to a greater extent than ever in the history of humanity" (this is Alex "largely quoting" Derrida).

So while endorsing the power of Derrida's denunciation of the deadening weight of the market, it is pointed out to us what is apparently a kind of rhetoric, one that is taken on approval because its effects, even if accidental, lead to positions that Callinicos approves. In spite of the sense which Alex obviously and rightly has, of Derrida's writing giving access to a future, it yet is almost immediately depreciated: it may be the means of a stage magician, since the positions are "conjured" into existence. Now, to say this is to rely on a distinction between style and content which is hardly plausible. Worse, by a slip of the pun, it transforms the political act of Derrida's "kind of counter-conjuration" into a kind of conjuring trick: acting under oath and as a group has been dissolved into a performance. We do not learn how it is that this "distinctive philosophical style" can open access to these positions nor bring about the changes in thinking needed to reach them, except as some kind of wizardry. Yet the constant resistance which Derrida's writing sets up *is* resistance to a kind of globalization: the globalization of thought, not one which beds down with politico-economic globalizations, but one which Callinicos never mentions, though it is one to a version of which he may subscribe. For Derrida's relation to language is poised between the universalizing force of language in general and the extreme particularity of the "irruption" into language at one point in time, in one place, in one natural language. (Rodolphe Gasché in particular has explored this.)

Language as a kind of resistance

However far the position I am attacking is from the obituaries in the *New York Times* and *The Economist*, it shares their attitude to Derrida's writing. Against these failures of analysis, I will try to push further: arguing, namely, that the distinctive philosophical style *is* one of the arguments; that the discomfort it sets up *is* one of the legacies; that the "arcaneness" is not a blemish or a curlicue which could be air-brushed out, leaving rugged wisdom and straight-forward exposition, marxist in Callinicos's case, anglo-saxon-positivist in the case of the newspapers. Nor is the "apparently self-referential character of Derrida's writing" an act of a conjuror. But if these are not to become a kind of brand-mark (as they tend already to be in more general discourse on him), if there is to be any kind of continuation of what he has done, it needs to be related to defined philosophical traditions, either as a working in or as an extension by contestation of them. This was the point made by the last speaker from the audience in the last session at the Tate, and although one can disagree with her choice of tradition, pragmatism, the remark stood and stands. The present article will try out the possibility of another tradition, that of philosophical irony.

To do this, and to clear away some misapprehensions, a feature, both obvious and disregarded, must be brought in: we all know that Derrida, all his life, earned his living by teaching philosophy. We also know that since Plato at least, philosophy has had an intimate connection with teaching, one that mathematics, for instance, or history, does not have. Now, in teaching, to check that someone has understood, we commonly use two methods: we ask them to put the points "in their own words" to affect a kind of translation on them. And then, we may ask them to summarize, to give us a précis of the matter being studied, to show that they master it as a whole as well as in detail, and judge of the importance of the different points being articulated into an argument. As a teacher, Derrida will have used these techniques. But it is not accidental that when he is defining himself against traditional work in philosophy, when saying "I wouldn't say I am not at all a philosopher", he says he doesn't speak from the position of philosophy, though "not necessarily from that of poetry either".[1]

So what *is* Derrida's relation to the kind of clarity or mastery that is given by summary, and to the kind of re-owning that is guaranteed by translation, and that many desire – for Alex Callinicos and Dominic Willsdon are two among many? We know that a lot in the way we live is reliant on this summarizing and this translation: we only need to think of what goes on when we computerize data for instance, and how much of our lives is governed by such data. The way we exist as a community and ensure its continuance relies on our learning from others and others learning from us, and summary and translation are at the heart of this. Do we not hand things on, and that helps us know where we ourselves are? Now Roland Barthes already in 1972 picked out something in Derrida's work that might be almost the contrary; not a continuing tradition, knowing where we are, but "une sorte de détérioration incessante de notre confort intellectuel". Is this a reaction to that "distinctive philosophical style" discerned by Callinicos some 30 years later? It seems so; it comes immediately after Barthes' mention of the new words, active words Derrida has invented: "ce en quoi son écriture est violente, poétique".[2] So is this discomforting writing, as not very translatable and not very summarizable, itself a kind of resistance to what is usually attributed to philosophy, and its "house style"? Well, I suppose it may be. Certainly other great philosophers, Hume for instance, have woken yet others up to a resistance to their own "dogmatic slumbers" and that was at first, and perhaps permanently, a loss of home comforts, as well as an enlargement of the philosophic tradition.[3]

Much of the spiky reception meted out to Derrida (famously, and for instance, the *New York Times* obituary of 10 October 2004) seems indeed due to a deterioration of comfort. But is that then the purpose or the effect, or both, of his way of writing? Take one of its striking features, lexical recklessness. He appears to make up words with some abandon, and collocates others freely. How about "chiasmatic invagination", for example? That makes one laugh, and was meant to, surely. Here then, baroque invention. Elsewhere there is word play which is often slightly off-key, intent on jarring us; *Legs de Freud*[4] for instance is a linguistically double allusion to Freud's construction of an institution based round his name and his work [*legs* = legacy], and the rhythm with which he discusses the problem of repetition [*legs* in its English sense]. Such surprises lie in wait at many turns of Derrida's phrase. But, if you work in a shop, you are taught to ask "what seems to be the problem?" Are we not meant to serve and be served laughter? Not supposed to find philosophy in writing funny? In discussion at the end of seminars, Derrida certainly owned up to this – it was not any more accidental than any free ride given by language. A resistance to the solemn deeded to his readers, one could say, rather than willed.

In Freud's analysis, laughter arises when comfort deteriorates, and then is suddenly augmented by release of tension. You can make a case – indeed Sam Weber has made the case[5] – that with the telephones that turn up at a certain period in some of Derrida's writings, he is parodying, or at least referring to Heidegger's tone of pathos in speaking of the "appeal" – the "call", *der Anruf*, or phone call in modern German. Do these examples stay with the bumpy ride of the send-up and then the relief of the put-down? I think not; they may have unsettling consequences but these continue. But are we then to be solemn about them? Do they have a "claim" to be a "resistance", and thus to be serious, slightly grandiose even, as they joke?

Well, Derrida has discussed, at some length, what "being serious" is or might be. When J.L. Austin wanted to show *How to do things with words*, he excluded certain types of acts which might seem to be doing things: acts performed by speaking when the words are said by an actor, for instance, or in a poem or in a soliloquy. These cases are precisely literary or related to literary cases.[6] Derrida argues that by excluding them, Austin works with an assumption that the "normal" utterance tends to unequivocal meaning, and thus excludes from the structure of his theory a fact he nevertheless recognizes, that words can always possibly be spoken "not seriously", that there is an "always possibly not seriously" which is a possibility essential to language and not an extrinsic accident. As in the case of *Anruf*, Derrida warns us of what we do not always wish to acknowledge: language brings with it a freight that we do not own or control. The admission is certainly desecurizing on our side: we can't have a single and simple homeland then, in particular a certain response to the relation to Heidegger in these texts, and thus, probably, a single and simple homeland in any Derridean text. But does the notion of "resistance" fit what Barthes was describing?

Can the pathos or the grandiose of "resistance" be avoided?

The example of "the call" above draws out a second consequence, one that goes beyond the borders of security and resistance to security; if we have to work between French and a German word that is allowed to be subjacent, one that is alluded to, not raised to the surface, we may need to be heirs "of more than one tradition" (as the discussions with Moroccan philosophers at Rabat, in1996 suggest),[7] it may be necessary to read Derrida not just with one eye on the language he wrote in, French, but with the other eye on other languages, those of the texts he is working on. That the way Derrida writes matters, and that it matters that the language he writes in is French, is left out of most reckonings, as when challenged Alex Callinicos explicitly did.

Behind this neglect is a kind of time-fold in the reception of Derrida's early work. Before 1990 when it was first published, it couldn't be taken into account by more than a very few that his first book-length work, *Le probléme de la génése dans la philosophie de Husserl*,[8] composed in 1953–4, worked on difficult texts, many on the philosophy of mathematics, several of which at that date lay untranslated in their original German, and even in an archive rather than in print. Composed as a thesis (*diplôme d'études supérieures*) it had been unexceptionally thesis-like in structure and in expression. It had involved both a developmental structure – or at least a genealogical one – *and* a weaving between two different languages, French and German. The enterprise of the then very young philosophy and literature graduate was to track the problem he discerned in Husserl, of how something can start up in a phenomenological structure when its components are by definition always already there. He carries this investigation right through, from the beginning of Husserl's work as a philosopher of mathematics, to the last texts on the nature of the rational mathematical tradition in human culture, the "*Origin of Geometry*".[9] In the brilliant *dissertation*, the reader discovers seeds that will be developed throughout Derrida's later writings: the work of the infinite, the development of contradiction and dialectic into something delayed and differential, and a suspicion of too ready a transforming of philosophical matter into themes. In spite of this, the older Derrida says his younger undertaking has "the imperturbable impudence of a scanner". And it is true that later he will not use chronological exposition at all, at least I can't think of an instance, nor the traditional style of analysis that his thesis clearly shows he has mastered. But what the writing of this dissertation must also have provoked in the young author is something not easily turned into words but perhaps only into works: an awareness that philosophy in German is not the same activity as philosophy in French, and yet that the very movement between the languages throws bridges forward, which by developing commentary on a German text can open out possibilities for a French one.

This movement between languages or movement between different areas of language within one natural language is rarely taken into account, unless to issue a mental rejection slip, and one can see why. It engineers a linking-up of aspects of Derrida's work many, not only Alex Callinicos, would prefer to keep separate: the "arcane" style and the evident public importance of many of the texts, for instance. If these links became active, that would in turn engineer a breaching of the homeland of institutional philosophy by a diffusive force, language, and even more important, the forces of different languages.

So far, so general. This article will act on the comments made by the last speaker from the floor at the "Derrida's Legacy" conference, mentioned above. It will seek to try out links to a philosophical tradition, but links of writing, rather than of themes. It will ask whether what Derrida does, the way he goes on, may be fairly called "irony".

Irony

To return to the article by J.L. Austin: doing something with words can be traced back to a context, usually one where the utterance was enunciated by a person who can say "I", who is speaking seriously and is thus neither quoting, nor speaking in a play, nor as a joke. For we are used to most utterances having a deictic anchoring, to their meaning being traceable back to their originator, and hence to a circumscribable context. Derrida denies this. Language, he argues, is always quotable, whether it is an action or not, and the intention and even the presence of an original utterer cannot suffice to tie its meaning down or exhaust it. Hence and in particular we may not be able to anchor this balloon, philosophy, back home to one language, nor likewise to trace a piece of philosophical discourse back to one person who emitted it, like a speech-bubble back to a character in a cartoon. So in this perspective, Derrida's own language would not always be referable back to a home. Given this, it isn't surprising that Derrida's writing might be ironic on occasions.

Though I would like to contend that the tradition of philosophical irony can help us with the language of his writings, I would hesitate to claim that these are ironic in a traditional sense. For irony is an intentional figure, like allegory, with which it was usually classified – by Quintilian for instance.[10] The classical definition of the figure is to mean one thing with our words, to feel otherwise about the matter "aliud verbis significamus, aliud re sentimus"[11] – the words lead to something other than the speaker's overt meaning. Both allegory and irony relied on this path being open for the listener or reader; both concentrate less on the structure of the figure (the taking of the part for the whole, for instance) than on suggesting characteristics of a representation, the way in which it aims at meaning. But in the classical oratorical tradition, the speaker did intend a pre-existing meaning.

"Allegory" means "other speech", a saying other than what one says. "Irony", and its Greek origin, *eironeia*, are sometimes derived from verbs meaning "to question". Cicero, quoted above, defines irony as not expressing that question, as meaning one thing with our words and feeling otherwise about the matter, A specification of allegory, in fact, in that the other meant by irony was in opposition, or at least in tension with the said. Yet there would exist some kind of alarm that something else was meant: either the delivery or the character of the orator, or the nature of the subject, warns the hearer not to take simply what he is hearing. Irony in this way was important in adversarial rhetoric, for its use implied that you were so convinced of your case, or of the sympathy of the public, that you could use the vocabulary of your opponent, and make an assumption of some weight: that the untruth of this sentence which used the language of your adversaries would become apparent through the saying itself or through the context.

In classical oratory, irony could largely take two forms: hiding what one means (*dissimulatio*) or putting forward as one's own a sense that one does not endorse (*simulatio*). The irony of *dissimulatio*, of hiding one's meaning, is sometimes in these ancient theorists linked with *urbanity*. It looks much like the slight lies, the manoeuvrings and tactical shadow boxing behind the social drive to conformity, to received opinion – much like the ironies which surround Henry James' characters, or Jane Austen's, for that matter. *Simulatio* is much more fraught. In classical as in modern politics, putting forward words whose sense one did not endorse was used by those underdogs, often great ones, who needed to evade the attentions of the powerful, who needed to avoid the latters' *coniectura animi*. Freud's exit from Austria is a modern example of the type – to the Nazi official giving him the permission he needed to leave, but on condition he signed a paper acknowledging Nazi courtesy, and suspecting what would befall others left behind, he handed back the paper by which he agreed that he had been well treated by them, having added the ironic hyperbole, "I can recommend them to anyone".

The ancients distinguished figures as figures of speech and figures of thought. But irony constantly fails to be a figure of speech and becomes a figure of thought; it leaks out beyond any containing in ideas of "style" or "expression" because it cannot be contained in one word, but impresses its tone, its quizzical colouring, on the words and the phrases which are around it. It raises very acutely problems of the limits of its intention, its homeland borders – where does it stop? Flaubert's *Madame Bovary* is the prime modern example, in which apparently ironic passages merge into others where the irony is less clear. In other words, some irony may induce a general unease. In that way it is often presented by reported speech, by what ancient orators called *sermocinatio*, a discussion excerpted from the thought world of the opposite party, and used to characterize it – held up for inspection, so to speak, put into quotation marks. The effect of the figure of thought, this holding up in quote marks, this taking between pincers, worked for the ancient rhetoricians because the pragmatic context made quite clear what the meaning intended was: the orator is engaged in a clearly defined public debate, over against his antagonists. Now Derrida's French often uses the conditional of reported speech, without marking off that speech, and indeed, meaning for him in general cannot be circumscribed by the context of utterance, it doesn't incorporate natural facts about speech, and there is nothing non-semantic in the speaker's situation which determines completely what they mean. So while I would hesitate to claim that Derrida's writing is ironic in a traditional sense, perhaps his is an irony which might be elucidated by relating his work to philosophers who have practised it.

Irony and philosophy

Take Pierre Bayle, for instance; sceptic, speaker up for tolerance, and for a virtue connected with tolerance, scruples and care in the way ideas are put forward. It is not at all clear even now what his religious views were, so hedged around with irony was their expression. This may partly be a sign of his times, a need for caution; partly his own delight in a teasing ogling way of writing, but even so, it is astonishingly difficult to get to his meaning, and that may indeed be ultimately what the meaning is – you must work through argument and counterargument, without ever quite managing to resolve them into the faith of belief, or the convinced doubt of agnosticism.

We all recognize an appropriate home for irony in literature. But should not philosophy say what it means, and mean what it says? There is, much earlier than Bayle, an example that overshadows the whole of Western philosophy: Plato's Socrates. "He who would explain to us when men like Plato spoke in earnest, when in jest or half-jest, what they wrote from conviction and what merely for the sake of the argument, would certainly render us an extraordinary service and contribute greatly to our education." This is Goethe on Socrates.[12] It is Socrates, Gregory Vlastos has suggested, whose influence, whose person, caused a sea-change in what irony is in our culture. This may already have been noted by Quintilian,[13] who says that a man's whole life may be coloured with irony, as was the case with Socrates, called an ironist because he assumed the role of an ignorant man lost in wonder at the wisdom of others. His querying and questioning of his dialogue-partners certainly exposed their confusion; and just as certainly upset people – look what happened to the historical Socrates. His arguments, and this role, were not merely to expose confusion in his interlocutors, though they did that, but were there to explore through undermining certainty. So it isn't perhaps surprising that the earliest uses of *eironeia* in Greek are apparently all derogatory – in Aristophanes in particular, says Vlastos, they mean at the end of the day, saying something you do not mean. And it has been suggested that the ironist, the *eiron*, is in some circumstances for the Greeks a name for a particular role in interaction; it is he who always asks the questions, and never has to answer them, answer for them.[14] Indeed, some of this is shocking even now: of the archetypes in the *Phaedo*, Socrates says that they are things "much babbled about", and in the discussion of the Good in the *Republic*, when it finally appears as "beyond being and essence", an interlocutor, Glaukon, says "By Apollo, what a demonic hyperbole", ironizing the very statement of the good.[15]

The major modern interpreter, Vlastos, puts back together Goethe's puzzle; he integrates the shifting ironic tones through the historical person of Socrates. "He created something new for irony to mean, a new form of life realised in himself."[16] He both professed to have and not to have wisdom, to know and not to know the answers. That makes sense if one understands that one sort of knowledge is being disclaimed, but another one implied. So that, according to Vlastos, Socrates moves the meaning of the term *eiron* from "deceitful" to something else.

For what Socrates is building on is the fact that in almost everything we say we put a burden of interpretation on our hearer. When we speak a sentence we do not add a gloss on how it should be read – and any way, this wouldn't work, because it would be an infinite regress. (p. 44).

In this modern interpretation of Socrates, the personality provides a solution to his irony, to ensure that beyond the displacement operated in the hearers and the discomfort in us the readers, there is a maieutics, an educational purpose. In this interpretation, we are led forward by someone who *does* possess some kind of *key*, someone whose irony is that of overview.

Such has not always been the way of reading Plato's Socrates. Not much later than Goethe, but closer to the German romantics, to their view of irony and to Hegel, Kierkegaard thought differently. Platonic irony for him has to stay disquieting, remain unresolved:

> It is the nature of irony never to unmask itself – there is something deterring about irony, it likewise has something extraordinarily seductive and fascinating. Its masquerading and mysteriousness, the *telegraphic communication* it prompts because an ironist always has to be understood at a distance, the infinite sympathy it presupposes, the fleeting but indescribable instant of understanding that is immediately superseded by the anxiety of misunderstanding. All this holds one prisoner in an inextricable band.[17]

Vlastos, by the way, dismisses such a view as the "vagaries of a romantic novella", and obviously his genealogy is right; Kierkegaard's view *is* related to notions of Romantic irony. Kierkegaard in fact distinguishes two ironies, as he distinguishes two dialectics in Plato: there is irony that is a mere stimulus for thought, and there is the irony which is itself the aim towards which the ironist is striving.

Friedrich Schlegel, in a famous note, said of the ironist: "There lives in them a really transcendental Bouffonerie. In the inside, there is the mood, which oversees everything, art, virtue or genius; on the outside, in the presentation of the mimic manner there is the usual good old Italian clown".[18] The process is not constrained, but transcendental. It involves hovering over endlessly exfoliating layers of consciousness. Among some of the German romantics, irony took on a pattern like some uncontrollable dialectical process – Hegel was deeply antagonistic to it, calling it a "fear of reality". Indeed for Tieck, it has been said that "irony assists the self-dissolution of 'common reality'".[19] Comparable to a process of disillusion, appearance when viewed ironically shows its own negativity. It is not a harnessed negativity, as it will be in Hegel. Schlegel, in spite of a process of irony which treats nothing as final but dissolves it further, actually said "Irony is the form of the paradox" and his contemporaries, be it noted, complained about his incomprehensibility. There is a "transcendental" hovering – transcendental "bouffonerie" – moving between opposite poles which are allowed to relativize each other by being ironized. Yet the consciousness as it moves is always transcendental.

Derrida has suggested again and again that meaning is not controllable completely; that it goes well beyond what is conscious, or bound by the individual consciousness; that it inevitably and irreducibly brings with it reachings-out or "commitments" – to use the English philosopher, Tom Baldwin's term – to other meanings which aren't present to consciousness. But Kierkegaard's analogy of the telegraph is highly relevant to Derrida, and to the telephones which appear at a certain point in his writings, for it suggests a transfer across distance, often anxious and incomplete. There is then no totality of meaning, and hence no "ironic totality", to use Kierkegaard's phrase. The speaker is *always* quartered into language, he or she is a nodal point in a complex web of meaning that they don't control or own. So can this be called "irony"? Mustn't "irony" be something yet again, something more sporadic, more particularized? Or, if all language is like this, how can one say of Derrida in particular that his writing is ironic?

Derridean irony?

In some Derridean texts, no one voice is speaking and claiming transcendence over what is said, and thus there is no totality except that created by the covers of a volume (and even then). Take *Glas*, for example, an extraordinary work written on the death of his father. The title means "knell", death knell. The text appears at first to be a collage of quotations. It is composed in two columns, each of which contains a very extended quotation; into each column are let "hanging paragraphs" of commentary or quotation. This arcane and highly original form is not wilful – it has been related for instance to the rabbinic tradition of commentary. One column is "on" Jean Genet, long-term prisoner, homosexual and writer; it sits opposite a column on Hegelian dialectic, and on Hegel, especially on his view of the family and of Judaism. The columns "cross talk", to use a term from telecommunications, they cut across each other, there is interference. But the textual set-up consciously puts into practice, or reinvents, an eighteenth-century game or "cross-reading", reading across columns or batches of newspapers, instead of down the columns. There is in fact an OED article, "cross reading" and some "cross-readings" were actually published in London in the late eighteenth century, and were imitated by the German aphorist Lichtenberg; they link up with collage techniques used both in painting and in poetry in the twentieth century.

Nor does there seem to be any controlling voice in the article called "Dissemination", written as a review of a difficult novel by Philippe Sollers (the husband of Julia Kristeva), where the pronouns change and swerve, as if miming the changes in pronouns of the novel. This is a kind of parody, an approving parody, *parodos*, a path which goes alongside, to bend the etymology back to its first sense in Greek. But it is not just this: the whole article discusses the relation of the self to language, as does Sollers' novel, it brings up the problem of who the YOU, the WE and the I of the novel are, it enacts the question of whether every utterance can be traced to a source, tied down, like the words in a comic strip balloon, to an extra-linguistic source who once could have said "I" – the problem raised earlier apropos J.L. Austin.

> Un langage a précédé ma présence à moi-mîme. Plus vieille que la concience, que le spectateur, anterieure à toute assistance, un phrase "vous" attendait, vous regarde, vous observe, veille sur vous, vous concerne de toute part. Toujours une phrase s'est déjà scellée quelque part qui vous attend où vous croyez frayer un espace vierge.[20]

This is a very accurate account of the relation to language in Sollers' novel, but it spreads wider, becoming a possible version of those commitments to other meanings not present to awareness, in Tom Baldwin's formulation mentioned earlier. So in this case there is certainly not a voice, bearing what is said, and whom one could interpret as implying the opposite, or otherwise than what is said. In that way, what goes on can't be compared to Voltairean irony, for instance.

Syntactic irony

In texts like *Glas*, or "Dissemination", in a sense the genre itself allows for ironic contrast; it takes contrasts in charge as it does for instance in Diderot's *Rameau's Nephew*. But one must also look at the microstructures in Derrida's writing, at what goes on in some texts at the level of text. (Certain texts, once again, for some are much more plain sailing and plain speaking than others.) His interest in words with antithetical meanings has been much commented on: *pharmakon*, for instance, which means "drug" in ancient Greek, and therefore both "poison" and "medicine". He shows in the article "Plato's pharmacy" how both senses of the word function in the Platonic text. However, it has been much less remarked that Derrida develops *syntactic* double meanings, what might be called *syntactic* irony. This works a destabilizing effect on *syntax* rather than on semantics, on *relations* rather than on meanings, on the syntactic status, on the syntactic relation of words rather than on the individual word itself.

An example: he uses the homophony between "entre", the French preposition meaning "between", and the noun "antre", a cave.[21] In other words, he plays off what is technically a syncategoreme, expressing a relation and not a generic idea, and a philosophical *locus classicus*, the Platonic cave. In yet other words, a relation, a joining word, is being substituted for a place; a link is replacing a defined item or a unit. And commenting on a Mallarmé text, Derrida actually says that its peculiar swinging effect is produced by the syntax, which places the "entre", the "between", so that the suspension is operated by the way the words are placed and not by the words' content, their meaning. An accurate account of Mallarmé's prose. But it also points to effects in Derrida's own writing and my argument is that this is a making something new of the figure of irony. Irony because this oscillation in meaning in Mallarmé and in patches of Derrida's own writing has ironic effect, yes, but it is NOT one that is related to a human mind which has an ironic overview, a *transcendental bouffonerie* to use Friedrich Schlegel's phrase. On the contrary, it works off syntactic units which join together in unstable ways. It works in fact in provisional and unpredictable fashion.

For this word-play serves with Derrida, not to focus a double meaning and to confine it within a single word, as one can argue puns do, but to disperse it. The words played on stop functioning as foci, as centres, and start functioning as junction points. They don't assemble, they act like multiple dispatchers. Moreover, the dispatching may take on occasion an even more disturbing form still. A syntactic form. In his prose, in certain works, what one can't call word-play, but might call "two-way" phrases turn up quite readily. These "two-way" phrases are often barely translatable, exploiting to the full resources of one natural language, of *French*. Take, for example, the phrase Derrida uses of a Kantian argument: "faire l'économie du saut".[22] This could mean both "to economize on the jump" and also something like "to go through the hoop of the jump", "to go through the motions of the jump" (in Dominic Willsdon's words, to "do the jump") which suggests that by embedding contradiction in a circuit, Kant ultimately does without it. Such phrases are poised on the page, swinging in relation to the sentences adjacent to them, hijacking other grammatical functions, leaving the reader aghast and amused. The swings in ways of reading the phrase ripple suspicion around them, but the irony is local, not spread all over; it involves local insecurities and instabilities, not a constantly ironic tone. It is certainly not transcendental.

Let's be quite sure: the run of many Derridean texts *does* contain much more conventional ways of arguing. But this irony I am speaking of, when it occurs, works by turning units into relations, and semantic items into syntactical ones. And unsettles us with a meaning which is not quite present, with which we are not at home. Is this mere "come and get me", mere teasing? I think not. To quote the same letter of Roland Barthes once more: "Il y a enfin dans son travail quelque chose de tu, qui est fascinant: sa solitude vient de ce qu'il va dire".[23] In this incredibly and typically perspicacious remark, Barthes points to something very much less visible then than now: the messianic side of Derrida's writings, the extent to which he is not enrobing in words something already there, but pulling the thought down into the seas of language, reaching out to the barely anticipated but not-already-formulated. In this writing, the absent is the future of what he will say.[24]

So it looks as if some of Derrida's writings have developed, locally, partially and provisionally a considerable ironic force. But not always, not all the time. The language itself seems to be being ironic, rather than there being an author, a source behind it controlling what is going on. Such writing fits with the view of language not as controlled in its meaning by a conscious intention which is Derrida's. But is that then being serious? Perhaps there are more ways of "being serious" than most of us dream of.

A P.S. to this: you will have noted how important the *actual text* is in evaluating this kind of irony – it may be very largely lost, or at least strangely travestied in translation. What language you read Derrida in makes a difference to what you are reading. That is a situation familiar to students of literature. Does this matter in the present case? What does it mean for philosophy?

Let us remind ourselves:

- "Sans doute le sens de l'être n'est-il pas le mot " être " ni le concept d'être, Heidegger le rappelle sans cesse. Mais comme ce sens n'est rien hors du langage et du langage de mots, il est lié, sinon à tel ou tel mot, à tel ou tel systéme de langues (concesso non dato) du moins à la possibilité du mot en général".[25] The concession refused by Derrida here à propos Heidegger is crucial, and operates far more widely: philosophy is strung by a contradictory tension, between its desire for universality, or globalization in our current vocabulary and its inevitable relation to the particular language in which it is expressed, indeed to the particular state of the particular language at the particular time at which it is expressed. Yet philosophy has often been the "la thése de la traductibilite en un certain sens du concept de traduction, c'est à dire la traduction comme transport, non pas comme " herméneia " active, poétique, productrice, transforma-trice, mais transport d'un sens univoque, ou en tout cas d'une plurivocité maîtrisable, dans un autre élément linguistique".[26] For any meaning to be shared, there has to be a tendency to univocity; for any meaning to be shared, it has to be expressed in an actual language which of itself pulls and disseminates into plurivocity. We balance between the two.[27]

- So there emerges a possible reason for what I am trying out as "irony": that it, signals a kind of wobble between univocity and plurivocity, between sharing of meaning and searching for meaning. A symptom of this might be Derrida's constant use of terms from the language of the writer commented on, in other words, the constant hinting at the problem of translation, and indeed, in his professional life, the not inconsiderable time he spent working with translators and supporting translation as an activity. We can't climb out of the particular language we are speaking, writing, thinking in, just as we can't climb out of language in general. We can go ex-directory, we can not carry a portable telephone, but we can't go ex-language, either generally, or in particular. Yet by cutting across different languages, or within one language by occasionally ironizing, we can become aware of what the tensions and shapes are in the languages we do use, aware of what tenses and shapes us.

One of Derrida's most beautiful and most difficult texts, *Le monolinguisme de l'autre*, examines, probes and prods this discomfort. In it he speaks of the "otherwhere" towards which he was in advance ex-ported – the keeping open of what can't be anticipated. It is a desire without horizon, he says, "là où tendu vers ce qui se donne à venir, je sais enfin ne plus devoir discerner entre la promesse et la terreur".[28] For those who have seen that horizon move, a keeping of the self open to death.

Bibliography

Roland Barthes 1994 *Euvres complétes*, édition établie et présentée par Eric Marty. Paris: Editions du Seuil, 2 vols.

Derrida, Jacques 1962 [Husserl] *L'origine de la géométrie*, traduction et introduction par Jacques Derrida. Paris: PUF.

— 1967 *De la Grammatologie*. Paris: Editions de Minuit.

— 1972 *Marges*. Paris: Editions de Minuit.

— 1974 *Of Grammatologie*, corrected edition, trans. Gyatri Chakravorty Spivak, 1997. Baltimore and London: Johns Hopkins University Press.

— 1980 *La Carte postale de Socrate à Freud et au-delà*. Paris: Aubier-Flammarion.

— 1982 *L'oreille de l'autre: otobiographies, transferts, traductions*. Textes et débats avec Jacques Derrida, sous la direction de Claude Lévesque et Christie V. McDonald. Montréal: VLB éditeur. P. 185.

— 1988 *The Ear of the Other: Otobiographies, transference, translation*: texts and discussions with Jacques Derrida, translated by P. Kamuf and A Ronell. Lincoln NE: University of Nebraska Press.

— 1990 *Le probléme de la génese dans la philosophie de Husserl*. Paris: PUF, a thesis worked on in the academic year 1953–4, and not published until 1990.

— 1996 *Le Monolinguisme de l'autre*. Paris: Galilée.

— 1998 *Monolingualism of the Other; or, The Prosthesis of Origin*, translated by Patrick Mensah. Stanford: Stanford University Press.

— 1998 "Fidelité à plus d'un. Mériter d'hériter où la généalogie fait défaut", *Cahiers intersignes* [Editions Toubkal et Editions de l'Aube], *Idiomes, deconstructions. Rencontres de Rabat avec Jacques Derrida*, no. 13, automne 1998, pp. 221–65.

— 2004 *The Problem of Genesis in Husserl's Philosophy*. Translated by M. Hobson. Chicago: The University of Chicago Press.

Gasché, Rodolphe 1986 *The Tain of the Mirror*. Cambridge: Harvard University Press.

Lausberg, Heinrich 1960 *Handbuch der literarisechen Rhetorik*. M.nchen: Max Hueber Verlag.

Weber, Samuel 1984 The debts of deconstruction and other, related assumptions, in J.S. Smith and W. Kerrigan (eds), *Taking Chances: Derrida, Psychoanalysis and Literature*. Baltimore, MD and London: Johns Hopkins University Press.

Notes

1. *L'oreille de l'autre: otobiographies, transferts, traductions*. Textes et débats avec Jacques Derrida, sous la direction de Claude Lévesque et Christie V. McDonald, 1982. Montréal: VLB éditeur. P. 185. *The Ear of the Other: Otobiographies, transference, translation*: texts and discussions with Jacques Derrida, translated by P. Kamuf and A. Ronell, 1988. Lincoln NE: University of Nebraska Press. P. 140.
2. "A sort of incessant deterioration of our intellectual comfort"; "in which his writing is violent, poetical", in Roland Barthes, *Euvres complétes*, édition établie et présentée par Eric Marty, 1994. Paris: Editions du Seuil, 2 vols. Vol. II, p. 1417. Letter dated 21 March 1972, a reply refusing the request for an article for the Derrida special number of the journal *Les Lettres françaises*.
3. Kant, on Hume.
4. See *La Carte postale de Socrate à Freud et au-delà*, "Spéculer – Sur 'Freud'", section 2.
5. S. Weber, "The debts of deconstruction and other, related assumptions", in J.S. Smith and W. Kerrigan (eds), *Taking Chances: Derrida, Psychoanalysis and Literature*, 1984. Baltimore, MD and London: Johns Hopkins University Press. Pp. 33–65.
6. See Jacques Derrida "Fidelité à plus d'un. Mériter d'hériter où la généalogie fait défaut", *Cahiers intersignes* [Editions Toubkal et Editions de l'Aube], *Idiomes, deconstructions. Rencontres de Rabat avec Jacques Derrida*, no. 13, automne 1998, pp. 221–65. "Signature, événement, contexte", in Derrida, *Marges*, 1972. Paris: Editions de Minuit.

   It is important to realize that Derrida would only very rarely write about texts he had no sympathy with, and that it was because he was deeply interested in aspects of Austin's book that he commented on and disagreed with it.
7. See note 22.
8. *Le probléme de la génése dans la philosophie de Husserl*, 1990. Paris: PUF, a thesis worked on in the academic year 1953–4, and not published until 1990. Translated by M. Hobson, *The Problem of Genesis in Husserl's Philosophy*, 2004. Chicago: The University of Chicago Press.
9. Translated by Derrida and published with an introduction in 1962: *L'origine de la géomtétrie*, traduction et introduction par Jacques Derrida. Paris: PUF.
10. Quintilian, *Institutiones OratoriÊ* (1st century AD), VIII, 6, 44.
11. Cicero, *Pro Ligario*, quoted from Heinrich Lausberg, *Handbuch der literarisechen Rhetorik*, 1960. München: Max Hueber Verlag.
12. Quoted by Paul Friedlander, *Plato*, translated from the German by Hans Meyerhoff, 1958–69. NY: Harper and Row, 3 vols, vol. I, p. 137, quoting from Goethe, "Plato als Mitgenosse einer Christischen Offenbarung", 1796.
13. Quintilian, *Institutiones Oratoriæ*, VI, 2, 15.
14. Michel Narcy, *Le philosophe et son double: un commentaire de l'Euthydéme de Platon*, 1984. Paris: Vrin. Cf. Thrasymachos, in the first book of the *Republic*, who shouts at Socrates, in tones that may be familiar to some of us: "express clearly and precisely whatever you say. For I won't take from you any such drivel as that", Plato, *Republic*, Loeb translation by Paul Shorey, [1930]. 336 D.

15. *Republic*, 509 C. My translation.

16. Gregory Vlastos, *Socrates; Ironist and Moral Philosopher*, 1991. Ithaca: Cornell. P. 29.

17. Søren Kierkegaard, *The Concept of Irony, with continual reference to Socrates*, ed. and trans. by HV Hong and EH Hong, 1989, p. 48. Princeton, New Jersey: Princeton University Press.

18. F. Schlegel, 1798, quoted by Ingrid Strohschneider-Kohrs, *Die romantische Ironie in Theorie und Gestaltung*, 1960, p. 18. Tübingen: M. Niemeyer, Schlegel claims that philosophy is the true home of irony. I owe gratitude to Jeremy Adler for help in understanding the German romantics' notion of irony.

19. "Iron helps the process of self-dissolution of 'common reality'. It is, in Tieck's eyes, the incessant and inconsistent nature of finitude itself which convinces us of its vanity and at the same time directs us to the Absolute" (my translation); "Die Ironie assistiert dem Selbstauflösungsprozeß der 'gemeinen Wirklichkcit'. Es ist, in Tiecks Augen, die Unhaltbarkeit und der Unbestand der Endlichkeit selbst, die uns gleichzeitig von derene Eitelkeit überzeuge und ans Absolute verweisen", Manfred Frank, commentary on *Phantasus*, in *Schriften*, vol. 6, 1985, p. 1193. Frankfurt am Main: Deutscher Klassiker Verlag.

20. *La Dissémination*, 1972, pp. 378–79. Paris: Aux Editions le Seuil. *Dissemination*, translated by Barbara Johnson, 1981. London: Athlone Press, p. 340: "My own presence to myself has been preceded by language. Older than consciousness, older than the spectator, prior to any attendance, a sentence awaits 'you', looks at you, observes you watches over you and regards you from every side. There is always a sentence that has already been sealed somewhere waiting for you where you think you are opening up some virgin territory", p. 340.

21. *Dissémination*, p. 249; trans. p. 220.

22. *Glas*, 1974, p. 242. Paris: Galilée. *Glas*, translated by J.P. Leavey and R. Rand 1986, p. 216a. Lincoln NE: University of Nebraska Press.

23. "In the end there is in his work something unsaid [*quelque chose de tu*], which is fascinating: his loneliness comes from what he is going to say".

24. "Je fais passer dans le discours logique quelque chose qui ne l'est pas. J'anticipe encore le non-anticipatable", Jacques Derrida "Fidelité à plus d'un. Mériter d'hériter où la généalogie fait défaut", *Cahiers intersignes* [Editions Toubkal et Editions de l'Aube], *Idiomes, deconstructions. Rencontres de Rabat avec Jacques Derrida*, no. 13, automne 1998, p. 248. "I cause to pass into logical discourse something which isn't. I anticipate once more the non-anticipatable".

25. *De la Grammatologie*, 1967, Paris: Editions de Minuit, p. 34. "But as that sense is nothing outside of language and the language of words, It is tied, if not to a particular word or to a particular system of language (concesso non dato), at lease to the possibility of the word in general", *Of Grammatologie*, [1967], corrected edition, trans. Gyatri Chakravorty Spivak, [1974], 1997. Baltimore and London: Johns Hopkins University Press, p. 21.

26. *L'oreille de l'autre*, see fn. 1, p. 185; "When I said that philosophy was the thesis of translatability, I meant it not in the sense of translation as an active, poetic, productive, transformative 'hermeneia', but rather in the sense of the transport of a univocal meaning, or in any case, of a controllable plurivocality, into another linguistic element", translation, p. 140.

27. See the work of Rodolphe Gasché, e.g. *The Tain of the Mirror*, Harvard, 1986, but many other articles, for a deep examination of this.

28. *Le Monolinguisme de l'autre*, 1996, p. 136. Paris: Galilée. "There where, striving for what is given to come, I finally know how not to have to distinguish any longer between promise and terror", *Monolingualism of the Other; or, The Prosthesis of Origin*, translated by Patrick Mensah, 1998, p. 73. Stanford: Stanford University Press

11 Presence, truth and authenticity

Thomas Baldwin

In 1991, prompted by intellectual curiosity, I ran a graduate seminar on some of Derrida's early writings at Cambridge where I was then a lecturer in the Philosophy Faculty. The seminar went well and the students and I felt that we had found it rewarding, as well as challenging, to work through *Speech and Phenomena*[1] and *Of Grammatology*.[2] So when the news emerged early in 1992 that the university proposed to award an honorary degree to Derrida, following his nomination for this award by Gillian Beer, a distinguished Professor of English, I was pleased – but also a little surprised since it would have seemed sensible to consult the Philosophy Faculty about the proposed award. Among others, however, in both the English and the Philosophy Faculties, the reaction was not surprising but outrageous and there followed the notorious 'Derrida affair'. The university's proposal was formally challenged in a way which necessitated a vote among Cambridge academics on the issue; and in the run-up to the vote there was an extraordinary public debate about Derrida's work in which several distinguished philosophers with no knowledge of Derrida's writings denounced him as an intellectual charlatan. Fortunately for Cambridge's reputation, a substantial majority of its academics were not swayed by the vituperative critical rhetoric directed at Derrida and listened instead to the case made by those who supported the proposed award.

So what was it about Derrida's philosophy that excited so much hostility? The accusation was similar to that which Socrates faced, that he was corrupting the youth by propounding a sceptical nihilism about truth and value. It is this accusation that I want to examine here, so that one can understand both why it arises and why it is misplaced.

In the book which remains his most important, *Of Grammatology* (1967), Derrida provides the following account of his 'final intention':

> To make enigmatic what one thinks one understands by the words 'proximity', 'immediacy', 'presence' (the proximate [*proche*], the own [*propre*], and the pre- of presence), is my final intention in this book. This deconstruction of presence accomplishes itself through the deconstruction of consciousness, and therefore through the irreducible notion of the trace (*Spur*), as it appears in both Nietzschean and Freudian discourse. (p. 70)

One may well find this statement itself somewhat 'enigmatic'; in order to elucidate it, I shall concentrate on the phrase 'deconstruction of presence'. Derrida indicates the meaning of his talk of 'presence' when he writes that presence 'orders all objectivity of the object and all relations of knowledge' (p. 57). So, if presence is the mark of objectivity, one might well suppose that the 'deconstruction of presence' is the rejection of the possibility of knowledge of objective truth. That would seem to come close to the sceptical nihilism of which he is accused. But there is an alternative hypothesis, namely that Derrida seeks only to call into question and then correct one traditional but deeply rooted way of thinking about objectivity.

At the start of *Of Grammatology* (p. 12) Derrida mentions several ways in which 'logocentric' conceptions of the 'meaning of being as presence' have been developed, including:

> presence of the thing to sight as 'eidos' (form),
> presence as substance/essence/existence,
> self-presence of the cogito,
> consciousness.

What makes these conceptions of being as presence seems to be the fact that they aim to provide an account of objective knowledge on the foundation of some immediate intuitive relationship between a person and something else whose significance is made manifest to her through this intuitive relationship and which enables her to go on to develop an objective understanding of the world. Derrida's first example – 'presence of the thing to the sight as "eidos" (form)' – is clearly intended to remind the reader of Plato's theory of forms, and this example readily fits the model. The next example seems intended to remind the reader of Aristotle's conception of substance and his theory of science as based on knowledge of the essences of things. Derrida's allusion to it here seems to involve the presumption that, for Aristotle, we have intuitive knowledge of the essences of things; I doubt myself if this is an appropriate way to interpret Aristotle, but this is not the place to argue the point. The next case is, however, straightforward; for here we are clearly reminded of Descartes and the way in which through consciousness of our own thoughts we are supposed to be able to find a foundation for knowledge of the world. Finally, the mention of 'consciousness' by itself seems to be a reference to Husserl, who held that through the phenomenological method we are able to gain an immediate insight into the structure of our own consciousness and thereby grasp the foundations for the acts through which meaning is given to experience in such a way that objective knowledge is possible.

Thus each of these cases, except, arguably, that of Aristotle, involves a model of understanding whereby the knowing subject is presented immediately with an object that is thereby understood for what it is. So the logocentric conception of presence is one according to which the possibility of objective knowledge is thought to be founded on the immediate cognitive presence of an object to a subject. And lest anyone imagines that Derrida is here tilting only at philosophical doctrines which are either long dead or alien to our own tradition, it is worth noting that the conception of knowledge by acquaintance developed by Bertrand Russell in his immensely influential book *The Problems of Philosophy* (1911) provided a classic formulation of a position of this kind for twentieth-century British philosophy.

So what might it be it to 'deconstruct' presence so understood? I take deconstruction to be more a matter of '*re*construction' than is suggested by its verbal similarity with 'destruction'. For, as practised by Derrida, deconstruction is typically a reconceptualisation of some phenomenon in the light of a more complex understanding of its structure and relationships. Although it starts from the denial that some phenomenon is as it has been supposed to be, the aim is to achieve a better understanding of it, usually by seeing how it is in fact similar to or dependent upon something which has traditionally been unfavourably contrasted with it. Hence deconstruction is best thought of as the deconstruction of a distinction rather than of a single type of phenomenon, and the 'deconstruction of presence' turns out to be a deconstruction of the distinction between presence and absence.

A good example comes from Derrida's early work in which he seeks to deconstruct the romantic conception of speech as a privileged and immediately meaningful expression by a speaker of her thoughts and feelings. On this account of the matter speech is contrasted with writing, which is conceived as a derivative phenomenon, a public record of speech that is only indirectly connected with thought and feeling via a system of repeatable signs for spoken words. Derrida argues that once one considers what makes meaningful speech possible, one is led to recognise that it crucially depends on the use of words on a variety of occasions by a variety of speakers. Hence, he infers that speech cannot have the kind of immediate meaning characteristic of the romantic conception of it; instead, just like writing, it depends on a speaker conforming to the general practice of using language which is subject to rules that are not of the speaker's own making. Thus although Derrida does not of course deny that there are significant differences between speech and writing, his deconstruction of this distinction aims to suggest that these phenomena are not as different as one might think, and that we get a better understanding of speech by thinking of it as essentially similar to writing, which obviously depends on the use of repeatable signs, than by thinking of it as an immediate and self-sufficient expression of thought.

For Derrida the case of speech and writing is a model for other cases of deconstruction, such as deconstructing the traditional distinction between mind and body. As with speech, 'mind', the capacity for self-conscious thought, has traditionally been regarded as something which provides each of us with a sense of our own identity, and this leads to the thought that our body is not something of a similar value, that it is just a natural phenomenon on which we are causally dependent but which is not integrated into our sense of our own identity. So Derrida's deconstruction of this distinction is intended to lead to a reconceptualisation of the mind via a critical re-evaluation of its relationship with the body; and he argues that once one appreciates the preconditions for the role of meaning in the articulation of thoughts and feelings, one will see that mental phenomena cannot be sharply divorced from bodily phenomena. For him, as the passage cited earlier from *Of Grammatology* (p. 70) indicates, the fundamental concept here is that of a 'trace'; it is the existence of networks of traces that provide the meaningful contents of thoughts and feelings. Just what Derrida means by 'traces' is obscure; he thinks of them as phenomena that are antecedent to the mind/body distinction. But we can approximate his position by drawing on the previous discussion of speech as the expression of thought to reiterate that the achievement of meaning, and thus thought, is essentially achieved by means of bodily speech-acts which involve the use of repeatable gestures and vocalisations.

Another case which is prominent in the latter half of *Of Grammatology* concerns the distinction between nature and culture, especially as it is deployed by Rousseau. For Rousseau, nature is a privileged source of meaning and value while culture is conceived as a system of rule-governed institutions in which the spontaneous meanings of our gestures are lost and our sympathetic feelings become corrupted by competitive *amour propre*. And yet, as Derrida observes, as soon as Rousseau writes about natural feelings and practices, institutions and rules are tacitly presupposed in the 'discourse' through which these natural forms of life are articulated and expressed. Derrida formulates this point in his own, characteristic, idioms which it is worth quoting briefly:

> What does Rousseau say without saying, see without seeing? That substitution has always already begun; that imitation, principle of art, has always already interrupted natural plenitude; that, having to be a *discourse*, it has always already broached presence in differance; that in Nature it is always that which supplies Nature's lack, a voice that is substituted for the voice of Nature. (p. 215)

So, again, the conclusion is that the distinction between nature and culture needs to be deconstructed, that is to say reconceptualised, without being altogether obliterated. We need to locate the distinction within the space of meaningful discourse in which there are rules permitting 'substitutions' of equivalent signs instead of perpetuating the illusory ideal of a form of life that has not shared rule-governed practices at all.

Whatever one thinks about Derrida's discussion of these particular cases, it should, I think, be reasonably clear now what, in outline, his 'deconstruction of presence' will involve. The aim will be to provide a better way of thinking about 'presence', i.e. the kind of meaningful experience of the world which makes knowledge of it possible, by elucidating the way in which such experience makes reference to phenomena that are not currently being experienced by the subject. Derrida does not seek to deny the possibility, indeed the importance of 'presence', conceived simply as our experience of things; what is rejected is the 'logocentric' conception of presence as an immediate and self-sufficient source of meaning and truth which is distinctively privileged in comparison with 'absence', our relationships to things which are not currently being experienced. Instead, once the internal relationship between presence and absence is properly understood, it will become clear that our experience of the world needs to be understood in the context of a much more complex network of relationships involving things which are 'absent'. So if anything is fundamental here, it is not presence by itself but the 'play' of presence and absence.

Derrida's arguments for this thesis build on the considerations already introduced. Again, although he takes the notion of a 'trace' to be fundamental, we can set this to one side and concentrate on the concept 'differance' which is employed in the passage quoted above concerning Rousseau. For meaningful experience exemplifies 'differance' and by understanding what Derrida has in mind here we will be able to understand how it involves a play of presence and absence. Derrida coins the term 'differance' in order to label the conjunction of two theses involving two different kinds of 'différence' (as expressed in French) which are, he argues, together central to the possibility of meaning. One thesis draws on Saussure's work and affirms that we use words not to label objects and properties that can be identified by themselves but to mark salient points within a network of connected but different features that form an essential context for understanding. Thus colour words pick out, not isolated colours, but segments of the spectrum and to understand what colour 'red' is, is to understand how it differs from other colours. Similarly to understand what a 'table' is, one has to understand how it belongs in the familiar domestic environment which is composed of different items of furniture; and so on. The second thesis draws on the fact that in French (but not English) the verb 'différer' means not only, as we say, to differ but also to defer, in a temporal sense. So 'différence' also means deferral, and Derrida uses this aspect of its meaning to express the fact that meaning something by a speech-act on one occasion depends on the possibility of using the same words, often in different sentences, on other different occasions. For what one means by the words one utters on one occasion is dependent on the use of the same words on other occasions, typically by other speakers:

> A sign is never an event, if by event we mean an irreplaceable and irreversible empirical particular. A sign that would take place but 'once' would not be a sign.... <A phoneme or grapheme> can function as a

sign only if a formal identity enables it to be issued again and to be recognised. (*Speech and Phenomena*, p. 50)

Thus where the first thesis affirms that the meaning of a word is a matter of its use to identify a distinguishable feature ('a difference') within a broad synchronic context of related features; the second thesis affirms that meaning is dependent on the diachronic context of the 'deferred' use of the word on different occasions by different speakers.

It is these two connected theses that Derrida brings together in his conception of meaning as 'differance'. It follows from this that meanings cannot be fixed simply by the content of a speaker's 'present' state of consciousness; they are always dependent on elements that are 'absent' – both on features of the world that are absent from the speaker's current situation but help to give significance to that aspect which the speaker seeks to identify, and on other speakers, speaking at other times, who use the same words. It does not follow that meaning, so far from being a matter of presence, is altogether dictated by what is absent. For that would imply that what is meant here and now is uniquely determined by what has been said by the use of the same words in the past, and that the relevant feature of the speaker's context can be uniquely determined by the network of relationships within that context. But neither of these claims is correct. What undermines the first is the fact that particular situations are always unique, and thus that the application of past practice to new cases is bound to be potentially indeterminate in some respects; although meaning is essentially 'deferential' it is equally a matter of setting new precedents.[3] And the second point is equally undermined by the familiar point that singular identity is never just a matter of a pattern of general similarities and differences, for patterns are inherently repeatable. So meaning, and thus experience, feeling and thought, involves the speaker's present situation along with features and practices that are absent; it depends, therefore, on the interplay between presence and absence.

If this line of thought is correct, it undermines the logocentric conception of presence and thus the foundationalist account of objective truth and knowledge that relies on some form of presence as a foundation. This conclusion is not novel: it was affirmed in the 1870s through a similar line of reasoning by the great American pragmatist philosopher C. S. Peirce[4] (it is worth noting that Peirce is, to the best of my knowledge, the only American philosopher whom Derrida quotes with approval, though not in fact on this point). The issue that now arises is whether this conclusion undermines the possibility of objectivity itself. This was certainly not Peirce's view: he famously held that objective truth requires, not an absolute foundation, but an absolute goal, since it is to be identified as 'that opinion which is fated to be ultimately agreed by all who investigate'. Most contemporary philosophers hold that this position is unattractive, since it relies on the speculative ideal of an 'ultimate agreement'. Instead they argue that objectivity requires the possibility of gaining external confirmation of one's beliefs and that this is achieved through intersubjective agreement with those whose criticisms and corrections of our own beliefs we acknowledge to be justified. Donald Davidson, the great American philosopher whose recent death has more or less coincided with that of Derrida, captured this conception of objectivity nicely by suggesting that we think of it as the outcome a process of triangulation in which as thinkers we seek to connect our own beliefs both to the world and to the beliefs of others.[5]

What, however, about Derrida himself? Did he take the view that without a logocentric foundation in presence the very idea of knowledge of objective truth should be abandoned? It has to be acknowledged, I think, that in some of his remarks in *Of Grammatology* he seems to make this suggestion. For example, when he is writing about the belief that speech is not subject to mundane conditions of differance and can be an immediate vehicle of meaning he suggests that a belief of this kind, although illusory, is essential to 'the very idea of truth':

> This experience of the effacement of the signifier in the voice is not merely one illusion among many – since it is the condition of the very idea of truth. (*Of Grammatology*, p. 20)

If this were indeed all that Derrida had to say on this matter, then it would be right to conclude that he was indeed a sceptic about objective truth. That would not, in my judgement, be a reason for repudiating the insights of his conception of meaning as differance; it would just be a reason for thinking that he had drawn from the wrong conclusions from it, from his 'deconstruction of presence'. For it is a mistake to hold that objective truth is an inherently logocentric concept.

Once one looks to Derrida's later writings, however, one finds an emphatic repudiation of this mistaken view:

> I have never put such concepts as truth, reference and the stability of interpretive contexts radically into question if 'putting radically into question' means contesting that there *are* and that there *should be* truth, reference, and stable contexts of interpretation. I have – but this is something entirely different – posed questions that I hope are radical concerning the possibility of these things, of these values, of these norms, of this stability (which by essence is always provisional and finite). (*Limited Inc*,[6] p. 150)

I think we should take Derrida at his word here and accept that he never intended to 'put such concepts as truth, reference and the stability of interpretive contexts radically into question'. But there does now arise the question as to what he was trying to do in passages such as that quoted above from *Of Grammatology*. My suggestion is that we can make sense of the dialectic here by distinguishing objective truth, which is truth from no special point of view or perspective (and which can therefore be contrasted with perspectival 'subjective' truths), from 'absolute' truth, conceived as a kind of truth that is subject to no conditions at all. With this distinction in place we can allow that objective truth does not require absolute truth: objective truths are those whose truth is available to any thinker. But it does not follow that they are absolute truths, since it may be that the possibility of thinking them has some presuppositions. The classic case of a philosopher using this distinction was Kant, who held that the natural sciences furnish objective knowledge despite the fact that this knowledge is dependent upon 'a priori' categories and intuitions; so, for Kant, scientific truth is not absolute truth concerning things 'in themselves'. I suggest that we take Derrida to be developing a similar line of argument in *Of Grammatology*, arguing here against the possibility of absolute truth in the light of the conditions for the possibility of meaningful discourse.

The most important conditions that any such 'absolute' truth would need to evade are those inherent in the way in which a fact is represented by that which is true; for any ordinary method of representation (linguistic, mental or pictorial) imports certain conditions. Yet even an absolute truth has to be a representation of some kind, since a truth is something which is true and the facts or states of affairs in virtue of which something is true are not themselves true. So they themselves are not truths (unless they are themselves representations); it is a misunderstanding to think that facts themselves could be absolute truths, and equally a mistake to suppose that someone who denies that there are absolute truths denies that there are facts. Thus insofar as an absolute truth is to be unconditioned, it will have to be a completely unconditional representation of a fact, and I suggest that it is this conception which is Derrida's target when he is discussing the critical implications of his account of meaning for 'the very idea of truth'. For, one might say, the very idea of absolute truth depends on the availability of a 'transparent' mode of representation which brings about 'the effacement of the signifier in the voice'. Since, according to Derrida, this requirement turns out to be an 'illusion', to be, indeed, a profound mistake about representation, it does then follow that the very idea of absolute truth is also an illusion.

What then contrasts with 'absolute' truth? Presumably it is 'relative' truth. Hence the accusation that Derrida is a relativist, and thus an underminer of all serious truths and so on. But there is a terrible misapprehension here. For Derrida truth is inescapably dependent upon the work of differance and thus typically relative to a language because truths are primarily statements made in a language. So the sense in which truth is 'relative', and not absolute, is just that because truths are representations of facts, and there can be no representation of facts without language or something essentially similar; it follows that truths of any kind are subject to the conditions under which meaningful language is possible, which for Derrida are summed up in his conception of differance. It does not follow from this that truth is inherently relative to the point of view of the speaker, or to the speaker's culture or whatever; these kinds of relativity are incompatible with objectivity, but there is nothing in Derrida's conception of truth as the truth of sentences of a language to entail that truth so conceived is not objective. On the contrary, as Derrida puts it in the passage quoted above from *Limited Inc*, as long as there are 'stable contexts of interpretation', and thus stable meanings, there is every reason to expect truth to be objective. For it is precisely where there is this kind of stability that it is reasonable to expect that the process of triangulating beliefs and the world described by Davidson will yield objective truth.

I have perhaps laboured this defence of Derrida, but my reason for doing so is that it became clear to me, both during the Cambridge affair and subsequently that there has been a widespread misunderstanding of Derrida's position on this issue. The position I have attributed to him is of course not indisputable, but I shall not attempt to elaborate or defend it here. But I shall end with a few remarks about his approach to questions about values since the popular mythology has been that, as well as being a sceptic about truth, he is a nihilist about values.

The line of thought I have been setting out concerning the possibility of knowledge of objective truth indicates how one might approach questions about the possibility of objective values. But it is notoriously much more difficult to vindicate this latter possibility because there is much less consensus concerning questions of value, and the internal connections between values and cultural practices imply that objectivity, if available at all, should not be thought of as comparable to scientific truths which can draw on relatively stable 'contexts of interpretation'. I think the best way to capture briefly Derrida's approach to these issues is to look at his attitude to 'authenticity', the ethical ideal which had been central to the previous generation of 'existentialist' philosophers such as J.-P. Sartre. To the best of my knowledge Derrida nowhere discusses this ideal explicitly; but he does discuss 'le propre' of man – that which is 'proper' to man, and it is, I think, not tendentious to interpret him here as implicitly commenting on conceptions of authenticity. For this 'jargon of authenticity' starts off from Heidegger's use of the German term 'Eigenlichkeit' which literally denotes the property of something being one's own ('eigen') or being 'proper' to one. So Derrida's use of the term 'le propre' is a way of getting back to the root of the conception of authenticity so that he can discuss it while detaching himself from the significance it subsequently acquired in the work of philosophers such as Sartre.

Early on in *Of Grammatology* Derrida associates 'le propre' with presence (see the passage from page 70 quoted earlier). This association is just what a logocentric conception of value would lead one to expect, and the position could then be filled out in a variety of ways – we might think of the Platonic conception of our capacity for intuitive sight of the form of the Good and equally of the existentialist thought that moral ideals are to be found through a discipline of purity of heart. But once the deconstruction of presence has been accomplished, an alternative, non-logocentric, conception of 'le propre' should become available; and towards the end of *Of Grammatology*, in the context of his discussion of Rousseau, and drawing on Rousseau's references to the ways in which writing is a 'supplement' to speech, Derrida makes a proposal to this effect: 'Thus supplementarity makes possible all that constitutes "le propre" of man: speech, society, passion etc..' (p. 244). This 'supplementarity', he goes on to explain, is 'precisely the play of presence and absence'; so it is basically differance as explained already that is 'le propre' of man. In the light of what was said earlier about differance it is easy to see the basic thought here about the way in which human life is constituted through involvement in 'the play of presence and absence'. But what are the ethical implications of this position?

The negative implications are easy to identify: values cannot be founded either on pure subjective presence – e.g. purity of heart – or on absence, some external matter of fact such as a fixed code or law. The positive story is not so clear: ethical value will have to belong within the fundamental tension inherent in the conception of human life as located within an irreducible play of presence and absence. Derrida's discussion of Rousseau suggests the possibility of an interpretation of this in terms of the contrast between individual and community; as thus interpreted, 'le propre' for man (authenticity) will require a creative exercise of judgement through which one finds ways of negotiating the tension between one's own immediate moral convictions and one's responsibilities to the community without which one's life as a moral agent would not be possible.

This suggestion is not developed in *Of Grammatology*. But in some of Derrida's later writings in which ethical concerns are more prominent this thought is explored, most notably in his discussion in *The Gift of Death*[7] (1992) of Kierkegaard's well-known exploration of existential choice in *Fear and Trembling*. Derrida characterises the situation of Abraham, the protagonist of Kierkegaard's meditation, as one which exemplifies the inescapable 'aporia' (dilemma) of responsibility:

> Such is the aporia of responsibility: one always risks not managing to accede to the concept of responsibility in the process of *forming* it. For responsibility (we would no longer dare speak of "the universal concept of responsibility") demands on the one hand an accounting, a general answering-for-oneself with respect to the general, and hence the idea of substitution; and, on the other hand, uniqueness, absolute singularity, hence nonsubstitution, nonrepetition, silence and secrecy. (p. 61)

Thus, for Derrida, our personal responsibility requires us to mediate between two unconditional demands: the demands of our own individual conscience and the general requirements of justice and similar public virtues. We may not altogether agree with this; Derrida's view seems to be that the tension inherent in these conflicts of value always give rise to insoluble practical dilemmas, whereas a more sober view would be that while the possibility of such dilemmas can never be excluded, it is a legitimate aim of ethical thought and practice to seek to minimise such occasions. But while to disagree with Derrida on this issue is to judge him to be unduly sympathetic to the existentialist conception of life as a succession of predicaments, it is plainly not to take him to be a nihilist about values. That accusation is as misconceived as is the accusation that he is a sceptic about truth. In both cases, the fact that he rejects traditional 'logocentric' accounts of the foundations of knowledge and of ethics is misunderstood as a rejection of the very idea of truth and of value.

I hope that I have been able to demonstrate here how this misunderstanding arises and why we should get beyond it.

Notes

1. *Speech and Phenomena*, transl. D. Allison, Northwestern University Press, Evanston, IL, 1973. This is a translation of *Le Voix et le Phénomène*, Presses Universitaires de France, 1967.
2. *Of Grammatology*, transl. G. Spivak, The Johns Hopkins University Press, Baltimore, MD, 1974. This is a translation of *De la Grammatologie*, Les Editions de Minuit, Paris, 1967.
3. Those familiar with Wittgenstein's 'rule-following' considerations will recognise the argument here. Indeed it will be obvious that my approach to Derrida is much indebted to Wittgenstein's discussions of rule-following. I make no apologies for this.
4. See Peirce's paper 'How to Make Our Ideas Clear', reprinted in *The Writings of C. S. Peirce* vol. 3, Indiana University Press, Bloomington, IN, 1982–. As it happens Peirce's paper was originally written in French for the *Revue Philosophique* where it was published in 1879.
5. see D. Davidson 'The Emergence of Thought', reprinted in his collection of essays *Subjective, Intersubjective, Objective*, Clarendon Press, Oxford, 2001; esp. pp. 128–9.
6. *Limited Inc*, Northwestern University Press, Evanston, IL, 1988.
7. *The Gift of Death*, transl. David Wills, University of Chicago Press, Chicago, IL, 1995. This is a translation of Derrida's long essay 'Donner la mort' which was published in his collection of essays *L'Ethique du don*, Transition, Paris, 1992.

12 Derrida's America

Michael Naas

The topic is indeed "Derrida's America," not "Derrida's Algeria," "Derrida's France," or "Derrida's Europe," and it is being addressed by someone who not only resides in America but is American born and bred. Yet another example, it might be thought, of American hegemony, of America extending its empire over things not just military, political, economic, and cultural but academic and intellectual, right down to the reception, interpretation, dissemination, and, now, the legacy of Jacques Derrida. Unless, of course, it is simply an acknowledgment that, as Derrida himself once put it, "no theoretical work, no literary work, no philosophical work, can receive a worldwide legitimation without crossing the [United] States, without being first legitimized in the States,"[1] an acknowledgement that while Derrida lived the first eighteen years of his life in colonial Algeria, while he attended university in France and subsequently taught for over forty years in Paris, it was really only in America, or only through his success in America, that Jacques Derrida, professor at the Ecole Normale Supérieur and Ecole des Hautes Etudes in Paris, came to be known, indeed renowned, throughout the world, as "Jacques Derrida, the founder of deconstruction."

In what follows I would like to remember Derrida by recalling his time in America so as, first, to confirm the importance of his thought and work in and for America but then, also, so as to question some of the myths with regard to that importance. I will thus try to consider in the most straightforward way possible the impact or influence of Derrida's thought on or in America, the fate, therefore, of "deconstruction in America," but then, also, America's influence on Derrida, the way in which Derrida marked but was also himself marked by American friends, thinkers, institutions, and issues. Finally, I will take up Derrida's reading *of* America, his thoughts about America, and, in the very end, his way of relaunching the promise of "America," his unique way of reinscribing "America"—and "America," as we will see, always in relation to a certain "Europe"—as the name of a promise.

The topic is thus indeed "Derrida's America" or "Derrida in America" or "Derrida's American Question."[2] As a certain kind of American, then, I shall try to address this question by answering in what I would call a singularly "American" mode, that is, with a series of unequivocal, unilateral if not preemptive affirmations, a series of firm and unwavering "yeses." But then, each time, and in a second moment, I will, as a certain kind of American, try to temper my affirmation and enthusiasm with a more "European" "yes, but," and, later, a "no, and yet"—a kind of bilateral thinking that, I believe, and I think Derrida believed, was the only way of thinking responsibly today, the only way of thinking responsibly whether in Europe *or* in America.

I. Derrida in America

Let me begin, then, with what are widely acknowledged to be the facts regarding Derrida in America, by which I mean, in this context, Derrida in the United States. Like many middle class boys growing up in the 1930s and 40s in colonial Algeria, Derrida was no doubt exposed early on and often to American culture, and particularly American movies. Indeed his real or given name was, in fact, not Jacques but "Jackie," after the California-born child actor of the 1920s "Jackie Coogan." Like many young Algerians, then, he was familiar with a certain America or a certain image of America, and he would have no doubt come into contact with Americans in the early 1940s during the North African Campaign to free Algeria from Vichy France.

But what Derrida once called his own *débarquement*, that is, his own "landing" in America, did not take place until 1956–57 when Derrida, aged twenty-six, having just passed the *agrégation* exam in France, boarded a ship named the *Liberté* for his first trip to America.[3] Having been granted a fellowship to Harvard University on the, as Geoff Bennington puts it, "somewhat fictitious pretext of consulting microfilms of unpublished work by Husserl,"[4] Derrida traveled to New York and then made his way to Cambridge, Massachusetts, where he would spend the year reading philosophy and literature, particularly Joyce, and, we can assume, working on his English.[5] Though he would remain virtually unknown in the U.S. for another decade, this year appears to have been decisive in the personal life and professional or intellectual development of Jacques Derrida.[6] For this year abroad no doubt made it easier for Derrida to accept an invitation some ten years later that would mark his grand entry onto the American intellectual scene. The story, now legendary, is that in 1966 Derrida was invited by René Girard to participate alongside other important French intellectuals such as a Rolland Barthes, Jacques Lacan, Jean Hyppolite, and Jean-Pierre Vernant in a conference at Johns Hopkins University in Baltimore on "The Structuralist Controversy: The Languages of Criticism and the Sciences of Man." Derrida there delivered a paper, later published as "Structure, Sign and Play in the Discourse of the Human Sciences," that at once leveled a devastating critique against structuralism, the reigning thought of the time, and laid out much of what would come to be known as Derridean "deconstruction."[7] Within this star-studded field of French theorists, Derrida's star shone bright and his reputation quickly spread. When he published the following year no fewer than three major books,

Of Grammatology, Speech and Phenomenon, and *Writing and Difference,* that reputation was solidified within the American academy and his work began to be widely disseminated throughout the U.S. Not long thereafter, Derrida was invited to teach a couple of weeks a year at Johns Hopkins, and, in 1975, alongside Hillis Miller and Paul de Man at Yale. By the mid 70s one thus began to speak of a "Yale School" of literary criticism,[8] a school that would find itself, and Derrida most prominently, at the center of furious "debates and [culture] wars around the so-called 'invasion' of 'deconstruction in America.'"[9]

Derrida in the late 1970s and throughout the 1980s thus became the most visible and arguably the most influential figure in a wave of French theorists that included Barthes, Foucault, Lyotard, Deleuze, Levinas, Lacan, Kristeva, and others. By all the most obvious measures—publications, colloquia, curricular and institutional influence, and, though more difficult to measure, just sheer enthusiasm—this would prove to be the heyday of "poststructuralism," "postmodernism," or, more generally, "French theory" in America. Though Derrida remained popular and significant throughout the 1990s, continuing to publish widely and to teach a few weeks a year on both coasts, it is fair to say that interest in French theory generally waned during these years, with several of its leading figures, from Levinas to Lyotard to Deleuze, dying in the course of that decade. When Derrida himself died in October 2004 his death was thus perceived by many in the U.S. and elsewhere as something like the end of a most celebrated generation of poststructuralist or postmodern thought.[10]

II. Derrida's influence on America

These, then, are, to the best of my knowledge, the barest, essential facts, on the basis of which I will put forward my first unwavering affirmation concerning "Derrida's America"; as a result of the series of events just described, Derrida came to have as much notoriety and influence on the American academic scene as any single intellectual, whether American or other, from the mid-1970s through the 1980s, and perhaps even on into the 90s. From the mid-1970s onward, a steady stream of translations kept his thought in circulation throughout the English-speaking world, where it would have an enormous influence not only on philosophy, modern languages and literature departments, but also on disciplines as different as feminism, critical legal studies, critical race studies, art, architecture, theology, and many others. Through his more than 70 books, innumerable colloquia, and public speaking engagements, through his academic appointments, honorary degrees at places like Williams College, Columbia University, and the New School for Social Research, through at least two films,[11] one of which made its debut a couple of years ago at the Sundance film festival, Derrida became something of an intellectual celebrity throughout the U.S. and the one word with which he was most often associated, "deconstruction," something of a household word. Even if the word tends to mean in America little more than "to analyze" or "pick apart," or else to "negate" or "destroy"—all very inadequate ways of describing the work of deconstruction—the word has entered our parlance, and so shows up fairly regularly in the press and even in the occasional movie (like Woody Allen's "Deconstructing Harry"). All this seems to support the view, the tale or legend, that Derrida became an American intellectual "superstar," that is, a French intellectual made into a superstar in America—the most famous, most celebrated, most widely read and disseminated figure in a most famous and celebrated generation of French theorists in the U.S.

This reception of French theory in general and Derrida in particular did not, of course, occur in an intellectual and institutional vacuum. Among the many factors that no doubt contributed to Derrida and deconstruction finding a fertile ground in the U.S. are, surely, a growing institutional flexibility and interdisciplinarity in the American academy during this time, America's strong religious and theological tradition, particularly in the university,[12] certain movements, such as phenomenology, in American continental philosophy during the 1960s and 70s, the importance of New Criticism in literary theory and a concurrent interest in German romanticism,[13] a diverse but well-connected college and university system,[14] university-related and supported journals such as Glyph, SubStance, Boundary II, and Critical Inquiry, along with relatively well-supported and well-distributed university presses, beginning with the University of Chicago Press, which published many of Derrida's early texts. All these factors contributed to the growth and prominence of Derrida and deconstruction in America—making the latter a household name and the former an intellectual superstar.

But now it's time for my first "yes, but," time for a bit of "European reserve" or bilateral thinking to temper my American, unilateralist enthusiasm. For the tale I just told, while not without a certain truth, is misleading on many fronts, beginning with my rather glib and unthinking repetition of that journalistic phrase "American intellectual superstar." A first caveat would thus have to be raised concerning the extent to which Derrida's work has been disseminated and read in the U.S. Though Derrida is indeed well known in certain academic circles, I sometimes have to tell European friends, who often have greater misconceptions about Derrida's fame in America than Americans do, that one does not and did not during the 1980s ever see people on television discussing Derrida's analyses of Heidegger or his theory of metaphor, or beachgoers in Fort Lauderdale or Laguna Beach reading *Of Grammatology*, or people commuting to work in Chicago listening to book-on tape versions of *Glas* or *Specters of Marx*. In fact, from what I know, Derrida's books, published almost exclusively with academic or university presses, rarely sell more than between five and ten thousand copies in the U.S., that is, in a country where not only fiction but non-fiction and sometimes even academic works, such as

Allan Bloom's *The Closing of the American Mind*, can sell over a million copies. While the average academic book in the U.S. sells no more than about seven hundred copies, so that five to ten thousand copies qualifies as an unqualified academic bestseller, and Derrida had, to be sure, many of these, such sales figures justify, I think, Derrida's frequent claim that his books constitute something like a "quasi-private conversation," hardly, in any case, a mass phenomenon.

A second reason to be skeptical of this tale of American superstardom is that Derrida was just as well if not better received in many places outside the U.S., from Canada to Japan, Brazil to Romania, Portugal to Australia, indeed, even in France, where he was admired and read by many, even if it was often outside the university system. Though Derrida once declared the "state of theory" to be California, and "theory"—which would include "deconstruction"—an essentially American or "purely North American artifact,"[15] the fact is that, as Derrida also said, "There is no country of deconstruction."[16]

Third, if Derrida's success and status are to be attributed to America, we must reckon with the fact that nowhere else in the world was Derrida subject to more violent or more virulent critique than in the U.S. Nowhere more than in the U.S. did influential academic authorities try to discredit Derrida and those who read him with insinuation and insult rather than, as one might have hoped for in the university, thoughtful and engaged critique. And such campaigns were often carried out in well-known publications, such as *The New York Review of Books*, with a much wider distribution than Derrida's own work, the result being that many more people were no doubt exposed to Derrida through the critique of him and the intense debates surrounding him than through actually reading his work.[17] One thinks here of the so-called culture wars of the 1970s and 80s, of what came to be known as the DeMan affair,[18] of the Heidegger controversy,[19] or of the role played by certain American academics in the protest at Cambridge University over Derrida being awarded an honorary degree.[20]

If deconstruction was thus widely welcomed, praised, and ardently defended in many parts of the U.S., it was also terribly feared, reviled, and viciously attacked in many others. If Derrida's work received an enthusiastic reception in some quarters of the American academy, it was greeted with outrage, skepticism, or simple, persistent, or willful misunderstanding, in many others. For example, the tendency to understand deconstruction as a kind of linguistics, when it in fact mounted a critique against the reign of structural linguistics and its logocentrism, was nowhere more widespread than in the U.S., as was the tendency to hypostasize and capitalize "Deconstruction" despite Derrida's regular insistence that deconstruction is not a monolithic entity and that there are, in fact, only deconstructions.[21]

Finally, Derrida was suspicious, and so should we be, of the interests and motives of those in the U.S. and, perhaps especially, in France, who wished to develop this label or image of Derrida as an "American intellectual superstar" as a way of disparaging or discounting Derrida's work. Though Derrida had too much tact to draw out all the ugly implications, it is not hard to guess that what was often suggested by this French attribution of American super-stardom was the notion that only in America could someone like Derrida make it big, only in America could a flashy, flamboyant but ultimately shal-low thinker like Derrida be taken seriously, only in America could the glib simulacrum of genuine knowledge and erudition be taken for the real thing. Old Europe, according to the premise of the argument, had known better and had sent the imposter abroad. By presenting Derrida as some-thing of a pop star or cultural icon in the U.S., the French could at once snicker at a naive America taken in by the merry prankster of deconstruction and write off the prankster himself as "America's Derrida."[22]

If the word "deconstruction" thus did or does enjoy mass notoriety in the U.S., used by everyone from hipsters and advertisers to rightwingers who want to talk about the deconstruction, that is, for them, the destruction or undermining of American values and American cultural identity, I think it is fair to say that the person and thought of Jacques Derrida did not and do not hold such a place of prominence. If the word deconstruction and the name of Jacques Derrida are known to a certain cultural milieu, the thought of Derrida is restricted essentially to the university.[23] There are many admirers, students, faithful readers, and teachers of Derrida's work, to be sure, but no mass appeal, and, for here is yet another prejudice, no cult followers.[24] As someone who, I think, would know about a cult if there was one, I have often reassured people both in France and the U.S. that I've never heard of any Derridean dissemination rituals, never partici-pated in any breaking of the holy pharmakon, never learned any secret deconstructionist handshake.

III. America's influence on Derrida

Derrida marked America, to be sure, but perhaps not in the way we like to think, perhaps in ways that cannot even immediately be identified with him, that is, in more secret, subterranean, but perhaps all the more power-ful and transformative ways. But then what about the mark left by America on Derrida? It's time for another big, bold American assertion: Derrida was marked and transformed by the American scene in a way that few European intellectuals have ever been. Each year Derrida spent a few weeks teaching and lecturing in the U.S., so that America, and certain place names and personal names to begin with, came to mark his corpus and inflect his interests. At the very least, America came to be for Jacques Derrida an open series of proper names, of friends and colleagues and place names, that is, a vast network of intersecting singularities from New York, New Haven, and Ithaca on the East Coast, to Santa Monica, Laguna Beach, and Irvine on the West.[25] From the late 1960s on, innumer-able conferences and texts are marked by an American context and the places and names associated with them. The relatively recent text "The University Without Condition," for example, is marked from beginning to end by Derrida's experience in the American university system; *Specters of Marx* was written for a colloquium at the University of California Riverside and cannot be read without some understanding of its American context and audience; and then there is Derrida's piece on the American "Declaration of Independence," a text Derrida no doubt would have never written were it not for an invitation to speak at the University of Virginia during a conference marking America's bicentennial in 1976.[26] One could cite a long list of texts that were either first delivered in the U.S. or else written for and within an American academic context. So, yes, Derrida was profoundly marked by America, by *his* America, and Derridean deconstruction was marked, translated, transformed by the American context, often taking forms that Derrida could not have predicted and might have even had difficulty recognizing.[27]

And yet, and here's my more measured, European counterpoint: Derrida remained through it all, and despite this American influence, *profoundly European*. Though he marked and was marked by America, he remained a European intellectual, though, as always, in his own way, that is, as a European who claimed to be European by *not* being European *through and through*. Near the end of *The Other Heading* in 1991, Derrida himself declared:

> I am European, I am no doubt a European intellectual, and I like to recall this, I like to recall this to myself, and why would I deny it? In the name of what? But I am not, nor do I feel, European *in every part*, that is, European through and through.[28]

For all our talk of Derrida's America, or of Derrida in America, Derrida's corpus bears witness to a European provenance and orientation, to elective affinities that are essentially European in name even if Derrida used them to rethink and critique Eurocentrism. In an interview in 1991 Derrida says it so happens that he was "*born* .... in the European *preference*, in the preference of the French language, nation, or citizenship, ... and then in the preference of this time, of those I love, of my family, of my friends—of my enemies also, of course, and so on."[29] Hence Derrida taught regularly in the U.S., indeed every year, but it is important to recall that he never emigrated to America or took up a full-time position there and continued throughout his career to teach full time in France.[30] Equally revealing, perhaps, is the fact that while certain English phrases such as "double bind" or "speech act" entered Derrida's vocabulary quite early on, French remained the only language Derrida wrote in and his preferred language for delivering addresses and answering questions. This was more than just a question of comfort or competence, for Derrida spoke excellent English,[31] but a matter of responsibility and, indeed, of passion—of a preference and passion for European languages, German, Latin, Greek, but, especially, French. In literature, too, Derrida's tastes and interests were largely European, indeed Western European: French—Artaud, Baudelaire, Blanchot, Genet, Mallarmé, Ponge, Sollers; or Germanic—Celan, Hölderlin, Kafka; or English—Shakespeare, Defoe, Swift, Blake, Shelley, Joyce, Hopkins but scarcely American. Beyond a couple of short stories by Poe, most notably "The Purloined Letter," already analyzed by Lacan, and Melville's "Bartleby the Scrivener," along with passing references to Faulkner or Stein, Wallace Stevens or William Carlos Williams, Derrida remained rather unmarked, it would seem, by the American literary tradition.[32] This is not terribly surprising from an Algerian-born, French-speaking and -writing thinker, but it does need to be pointed out to temper any hyperbole concerning the fate of Derrida or deconstruction in America.[33]

In terms of philosophers, there is the same decidedly European inclination; there are several references to Pierce in *Of Grammatology*[34] and allusions here and there to Thoreau and Emerson; there is the debate with John Searle over a reading of J. L. Austin,[35] and then, much later, a critique of Francis Fukuyama's book on the end of history, and then punctual references to recent works of Noam Chomsky or Jeremy Rifkin.[36] But Derrida was in the end a European thinker whose preferred philosophical texts ran from Plato and Aristotle to Descartes, Kant, Leibniz, Rousseau, Hegel, Husserl, Heidegger, Benjamin, Bataille, Levinas, and so on. In other words, his interests coincided in large part not with the dominant philosophy of the English-speaking world but with various concerns in the history of philosophy and in what is called contemporary Continental philosophy in the U.S. and elsewhere, a philosophy that is rather peripheral to the predominately analytic scene and that, it must be emphasized, was written for the most part in languages other than English. Indeed, as Derrida himself once observed, the hegemony of the so-called analytic, Anglo-American philosophy in the U.S., Britain, and in many other places throughout the world is perhaps not unrelated to the growing, global hegemony of the Anglo-American language.[37] It is thus perhaps not surprising that Derrida's work first entered America, and is *still* most often taught in America, not in philosophy departments but in French, German, Comparative Literature, Theology, and English departments. Even though there are today more and more books attempting to bridge the so-called Analytic and Continental divide, Derrida is still not a particularly popular or widely read figure in American philosophy, despite the fact that the vast majority of his books are original, rigorous, and provocative readings of canonical figures in the history of philosophy and that for almost forty years he taught philosophy in Paris.[38]

IV. Derrida on America

A colonial Algerian living in France, a French speaker within an Anglo-American idiom, a European within the American state, a Continental thinker within an essentially Analytic profession, Derrida—and here's another bold, American assertion—brought a certain Europe to America more than he brought America back to Europe.[39] Though he visited the U.S. regularly for almost forty years, he did not follow that French tradition, what he once called that "French specialty," that runs from Alexis de Tocqueville to Jean Baudrillard of writing a book about or entitled "America."[40]

And yet, one might counter, without writing a book on America, examples from America, the issues and problems raised by America, mark his discourse from as early as "The Ends of Man" in 1968, with its pointed reference to the Vietnam peace talks and the assassination of Martin Luther King.[41] Moreover, the contexts, tones, and growing frequency of Derrida's remarks about America over the last two decades mark a certain trajectory and, I think it is fair to say, demonstrate a growing dissatisfaction not with America *as such* but, as he would prudently put it, with a certain dominant ideology within the U.S. In 1982, for example, in "Of an Apocalyptic Tone Recently Adopted in Philosophy," Derrida remarked upon America's sensitivity to "phenomena of prophetism, messianism, eschatology, and apocalypse," to its use of religious language in political discourse.[42] Two years later, in the French-written but English-titled *No Apocalypse, Not Now*, he analyzed the Reagan administration's rhetoric concerning nuclear proliferation, deterrence, and war.[43] In *Specters of Marx*, he again returned to this apocalyptic aspect of American political culture and philosophy in a reading of Francis Fukuyama's *The End of History and the Last Man*, a work Derrida characterized as "neo-testamentary" or "neo-evangelistic" in its rhetoric.[44]

In the 1980s and 90s, references became more and more frequent and explicit to American hegemony and to that predominantly Americanizing process known as "globalization."[45] Derrida thus spoke of American hegemony in academics,[46] in the culture[47] and information industries,[48] and, especially, in the global spread of the Anglo-American language.[49] Because of the time he spent in America, the growing number of Americans he counted as his friends, colleagues, and students, and, of course, because America is not just one country among others on the global stage, American examples and issues became more and more common in his work during the last decades of his life. Thus in an analysis of television and media, Derrida turned to the Rodney King case[50]; in an analysis of perjury and lying in politics, he was drawn to the Clinton/Monica Lewinski affair and everything it teaches us about the American obsession with truth-telling and public confession.[51] And in the final decade of his life Derrida spoke often in his teaching and publications about the death penalty in

America, "the only Western-style democracy," as he once put it, "with a dominant Christian culture, to maintain the death penalty and to remain inflexible about its own sovereignty."[52] By aligning the U.S. with other states that maintain the death penalty, that is, with China and certain Arab-Muslim states, and opposing these to European states, the critique was clear, and even led to an open letter in 1996 to Bill and Hillary Clinton protesting the death sentence of Mumia Abu-Jamal. Derrida thus became a vocal critic of the death penalty in America as well as of the obvious racism involved in its application and in the American penal system more generally.[53]

Finally, during his last few years, Derrida spoke very critically of American hegemony and of the imposition of American sovereignty throughout the world. This criticism became most explicit in Derrida's 2003 *Voyous* or *Rogues*, which contains Derrida's most sustained analysis and critique of American foreign policy, particularly as concerns the U.S. government's use and abuse over the last two decades of the demonizing expression "rogue state" to further its own sovereign interests at home and abroad.[54] It is not hard in this and other works to make out a growing distance from and disaffection with certain tendencies within American political culture and discourse, for example, the privileging of clear binary distinctions and decisions, of unwavering and unreflective resolve, as opposed to more nuanced, more balanced, and more difficult analyses.

V. Deconstruction is/in America

But what, then, of deconstruction not *in* America but *as* America? What of that now infamous claim or, really, hypothesis that "Deconstruction *is* America"? Back in 1984, during a series of lectures at Irvine, Derrida confessed to being tempted by the idea of addressing the theme that I have broached here, namely, the theme of "Deconstruction in America." Derrida ultimately resisted this temptation, he says, for several reasons. First, "Deconstruction in America" is, he argued, a work or a phenomenon in progress, and so is still radically undecided, something that, let me add, is still true today, even after the death of Jacques Derrida. Second, one cannot just assume that deconstruction was something that once existed in Europe and was then simply transplanted or translated into America, since there were "original configurations" of deconstruction in America well before his work and multiple and sometimes ambivalent forms after the arrival of his work.[55] Third, since deconstruction has done nothing if not question the "classical assurances of history, the genealogical narrative, and periodizations of all sorts," it makes little philosophical sense to speak of a clearly delimited and isolatable epoch of deconstruction in America. And fourth, and finally, as we've already said, there is no one, single, monolithic thing called "deconstruction." [56]

Any responsible analysis of something like "deconstruction in America" would thus have to confront such objections before going on to take account of all the political, technological, religious, ethical,[57] and academic aspects of deconstruction's place or work in America—for example, to take just this last, the way in which "deconstruction has accompanied a critical transformation in the conditions of entry into the academic professions [in the U.S.] from the 1960s to the 1980s" (*M*, 16), the way in which it has accompanied a permeability of disciplinary boundaries and a change in the constitution and role of the canon in education.[58] It is thus in the context of all these objections, hesitations, warnings, and reminders that Derrida offered back in 1984 not a claim about America, not even a hypothesis regarding it, but, you will notice, a hypothesis concerning a hypothesis. Derrida wrote:

> Were I not so frequently associated with this adventure of deconstruction, I would risk, with a smile, the following hypothesis: America *is* deconstruction (l'Amérique, mais *c'est* la deconstruction). *In this hypothesis*, America would be the proper name of deconstruction in progress, its family name, its toponymy, its language and its place, its principal residence. And how could we define the United States today without integrating the following into the description: It is that historical space which today, in all its dimensions and through all its power plays, reveals itself as being undeniably the most sensitive, receptive, or responsive space of all to the themes and effects of deconstruction. (*M*, 18)

But just a couple of lines later, Derrida withdraws this hypothetical hypothesis, recalling that "we have learned from 'Deconstruction' to suspect these always hasty attributions of proper names." He then continues:

> My *hypothesis* must thus be abandoned. No, "deconstruction" is not a proper name, nor is America the proper name of deconstruction. Let us say instead: deconstruction and America are two open sets which intersect partially according to an allegorico-metonymic figure... This is why I have decided not to talk to you about "deconstruction in America." (*M*, 18–19)

Derrida thus offers a hypothesis but then quickly withdraws it; he offers it all the while knowing that he is going to withdraw it. He does so because, in addition to all the aforementioned objections and hesitations, and perhaps before all else, it is not clear what exactly is being identified with the name "America." Just before the passage cited above, Derrida writes:

> In order to speak of "deconstruction in America," one would have to claim to know what one is talking about, and first of all what is meant or defined by the word "America." Just what is America in this context? (*M*, 17–18)

If Derrida complained that, in America, deconstruction was often taken as a single, monolithic enterprise, Deconstruction with a capital "D," he himself was circumspect with regard to the name "America" itself, with regard to the American thing, careful not to hypostasize it or use it as a slogan with which to conceal a whole series of internal differences. In an interview given just weeks after 9-11 Derrida warned once more, just as he did in 1984, against an unthinking conflation of the name "America" or the "United States" with some single reality. Speaking no doubt in part in reaction to growing anti-American sentiments in France and elsewhere, Derrida instead advocated a

> philosophical "deconstruction" [that] would have to operate not against something we would call the "United States" but against what today constitutes a certain American hegemony, one that actually dominates or marginalizes something in the U.S.'s own history, something that is also related to that strange "Europe" of the more or less incomplete Enlightenment I was talking about.[59]

Seventeen years after that hypothetical hypothesis "Deconstruction *is* America," Derrida cautions us against the same thoughtless repetition of a name. And yet, seventeen years later, not everything will have remained the same. Notice that in the passage I just cited Derrida speaks of that "strange 'Europe' of [a] more or less incomplete Enlightenment"; he does not speak—as I think he might have been tempted to speak a couple of decades ago—of that "strange 'America.'" Indeed, I suspect that Derrida would have today hesitated even to offer so as then to withdraw this hypothesis of a hypothesis regarding America as deconstruction. He would have hesitated, I think, because of the more and more serious reservations he came to have about a certain America/reservations about its internal and foreign policies, about its jealously-guarded sovereignty and its apparent disdain for international law and institutions, reservations about an America that, as Peggy Kamuf so aptly puts it in her introduction to *Without Alibi*, has become but "the effective or practical name for the theological-political myth we call sovereignty" (*WA*, 14).[60]

VI. Derrida's "America," Derrida's "Europe"

Derrida continued to speak and would today continue to speak, I believe, of a certain United States or of something within the United States' own history and tradition that would resist the theological-political myth we call sovereignty; he spoke, and would continue today to speak, of a certain American tradition of "civil disobedience"[61] and of resistance to and within the dominant American order, but he would not, it seems to me, risk any misunderstanding about America as the "most sensitive, receptive, or responsive space of all to the themes... of deconstruction." America might well be the most receptive place in the world to the *effects* of deconstruction, the most vulnerable to certain auto-immune or self-deconstructive processes, but I think it would be hard to argue that it is today the most receptive to deconstructive themes or to their *thoughtful* engagement.

That is why Derrida, for good geopolitical and strategic reasons, it seems to me, tended in the last few years to situate not America but a certain "Europe" in the place of this resistance to the hegemonic order, "Europe" in its unique political, ideological, and philosophical position between the superpower of the U.S. and its others. It is perhaps more than a mere stroke of chance that one of Derrida's very last pieces, written in May and published in November of 2004, was entitled "A Europe of Hope," not "An America of Hope." Indeed in several texts over the past couple of decades, beginning perhaps with *The Other Heading*, Derrida continued to use the name "Europe," often in quotation marks, to signal a promise that was perhaps born in what is called Europe but that nonetheless exceeds every geographical designation or current political formation of ten, fifteen, or twenty-five member nations. In "A Europe of Hope," Derrida writes this of a French and European responsibility vis-à-vis America and the rest of the world: "We are thus called to assume, in the world as it is and as it announces itself, an irreplaceably French and European responsibility in the *altermondialist* [or counter-worldwide] movement, between American hegemony, the growing power of China, and Arab or Muslin theocracies."[62]

Fully aware of how Heidegger once situated Germany between the two superpowers of the U.S. and the U.S.S.R., Derrida recognizes that Europe, despite its numerous problems and inadequacies, despite the inadequation between its reality and its promise, nonetheless offers something of an alternative not only to the Far East and the Middle East but to the U.S. whose model of government, or at least whose current political regime, is even more tied than Europe's to a theological model of religious authority and sovereignty.

In his interview on 9-11—an interview that begins, of course, by asking about what happened to *America*, and, then, to the rest of the world on 9-11—Derrida explains why he continues to use the name "Europe" to refer to this promise that exceeds all geographical and political boundaries, so that the name "European" might refer even to those living far away from Europe proper, those living, perhaps, why not, in America, those who would thus not be Americans through and through, or who would be "Americans" precisely insofar as they are not American through and through. Derrida writes:

> I persist in using this name "Europe," even if in quotation marks, because, in the long and patient deconstruction required for the transformation to-come, the experience Europe inaugurated at the time of the Enlightenment...(*Lumières, Aufklärung, Illuminismo*) in the relationship between the political and the theological, or, rather, the

religious, though still uneven, unfulfilled, relative, and complex, will have left in European political space absolutely original marks with regard to religious doctrine... Such marks can be found neither in the Arab world nor in the Muslim world, nor in the Far East, nor even, and here's the most sensitive point, in American democracy, in what *in fact* governs not the principles but the predominant reality of American political culture. (*A*, 116–117)

How could one deny today that there is in the U.S., as Derrida put it in 1985, a certain "resistance to theory. Resistance to things European. Not only to individuals from Europe, but even to Americans who are more 'European' than others"?[63] This twenty-year-old rhetorical question of Derrida's could not be more current or more pressing for us today. It goes far beyond the simplistic, binary acceptance or rejection of Europe or America, far beyond Eurocentrism or American chauvinism, far beyond anti-Americanism or Francophobia, for Derrida suggests that America's resistance to a certain Europe signals a resistance to something essential about America itself.

My conclusion thus surely is not, or is not quite, that Derrida left or turned away from America and turned back to Europe during the final years of his life. What Derrida taught us, whether we are talking about that strange "Europe" of the Enlightenment to come or about a certain "America," is that it can never simply be a question of saying "yes" to Europe or "no" to America, of unilaterally affirming the one while eschewing the other. Near the end of "A Europe of Hope," Derrida says he dreams of "A Europe that serves as an example of what a politics, a reflection, and an ethics might be, ones that have inherited from a past Enlightenment and that bear an Enlightenment to come, a Europe capable of non-binary forms of discernment," that is, I think, a Europe capable of forms of reflection where one can criticize a certain America without being anti-American and speak in the name of a certain "Europe" without Eurocentrism.[64] Though no country or continent could possibly have a monopoly on such a way of thinking, "European" is today, Derrida suggests, the best name for it— though it might well be otherwise tomorrow. It is a way of thinking that does not force us into believing that moral clarity always requires saying simply yes or no, a way of thinking that allows one the freedom of critique and honest interpretation to say "yes, but," "no, and yet," a way of thinking that keeps us from acceding to the belief during politically divisive times that nuance, measure, and honest self-critique are signs of a lack of moral purpose or resolve.

It is this form of reflection that allows one to say that, *no,* Derrida was not American, *and yet* he was a friend to a certain "America" and, I can attest, to certain extremely privileged Americans; *yes,* he was European, *but not* European through and through, European, then, always in his own way; *yes,* he was north African, *but* only in a certain way,[65] one that could not be

thought without taking into account the whole history of the Jewish dias-
pora and of modern colonization. He was thus a foreigner to America, but
also to France and even to Algeria, but, again, always in his own way, a
foreigner who brought a certain European tradition—as well as what
exceeds it, since he taught us that the tradition always exceeds itself—to
America, and a certain America—one that exceeds our common images of
it and the predominant culture within it—back to Europe. It was, it is, it will
remain an extraordinary itinerary, an inimitable, singular, quite literally
impossible itinerary, even if it took place, over here *and* over there, in
Europe and in America, an itinerary and a life for which, to speak not out
of American enthusiasm but with a form of affirmation I have learned from
Jacques Derrida, we cannot but feel *absolutely grateful.* This time, this one
time, without the slightest "yes, but."

Notes

1. See the "Roundtable Discussion" with Derrida in *Ethics, Institutions, and the Right to Philosophy*, ed. Peter Pericles Trifonas (Oxford, England: Rowman & Littlefield, 2002), 29. Derrida comments on this subject in *Applying: To Derrida*, eds. John Brannigan, Ruth Robbins, Julian Wolfreys (St Martin's Press, 1996), 224–225, and in "Deconstruction in America: An Interview with Jacques Derrida," with James Creech, Peggy Kamuf, and Jane Todd (*Critical Exchange* #17 (Winter, 1985), 1–33. Hereafter abbreviated "DA."

2. Derrida himself broaches the question of his own "American Question" in *Counterpath*, with Catherine Malabou, trans. David Wills (Stanford, CA: Stanford University Press, 2004), 27, 29. For an excellent analysis of Derrida's engagement with the U.S. context, see Peggy Kamuf's introduction to *Without Alibi* (Stanford, CA: Stanford University Press, 2002), 1–27. Hereafter abbreviated *WA*.

3. See *Tourner les mots*, with Safaa Fathy (Paris: Editions Galilée, 2000), 96, and *Counterpath*, 25.

4. Geoffrey Bennington and Jacques Derrida, *Jacques Derrida* (Chicago: University of Chicago Press, 1993), 329.

5. In the following years Derrida would publish two French translations of English texts, "Les frontières de la théorie logique," by W. V. Quine (with R. Martin) in *Les Etudes philosophiques*, no. 2, 1964, and "Le monde-de-la-vie et la tradition de la philosophie américaine," by M. Farber, in *Les Etudes philosophiques*, no. 2, 1964.

6. This was also the year of Derrida's marriage to Marguerite Aucouturier.

7. Derrida recalls this conference in several places. See, for example, *Counterpath*, 274–275. See "Structure, Sign, and Play in the Discourse of the Human Sciences," in *Writing and Difference*, trans. Alan Bass (Chicago: University of Chicago Press, 1978), 278–293.

8. The publication in 1979 of *Deconstruction and Criticism* (New York: The Seabury Press), with essays by Derrida, Harold Bloom, Paul de Man, Geoffrey Hartman, and J. Hillis Miller, did much to draw attention to this "Yale School." See also Jonathan Arac, Wlad Godzich, Wallace Martin, eds., *The Yale Critics: Deconstruction in America* (Minneapolis: University of Minnesota Press, 1983).

9. See "DA," 1–33.

10. Those are, in short, the facts, the kind of facts one would put in what Blanchot in a text written after the death of Bataille once called "the worst of histories, literary history" (Maurice Blanchot, *Friendship*, trans. Elizabeth Rottenberg [Stanford, CA: Stanford University Press, 1997], 290).

11. *D'ailleurs, Derrida* (1990), by Egyptian-born cineaste, Safaa Fathy, and *Derrida* (2002), by Kirby Dick and Amy Ziering Kofman. Parts of both of these were filmed in the U.S. The latter premièred at the Sundance Film Festival.

12. See "DA," 11–12. It is in religious studies and theology programs in the U.S. that some of the most interesting and engaging work on Derrida is taking place today.

13. As Derrida said in 1985: "it's in English departments that thing are happening more than in departments of French or philosophy" ("DA," 23).

14. Derrida says that because in the U.S. "everything is concentrated within the academic institution... there was right away a greater intensity of reception in the positive sense of the term, and also, just as great an intensity of reaction, of rejection...." ("DA," 5, 8)

15. "Some Statements and Truisms about Neologisms, Newisms, Postisms, Parasitisms, and Other Small Seismisms," trans. Anne Tomiche, in *The States of "Theory": History, Art, and Critical Discourse*, ed. David Carroll (New York: Columbia University Press, 1990), 71.

16. *Papier Machine* (Paris: Editions Galilée, 2001), 340.

17. Derrida responds in several places to the attacks made against him in the pages of *The New York Review of Books, The Times Literary Supplement, The New Criterion, Harvard Magazine*, and elsewhere. See, for example, *Memoires for Paul de Man*, trans. Cecile Lindsay, Jonathan Culler, Eduardo Cadava, and Peggy Kamuf (New York: Columbia University Press, 1989), 41–42 no. 5; hereafter abbreviated *M*. See also *Negotiations*, 58, where Derrida responds to a 1983 article by William Bennett criticizing deconstruction in *The Wall Street Journal*. See also *For What Tomorrow...*, with Elisabeth Roudinesco (Stanford, CA: Stanford University Press, 2004), 17, and an interview from 1981 with Richard Kearney in *Dialogues with Contemporary Continental Thinkers* (Manchester, England: Manchester University Press), 124. One might have thought these criticisms to be things of the distant past, but many resurfaced, rather shamefully, in several obituaries, including the one in *The New York Times*, after Derrida's death.

18. See the final essay of *Memoires for Paul de Man*, "Like the Sound of the Sea Deep Within a Shell: Paul de Man's War," 155–263. See also Derrida's comments at the end of *Limited Inc*, 153–154.

19. This was played out over the course of several weeks in the pages of *The New York Review of Books* from February to April 1993 with Richard Wolin and Thomas Sheehan. See *Points...: Interviews, 1974-1994*, ed. Elisabeth Weber, trans. Peggy Kamuf and Others (Stanford, CA: Stanford University Press, 1995), 422–454.

20. See "*Honoris Causa*: 'This is *also* extremely funny'," in *Points...*, 399–421.

21. See *Moscou aller-retour* (La Tour d'Aigues: Editions de l'aube, 1995), 125.

22. Derrida himself gives just such an interpretation in *Counterpath*, 29. On the "enormous prejudice" fostered in France regarding Derrida's superstardom in the U.S., see *Sur Parole* (Paris: Editions de l'Aube, 1999), 55, and *Points...*, 351.

23. See Derrida's comments on this subject in an interview with Peter Brunette and David Wills, "The Spatial Arts: An Interview with Jacques Derrida," in *Deconstruction and the Visual Arts: Art, Media, Architecture*, eds. Peter Brunette and David Wills (Cambridge: Cambridge University Press, 1994), 30.

24. Derrida responds in an interview in *Papier Machine* (339–340) to the claim that deconstruction developed into a sort of cult in the U.S.

25. Derrida writes in an essay devoted to Michel de Certeau (*Psyché. Inventions de l'autre* [Paris: Galilée, 1987], 639–640): "If I may be allowed just to whisper, just for me, a few place names. I remember the California sun, in San Diego or in Irvine. I remember Cornell, Binghampton, New York..." Derrida speaks of his special relation to New York City in *Counterpath*, 101, 119–120, and of his relation to California (to Santa Monica) in *Jacques Derrida*, 19 and *Counterpath*,

230–233, and (to Laguna Beach) in *Tourner les mots*, 23, and *Counterpath*, 276–278. California also provides the trope of tremors or earthquakes that became so prominent in Derrida's vocabulary. See, for example, "DA," 18 and *Divinatio*, 15, Spring-Summer 2002, 159. As for Derrida's many friends in America, from New York to California, I will not even begin to make a list, both because it would be extremely long and I would risk leaving out too many people.

26. "Declarations of Independence," in *Negotiations*, trans. Elizabeth Rottenberg (Stanford, CA: Stanford University Press, 2002), 46–54.

27. See "DA," 29.

28. *The Other Heading*, trans. Pascale-Anne Brault and Michael Naas (Bloomington, IN: Indiana University Press, 1992), 82. Hereafter abbreviated *OH*. Derrida concludes: "If, to conclude, I declared that I feel European *among other things*, would this be, in this very declaration, to be more or less European? Both, no doubt. Let the consequences be drawn from this. It is up to the others, in any case, and up to me *among them*, to decide" (*OH*, 83).

29. "A 'Madness' Must Watch Over Thinking," in *Points...*, 362–363.

30. See *Points...*, 189.

31. Derrida spoke and understood, it should be specified, American rather than British English. In an interview in *Applying: To Derrida*, eds. John Brannigan, Ruth Robbins, Julian Wolfreys (St Martin's Press, 1996), 215, Derrida explains why he did not take part in discussions about his work during a conference in England: "... I wanted to be with you, one amongst the others, listening, and sometimes not understanding what was going on because English is difficult for me. I understand American to some extent. But, for me, English is a torture. So, sometimes I keep quiet because I feel incompetent."

32. Derrida cites the famous line "I am dead" from Poe's "The Facts in the Case of M. Valdemar" as an exergue to *Speech and Phenomenon* (Evanston, IL: Northwestern University Press, 1973),1; Lacan's reading of Poe's "The Purloined Letter" is at the center of "*Le facteur de la vérité*" in *The Post Card*, trans. Alan Bass (Chicago: University of Chicago Press, 1987), 413–496; see also "For the Love of Lacan," in *Resistances of Psychoanalysis* (Stanford, CA: Stanford University Press, 1996), 39–69; "Mes chances," *Confrontation*, 19, Spring 1988, 26ff.; *The Post Card*, 43, 104, 148, 151; *Points...*, 21, 81; *Given Time*, trans. Peggy Kamuf (Chicago: University of Chicago Press, 1992), 105; *Politics of Friendship*, trans. George Collins (New York: Verso, 1997), 151; there is also a brief mention of Poe's "The Oval Portrait" in *Memoirs of the Blind*, trans. Pascale-Anne Brault and Michael Naas (Chicago: University of Chicago Press, 1993), 36.

Melville's "Bartleby the Scrivener" is also frequently cited; see, for example, *The Gift of Death*, trans. David Wills (Chicago: University of Chicago Press, 1995), 74–76, and *A Taste for the Secret*, with Maurizio Ferraris (Cambridge, England: Polity Press, 2001), 26–27.

There are many other references to American literature or literary figures, a brief mention of Faulkner and Stein in *Acts of Literature* (55, 59) and of Wallace Stevens and William Carlos Williams in Derrida's homage to Joseph Riddel in *The Work of Mourning* (Chicago: University of Chicago Press, 2001),127–132. American literature is thus not at all absent from Derrida's work. But, for all his time in America, there is no "Double Session" on Whitman's *Leaves of Grass*, no reading of Hawthorne or Faulkner, Bellow or Roth, to match his readings of Blanchot or Mallarmé, Kafka or Celan. This is not to say, of course, that there are not such treatments of American literary figures among Derrida's as yet unpublished works. My friend Thomas Dutoit, who has helped catalogue and organize Derrida's archives, tells me, for example, that in 1991–92 Derrida devoted several sessions of his seminar on the secret to Henry James' *The Aspern Papers*.

33. A good place to see Derrida's "elective affinities" is his interview with Derek Attridge in *Acts of Literature*, ed. Derek Attridge (London: Routledge, 1992), 33–75, where Derrida talks about (more or less in chronological order): Sartre, Camus, Rousseau, Gide, Nietzsche, Mallarmé, Joyce, Celan, Bataille, Artaud, Blanchot, Flaubert, Céline, Ponge, Genet, Kafka, the Bible, George Sand, George Eliot, Virginia Woolf, Gertrude Stein, and Hélène Cixous.

34. *Of Grammatology*, trans. Gayatri Chakravorty Spivak (Baltimore: Johns Hopkins University Press, 1976), 44 ff.; see also *Eyes of the University*, trans. Jan Plug and Others (Stanford, CA: Stanford University Press, 2004), 138.

35. See *Limited Inc* (Evanston, IL: Northwestern University Press, 1988), as well as Derrida's comments in *Eyes of the University*, 125.

36. Derrida cites contemporary American-born authors such as Noam Chomsky (see *Rogues*, trans. Pascale-Anne Brault and Michael Naas [Stanford, CA: Stanford University Press, 2005], 96, *For What Tomorrow...*, 132–134) and Jeremy Rifkin (see "The University Without Condition" in *Without Alibi*, 225–226), but in neither case is there anything like a sustained engagement with such figures.

37. See *Ethics, Institutions, and the Right to Philosophy*, 28–29.

38. Derrida's official title at the Ecole Normale Supérieure was "répétiteur" or, in the school's jargon, "caïman." In this capacity he was responsible for preparing students for the "agrégation" exam in philosophy. At the Ecole des Hautes Etudes his official title was "directeur d'études."

39. Catherine Malabou writes in *Counterpath*, 48: "How does Derrida traverse various countries, frontiers, cities, and languages? How does he set about his *experience* of traveling? It is possible to claim in the first place that Derrida has three countries: his native Algeria, France, and the United States. He divides his life, his teaching, his work, and his home(s) between the last two. We should say more precisely that his way of life in France owes its stability only to the turbulence of a tension, that of the thread tying, by means of a complex network, his country of birth (Algeria) and his chosen country (United States)."

40. See *Moscou aller-retour*, 55, and *Specters of Marx*, trans. Peggy Kamuf (New York: Routledge, 1994), 70–71, where Derrida expresses some skepticism regarding such undertakings.

41. "The Ends of Man" in *Margins of Philosophy*, trans. Alan Bass (Chicago: University of Chicago Press, 1982), 114.

42. "Of an Apocalyptic Tone Recently Adopted in Philosophy," trans. John P. Leavey, Jr., *Oxford Literary Review*, 6–2, 1984, 30. In *On Cosmopolitanism and Forgiveness*, trans. Mark Dooley and Michael Hughes (London: Routledge, 2001), 46, Derrida speaks of the use of religious language and oaths in American politics as well as the American sovereign's right to grant clemency.

43. "No Apocalypse, Not Now," *Diacritics* (Summer 1984), 20–31.

44. *Specters of Marx*, 56–60.

45. On "globalization" or what Derrida preferred to call *mondialisation*, see *Sur Parole*, 120 and "The University Without Condition," 223.

46. Derrida became an astute observer of the American university system. He spoke, for example, in a volume entitled *The Eyes of the University*, 145, of the many apparently external pressures on the American university system, the economic, cultural, and political constraints, the link between government funding and military programs and university research. See also "The University Without Condition," 202–237.

47. On the "homohegemonic" power of the American culture industry, see *Echographies of Television*, with Bernard Stiegler (Cambridge, England: Polity Press, 2002), 47, 54, 86–87.

48. Derrida spoke frequently of the worldwide presence of the American information industry, for example, of the CNN phenomenon: "In a digitalized 'cyberspace,'

prosthesis upon prosthesis, a heavenly glance, monstrous, bestial or divine, something like an eye of CNN, watches permanently..." ("Faith and Knowledge," in *Religion* [Stanford, CA: Stanford University Press, 1998], 70, no. 17); see also *Echographies*, 65.

49. The hegemony of the Anglo-American idiom was a common theme in Derrida's work over the past two decades. In *Ethics, Institutions, and the Right to Philosophy*, 28–29, Derrida writes: "the hegemony of the Anglo-American is all over the world, it is irreversible, something we shouldn't even try and resist. It's done. Everyone in the world will have two languages, his own plus Anglo-American. Then without trying to prevent this, we have to handle this differently." See also "Faith and Knowledge," 29, 43; "Mondialisation: la guerre ou la paix?" (*Divinatio*, No. 15, Spring-Summer 2002, 162); *The Other Heading*, 23; *Papier Machine*, 344; and *Applying: To Derrida*, 214.

50. *Echographies of Television*, 90–94.

51. *Sur Parole*, 110–120.

52. For an extended discussion of the death penalty in America, see *For What Tomorrow..*, 155–159; see also *Without Alibi*, 245, 263; *Negotiations*, 385–386; "Mondialisation: la guerre ou la paix?" 175–176.

53. See Derrida's comments on racism in America in *For What Tomorrow...*, 28, 154. See also "For Mumia Abu-Jamal" and "Open Letter to Bill Clinton," *Negotiations*, 125–129,130–132, and *Counterpath*, 325, no. 7. On apartheid as not just a South African but "an American problem," see "Critical Response II: But, beyond (Open Letter to Anne McClintock and Rob Nixon)," *Critical Inquiry* 13 (Autumn 1986), 170.

54. *Voyous* (Paris: Editions Galilée, 2003) [*Rogues*, trans. Pascale-Anne Brault and Michael Naas (Stanford, CA: Stanford University Press, 2005)]; Derrida speaks in *Without Alibi* (262) of "the principle of nation-state sovereignty, which the United States protects in an inflexible manner when it's a question of their own and limits when it's a question of others."

55. On the unique "translation" or "transference" of deconstruction in and to America, see, once again, "DA," 73, and "The Time is Out of Joint," in *Deconstruction is/in America* (New York: New York University Press, 1993), 27 and following.

56. Jacques Derrida, *Memoires for Paul de Man*, 11–17. The pages cited were written in January-February 1984.

57. I say "ethical" because deconstruction was often condemned for its "corrupting" influence on the academy. Derrida says in an interview given around the same time: "We can't understand the reception that deconstruction has had in the United States without background—historical, political, religious, and so forth. I would say religious above all." ("DA," 2).

58. See *Points*, 413.

59. "Autoimmunity: Real and Symbolic Suicides—A Conversation with Jacques Derrida," in Giovanna Borradori, *Philosophy in a Time of Terror* (Chicago: University of Chicago Press, 2003), 116–117. Hereafter abbreviated *A*. The quote begins: "What would give me the most hope in the wake of all these upheavals is a potential difference between a new figure of Europe and the United States. I say this without any Eurocentrism. Which is why I am speaking of a *new* figure of Europe. Without forsaking its own memory, by drawing upon it, in fact, as an indispensable resource, Europe could make an essential contribution to the future of the international law we have been discussing." On this "Europe" that exceeds its present configuration, see *The Other Heading*: "Something unique is afoot in Europe, in what is still called Europe even if we no longer know very well *what* or *who* goes by this name" (5). "Is there then a

completely new 'today' of Europe beyond all the exhausted programs of *Eurocentrism* and *anti-Eurocentrism...*" (12–13).

60. It should be said that Europe, which often does America's bidding, is not spared this same critique. In *Inconditonnalité ou souveraineté* (Athens: Editions Patakis, 2002), 42, for example, Derrida speaks of "Europe et son tuteur américain."

61. Derrida speaks of Thoreau's notion of "civil disobedience" in *Without Alibi*, 63–64.

62. "Une Europe de l'espoir," *Le Monde diplomatique*, November 2004, 3. Derrida's piece was written to celebrate the fiftieth anniversary of this publication.

63. "Deconstruction in America," 10.

64. In the issue of *Le Monde diplomatique* in which "A Europe of Hope" was published there is an article with the decidedly less nuanced title "Nous sommes tous anti-américains," "We are all anti-American," meaning, it seems, "we Europeans, or we Europeans of this political leaning, are today all anti-American." It is precisely this kind of non-binary reflection that "Europe" should give us some hope of escaping.

65. In *Who's Afraid of Philosophy?*, trans. Jan Plug (Sanford, CA: Stanford University Press, 2002), 103, Derrida refers to himself as a "sort of uprooted African."

13 The affect of America

Peggy Kamuf

My remarks are going to be somewhat personal.[1] I do not mean I am preparing to talk about myself, at least not much. Rather, I want to say something about Jacques Derrida's personal America. Many attempts have been made to characterize the intense relations that, forty years ago, began evolving between Derrida's work and his readers (or non-readers) in the US, relations mediated in very complex ways by the body of his writing, by its reception and translation, by the different institutions or traditions that welcomed or resisted it, and so forth. Instead of another attempt in that general direction, I thought I would try to address the topic in a less, or rather differently mediated sense by saying something about his affective relation to the US. Certainly this is hardly less complex, if only because affect can rarely be assigned to a positive or negative pole without admixture. But there is also the complication – if indeed one can call it that – introduced when someone presumes to talk about another's affective experience in order to say what this other feels or felt, the quality of his affect, what has affected him, and how. This ought to be not just complicated but impossible, practically and morally, or rather ethically. To think it is not impossible is to yield too complacently to the biographer's temptation, and to the belief that whatever obstacles there may be in the way of putting oneself in the other's place can be swept aside by dint of good will. Derrida is especially vigilant about the risk of this complacency; he never lets one forget that the others he writes about are constituted by that writing as *texts*, that is, as folded layers of sign-traces offered up to interpretation. To say that the other is encountered as text makes all ethics an ethics of reading, but one also thereby recalls that the other person is not, first of all or above all, a potential site of knowledge that I can appropriate, at least not without leveling all that makes that other other. Even with those who have been close companions of his life's intellectual adventures, Derrida never relaxes his vigilance in this regard and especially with those friends whom one might presume he knows well, he never ceases, for example, to wonder how they experience what affects them.[2]

And yet, it is also true that, as regards so many of his own experiences, Derrida speaks freely and, in his writings, even appears to seek a kind of absorption by language of an experiential excess that overflows the ordinary vessels of words, compelling him to reinvent the shared medium of meaning. Some such image has often described the gift of the poet, but in Derrida the poet cannot be distinguished from the philosopher, and likewise the gift or task of inventing a language cannot be distinguished from the work of formalizing, generalizing, conceptualizing that invention and its conditions. One could cite countless examples, indeed every text bearing Derrida's signature, for this is one of its principal characteristics. All the same, I'll mention just *Circonfession* or 'A Silkworm of One's Own' to index what I mean by an excess of experience, its unplumbable singularity or idiomaticity, that drives this writing constantly to let itself be reinvented within a general language.[3]

With texts like those just mentioned, Derrida has seemingly given a certain philosophical establishment ample provocation to dismiss what he's doing on the grounds that it is not philosophy but either autobiography, poetry or some unstable mixture of the two. For does not the singular experience of the philosopher himself or herself name the category of everything that the project of philosophy demands be set aside, bracketed, studiously ignored? And if it appears that someone writing as a philosopher has not ignored all this, well then, whatever he or she puts forward may be considered of little worth for those labouring in the fields of general, philosophical truth because it will have been corrupted or contaminated by the merely empirical, contingent, finite, or particular. Derrida, however, does not merely fly in the face of this prohibition but advances, in conceptual or quasi-conceptual terms, a thinking of contamination in general. He thus raises the stakes considerably for the profession of philosophy, which, even as he displaces what we can profess to hear and understand by 'profession', he never renounces, vigorously defends, and tirelessly renews through his teaching.[4] At stake from now on, for all those who have learned it from and with Derrida, is not only the possibility of distinguishing philosophy from all it professes to exclude (literature, poetry, autobiography, individual experience, the singular idiom and so on), but also the possibility of 'personal', that is, singular experience uncontaminated by repetition and generalization, by substitution and metonymy. For this is perhaps the greater scandal of Derrida's thought insofar as it flaunts the exclusion of singular experience or affect from the realm of general truth: his work shows us how to read that distinction as a barrier that has protected not just the idea of truth's generality but also – perhaps even above all, for each and every philosopher no less than anyone else – that of the propriety or property of one's own experience, of experience as, in the ordinary expression, irreducibly 'personal' and thus inaccessible to another. With his thinking of differance and general contamination, substitution and metonymy, Derrida makes or rather lets the distinction between self/not-self, ownness/otherness, as well as generality/singularity tremble and blur, a trembling and blurring that, he would argue, is the irremediable condition of what one wants to call, so as to appropriate it, one's 'own' experience.

But I seem to have been led off the track, and what is worse, to have backed into a blatant contradiction. For didn't I say that another's experience and affect have to remain unknowable in their singular unrepeatability? Yes, certainly, as such and by itself, by definition, the singular does not repeat; its time is 'one time only', without possibility of coming back, starting over, and over. And yet, by the same token, singular unrepeatabilty would always be lost, utterly and irretrievably, unless its trait *at the same time* can also be repeated, reiterated, remembered. This is true not only 'for the record', for example, the biographer's record of another's life experience, but also already and ineluctably for the 'one' (in quotation marks for it is indeed 'oneness' along with 'ownness' that is thrown into question by the necessary repetition of singularity) whose experience it supposedly *is*, but that it *is*, presently, only on the condition of coming back, returning, and repeating as the experience it never was in any past present. Readers of Freud's *Beyond the Pleasure Principle* and the studies of trauma spawned by that text (written in the immediate aftermath of the killing fields of World War I) may recognize in the description of such a temporal torsion or distortion, as well as in a certain compulsion to repeat, an essential affinity between what is identified and singled out as trauma and what is here being summarized about Derrida's thinking of experience in general. Experience is traumatic or has the structure of what can be analyzed as trauma, as Derrida has said somewhere pretty much in those terms. And this is true no less of a 'happy' experience – falling in love – than of a devastatingly 'unhappy' one.

The figure of singularity is thus what bids, appeals or calls for a repetition in order to 'be' the singularity that, therefore, it is – not. Close to the heart of Derrida's thought and work is the affirmation of this very contradiction, an inheritance in part from Nietzsche's affirmative thinking of the eternal recurrence of the same. Within Nietzsche's affirmation, Derrida hears and amplifies the call to repeat as having necessarily to be *addressed* to another, to others, and thereby dispatched into difference, dissemination, deferral, *without* guarantee of arrival at destination. It is this 'without' that Derrida affirms, not or at least not simply in its privative sense, but as the very condition of repetition. 'My' experience returns to me, recurs to me, if it does, as the experience of another, at once another 'me' and absolutely other, uncanny therefore. After Derrida, the category of the uncanny, no less than that of trauma, spreads and thus dissolves into the general structure of experience as extra-ordinary, where 'extra-' marks an irreducible extra-dition or extra-diction outside the self, an extra-vagance, if you will, but one that would not so much exceed a pre-existing self's balanced economy as instigate and re-instigate what is called self.

These remarks are far too compact and elliptical. But they are meant merely as prologue. For I set out in what follows from the fact that, with his friends or even with strangers, many of whom would soon become friends,

Derrida often confides details about his 'own' experience. But it is rare to find reference in his writings to anything from his complex and long (almost 50-year) experience of or in 'America',[5] a fact that contrasts sharply with his frequent, painstaking and often painful evocations (especially in *Circumfession,* but also see *The Monolingualism of the Other* or 'A Silkworm of One's Own') of childhood, adolescent and family experiences in his birth-place, Algiers, which he left for the first time at age 19 in 1949. One might well say that this is natural or normal, given that infancy, childhood and youth leave a deeper or more traumatic mark than adult experiences.

I should make clear that it is not some American trauma, however one chooses to understand this term, that I am trying to reconstruct. Having accepted the assignment 'Derrida's America', however, I could not help hearing a very wide range of the title's or topic's possible meanings, and thereby the mandate to choose from among them. In the circum-stance, it is Derrida's own not-so-private America that came to the fore of my recollection, but at the same time, unavoidably, a hesitation, a scruple. For how can one justify repeating another's account of his experience, especially once he himself can no longer correct as need be any misunder-standings, exaggerations, *malentendus,* not to mention deliberate distortions or even wholesale inventions? Hence this prologue. Which, however, provides no guarantee that my recollections are not somewhere mistaken. Everything that follows should therefore be read under the sign of 'perhaps'.[6]

I have the good fortune of following my friend Michael Naas, who has just recalled a great many of the most pertinent facts about Jacques Derrida's career in America as a teacher, lecturer and colleague. There seems little left to add. Nevertheless, one might ask if it is indeed possible to set a limit on 'facts' here, that is, on the facts of a relation-to-America that someone would likely have had or been subjected to had he been born in 1930, especially anywhere within the sphere of 'old Europe' and its old colonial powers. Like everyone, which is also to say unlike anyone else, Jacques Derrida begins to have a relation-to-America long before he happened to set foot there, in 1956, in Cambridge, Massachusetts, not far from the landfall of some earlier European pilgrims.

In 1943, when he was 13, Americans arrived in Algeria, part of the Allied forces that liberated Algiers, his native city. When Derrida speaks of witness-ing these events, he seems a little bemused by the image of himself in this very-soon-to-be cliché-picture of the Yanks bringing baseball and chewing gum to the populations under their occupying authority. He recalls that his family became friendly with one G.I., who was invited to their home a number of times and with whom letters were exchanged after the war, but then they stopped. I think he even still remembers the G.I's name, but I can't recall it.

His bemusement at these recollections is not easy to read. In 1942, right before the Allies landed and began to retake North Africa, he had been excluded from his *lycée* as a Jew, the result of an application of the so-called

'Jewish laws' by the Vichy loyalists in Algeria. The Allied liberators, along with the new Free French regime they installed in Algeria, took their time cancelling and reversing the effects of these laws. So perhaps he saw the liberators rather quickly, at age 13 (I now realize that these events would have coincided with the year of his Bar Mitzvah) as somewhat compromised heroes, at least in their – witting or unwitting – complicity with injustice. He has talked about the experience of his expulsion from school in so many different texts that there is little doubt about how deeply and lastingly it affected him. And it would have been from the place of this wound that he witnessed and judged the promise of a new world.

But, of course, well before these events the New World had already sent some spectacular proxies to represent it and not only to Algiers or to Europe: I mean of course American movies. When he talks about going to the movies in his youth, however, his memory seems to evoke less the films he might have seen than the places, the 'movie palaces' that, like so many Western cities, Algiers saw sprout up between the wars. He especially remembers the names of the movie theatres, which I cannot recall but they were not unlikely the names one would have found in other cities and that were so many exotic clichés: Rialto, Rex, El Dorado, etc. He likes to recollect the names but, it seems to me, they come back with the taste of a city divided by its colonial history and reality, where those 'palaces' were located in a 'European quarter' more or less officially off limits to the majority of the city's inhabitants.

Yet, if one were to try to reach all the way back to some first 'fact' of Derrida's relation-to-America, then it would be necessary to back up even before the beginning of his own experience of America, whether through proxies or not. Indeed, one would have to reach back even before his birth. And it would be necessary to put a name to this fact, and even to locate it in a name, his name, not Jacques but Jackie, spelled like that, despite several rules of French onomastics. As he explains in *Circumfession*, in the milieu of his family between the wars, there was a vogue for giving children English (not particularly American) names, which were often nicknames in the culture they came from. Hence, Jackie Derrida. As with the names of the movie palaces, this given name would have been mixed up with the marks of social division, which is not to say he ever complains about it, not to me at least, even when we have conversations about the fact that I too was given a diminutive for a first name, which unlike Jackie/Jacques, I didn't have the good sense to set aside once I began signing things for publication. But I also notice that he does not seems ready to admit that his name has any link to the American child actor Jackie Coogan, although this reluctance may be just as well his caution at the idea that anyone's name ever comes from an identifiable donor or model. But of course one's parents have their own ideas about such things and act on their own impulses, perhaps never more so, as parents, than when they give their child a name.

Thanks to a brief sequence in the film *D'ailleurs Derrida*, which was first shown in 2000, it may be that one has now something like an image of the impulsive desire that accompanied this strange and fateful naming gesture, which would have taken place some time around 15 July 1930. The sequence is shot in the house in El Biar, a suburb of Algiers, where Derrida spent most of his childhood and youth. It is the same house his family had to abandon, with almost all its contents, in 1962 after the declaration of Algeria's independence. When it enters the house in 1999, the camera uncovers a few remnants of this abandonment that surprisingly have survived intact: above all, the mother's piano and hanging above it, most improbably, the framed movie poster of Charlie Chaplin's 1921 silent film *The Kid*, showing the little tramp towering protectively over the boy actor Jackie Coogan, who played the eponymous kid. The framed, enshrined poster clings to the wall like some miraculous castaway of a shipwreck, as if the house itself had kept safe the memory of a possible namesake, Jackie Derrida, and had issued to all who subsequently found shelter there an obscure command to preserve this image artifact.

In signalling towards this mark of a certain relation-to-America that he must inherit or accept as one accepts a given name, I am suggesting that one has perhaps to retrace the 'facts' to unconscious drives of prior generations. Derrida would doubtless be the first to encourage such a procedure. If so, then it becomes hard to think that there wasn't put in place in his very own name, a kind of *draw* to America, if only unconsciously. I don't know why I say only unconsciously, as if there could be any more powerful force drawing one towards or away from the choices of a life.

To come back to 1956, which is where Michael Naas began his account with 'just the facts': Jacques (who at the time, I suppose, was still called Jackie by everyone and not just by close family) recounts some travelling he did that year, when he and Marguerite rented or borrowed a car and drove through the American South towards I forget which destination. The Southern United States in the mid-1950s was still a very segregated place, although the US Supreme Court had begun to rule against the constitutionality of Jim Crow laws. Nevertheless, below the Mason-Dixon Line, public space remained very clearly and obviously segregated. Certainly anyone travelling there, but especially Europeans unused to these primitive customs and most especially those whose sensibilities had been sharpened by Algerian apartheid, would have remarked it. He remembers that they picked up an African-American hitch-hiker, a sailor or soldier I think, in North or South Carolina I believe it was. The man they stopped for must have been quite astonished to be offered a ride by a white couple. Their hitch-hiker seemed nervous, ill-at-ease in ways that Jacques and Marguerite weren't sure they knew how to read. As I recall the story at least, no misfortune befell them, but doubtless their hitch-hiker was quite aware that the trip could have turned out very badly if, for example, they had had a run-in with the local police. When Jacques returned to Cambridge and told his

American friends about the experience, they let him know he had taken a considerable risk.

Following a kind of unconscious thread, I connect this story about the hitch-hiker to a remark he says Paul de Man made to him at some point during their friendship, which began well after the driving trip through the South in'56 or'57. To judge by his laughter, he likes to repeat this remark, as if it flatters some idea he has of himself, in addition no doubt to the pleasure he takes in reviving the speech of his friend. Paul de Man told him that he, Jacques, spoke English 'like a black sailor'. I ask and he doesn't deny that what he especially likes is to be told he does not have a typical or caricatural French accent when he speaks English as he so often must. Speaking English in public remains clearly a special kind of torture for him. There is above all the irreparable loss of his idiom, but also, despite his remarkable fluency and ease in the learned language, a sense that his non-native accent exposes him, denudes him. It's very difficult, impossible in fact, to reassure him on this score. (Whenever he hears a fellow Frenchman speaking English with a typical, Maurice-Chevalier accent, he turns to whoever he is with and says 'I don't sound like that, do I?'.) But finally perhaps it is not reassurance he seeks so much as an understanding of the generalized condition that he has called 'the monolingualism of the other' and that he pins down in one of those incomparable aphorisms or watchwords for which he has always had a special genius: 'I have only one tongue [or language], it is not mine'.[7]

Even though it is not the language he prefers to communicate in by any means, he has a keen ear for American English, for the idiomatic in our language that, as habitual speakers, we cease remarking. I think of two expressions in particular that he often isolates from the most humdrum conversations and reflects back to his interlocutor, as if he has a particular fondness for them and wants to restore the force of what they, what we are saying. First, to 'look forward to' something. This expression almost always elicits from him a smile. It's true that in French there is no equivalent idiom for saying one's eager anticipation of something promised, some-thing to come. To be turned thus by a turn of speech towards the future is doubtless what he savours and wants to save for the unthinking native users of the language. Another turn of phrase that he frequently fishes out of our current of everyday exchange is the expression 'take care', the phrase one often says upon leaving someone, as a sign-off in a letter, or at the end of telephone conversation: 'Take care'. Derrida remarks it, repeats it and reflects it back, prompting each time a reflection on what exactly one is saying thereby: take my care with you? Take it away from me?

To his fondness for these commonplaces of language, I would add a few words about Derrida's love of places in the US. Not just in the US of course, but his relation to America stands apart from the relation to other locales by virtue of the regular, annual repetition of his migration to the same places. Through long-standing associations with several universities, which cause him each year (and after a certain point, more than once a year) to return to the same places, his relation to America is rhythmed by a movement of return, of revisiting that which he has already found to be to his taste, of re-tasting, re-finding what was once found: *des retrouvailles*, as he might say. This taste for return, for *retrouvailles*, is such that it cannot be satisfied in the abstract, in the mere knowledge that one is once more in a place called Baltimore, New Haven, New York, Irvine, Laguna Beach, Los Angeles, or Santa Monica. Instead, it requires a movement towards concrete landmarks, although these are only rarely marked in any tourist's guidebook. Rather, they are the same restaurants, the same corners in Central Park, the same cafés, the same streets or even the same shops in the same shopping malls.

Most frequently, I meet him in Irvine, California, where he began giving his annual seminar in 1987. Jacques often invites friends to dinner after the seminar, but there are not many restaurants to his liking in the vicinity of the university. There is one, however, to which he gladly returns and brings his friends: a Japanese restaurant called Koto not far from the campus. Few indeed are his visitors who are not brought to this pleasant place, to its interior courtyard with a koi pond and waterfall. Calm and inviting, quiet enough for conversation.

On 3 December 2004, a memorial took place in the same auditorium at UC Irvine where Derrida returned to give his seminar every Spring since 1987. Afterwards, Elisabeth Weber and I have the same impulse: to go back to Koto. We drive the short distance there ... and find it closed. Out of business, by the looks of it. We cannot help thinking there is a certain justice in that.

Derrida is, in general, a very keen observer of the American public scene, of its politics, university, legal system, judicial system (one of his last seminars is on the death penalty and makes constant reference to capital punishment in the US), of religion in America, but also its eating habits (which he mostly deplores), child-raising customs, television, movies, violence, journalism, and so forth.

He is fascinated – I don't think the word is too strong – with the practice in the US of televising congressional hearings, with this particular form of public testimony. He watched hours of the so-called Iran/Contra hearings, broadcast I believe in 1987, thus at the end of the second Reagan administration. The hearings concerned the very shady financing of the Nicaraguan 'Contras' and their rag-tag rebellion, propped up by CIA-filtered American money, against the legitimately elected Sandinista government. The scheme involved illegal arm sales by the US government to Iran in exchange for the release of American hostages in Teheran, with the proceeds going to the Contras for the purchase of weapons. In short, a remarkably sordid affair, on which the televised hearings shed a certain amount of light. And from the way Jacques talks about the experience, it would seem he watched these broadcasts both with admiration for this very open democratic process, which exposes for all to see a government's crimes and deceptions ('Such hearings could never happen in France', I recall him saying), but also with a sense of the naïveté of American faith in legal procedure as a guardrail against the corruption of power.

These observations of a pervasive legalistic culture in America no doubt are fed into his own increasing reflection on concepts that straddle the domains of law, ethics, philosophy and literature, such as truth-telling and testimony (and thus perjury or lying), pardon and forgiveness, as well as capital punishment. These concepts not only set the programme of his later seminars, but also numerous texts written in their vicinity. A few years ago I realised I had translated in a fairly short interval several essays by Derrida that dealt with lying, perjury, forgiveness, excuses, cruelty and the death penalty. I edited them in a volume that was eventually titled *Without Alibi*.[8] The title comes from the volume's final essay, 'Psychoanalysis Searches the States of Its Soul', which is scanned by a repetition of that phrase. All the essays make significant reference to the US: for example, 'History of the Lie' devotes a long analysis to Hannah Arendt's writing on lying in politics and her famous article on the Pentagon Papers, while the essay titled '*Le parjure*' – perjury or the perjurer – deals principally with a novel by the French writer Henri Thomas that is set in America and models its principal character on the young Paul de Man in the first years after his arrival in the US. For these reasons, I had originally considered as a title for this collection: *What Lies in America*. My editor at the press was adamantly opposed, and no doubt rightly so, to my too-clever-by-half equivocation. Perhaps, however, it is not inappropriate to let that abandoned title come to rest (or lie) here, in these reflections on 'Derrida's America'.

Michael Naas has already underscored the important place Derrida allowed for religion in any understanding of 'America', above all in its difference from the pervasive secularism of Europe. What always impresses itself upon him is that this place has regularly to be marked and reaffirmed by its elected officials. Long before a second President Bush began to play 'the religion card' even more baldly than Jimmy Carter had dared to do, Derrida is heard to remark to American audiences or to friends in conversation that it is simply unimaginable for anyone to be elected President of the United States who is an *avowed* non-believer.

I emphasize the avowal, confession or profession of faith – that is, the performance of a certain speech act – because I believe that this remark points above all to the pertinence he grants to categories of speech act theory for the analysis of politics, in America or elsewhere. Concepts from speech act theory become a nearly constant reference in his writings after 1971, the date of his famous essay on J.L. Austin, 'Signature Event Context', whose seriously comic aftermath, *Limited Inc, abc*, is provoked by a dyspeptic reply from the American philosopher John Searle. (Now that I think of it, *Limited Inc* offers one of Derrida's most sustained responses to 'America', at least as impersonated by Searle in his earnest misprision of what is at stake in the deconstruction of certain of Austin's categories and assumptions.) Another American philosopher, Richard Rorty, will have been one of the few to acknowledge the proximity of Derrida's thought to that of American pragmatists. And yet it is with reference more to Nietzsche than to Peirce, James or Dewey that Derrida accepted on several occasions to call his thinking *pragmatics*, leaving the 'ism' of pragmatism to whoever finds it indispensable to adjudicate between schools of philosophy, which is a gesture that never interests him very much.

He is fascinated as well by the phenomenon of Christian evangelists on American television. He watches these programmes whenever he can, a habit that seems often to puzzle some of his American interlocutors. In 1995, in an important essay on religion, 'Faith and Knowledge: The Two Sources of "Religion" at the Limits of Reason Alone', Derrida advances a complex argument regarding an essential non-contradiction between religious faith and scientific technology or knowledge. I don't recall his making any explicit reference there to televised evangelism, in America or elsewhere, but his argument in this essay, concerning religion's positive and productive relation to technology, can easily be connected to his interest in that phenomenon. This argument, which obviously I am pointing to in a minimal fashion, engages with a certain interpretation of Enlightenment and counters the presumed historical antagonism between 'faith and knowledge', to repeat the terms of Derrida's title or, to put it another way, the axiom according to which wherever scientific enlightenment advances, religious belief retreats and so forth. Certainly the American everyday and political culture Derrida observes closely, but with the benefit of a certain abstraction from its ordinary preoccupations, gives the lie to this axiom by mobilizing every technological advance also to spread religious belief.

This is certainly not to say that he ever gives up his own faith in enlightenment and reason, although he insists that the understanding of 'reason' is severely impoverished whenever it is restricted to pure logical calculation.[9] He is even above all, I would say, a thinker of the irreducible tie between faith and reason or enlightenment. There is, he insists, no reason, no relation in language, no understanding that does not rely on faith or belief, on faith, for example, that the other is speaking the truth and not dissembling, lying, perjuring. It is this irreducible belief that is on display in practices of testimony, whether in a judicial legal context, in that televised testimony I referred to earlier, or in the most intimate confessions between lovers. Derrida's profound reflection on testimony is always guided by and brought back to a line from a poem by Paul Celan: 'No one bears witness for the witness', which states the inviolable secrecy of the witness's act and thus its irreducible appeal to belief.

I also believe he sees America's religious traditions as forestalling for a long time yet the new enlightenment of a faith placed not in some all-knowing God or in His providence but in the conditions of the relation to singular others, who are each one absolutely other. Indeed, I would say that he foresees not only a continuation but a further extension of American belief in its own sovereign right to know, its own right, that is, to enforce 'truth' as revealed to it by God. Hence the unshakable American belief in the necessity of capital punishment, hence a current US government that disregards international conventions prohibiting torture, hence the retreat of hospitality for non-citizens and the abrogation of civil rights for citizens in America today.

Derrida's America. Just as the US responded strongly to Derrida's work, he has responded to 'it' – or rather to many things marked by or as American. It has been a selective response and also a non-totalizing one. (Unlike some other prominent European intellectuals one can think of, Derrida has always been careful to avoid monolithic judgements of 'America'.) His critique of US policy, especially post-9/11, is thoroughgoing and severe.[10] I would thus tend to agree with Michael Naas that in the last decade or so Derrida's thinking has been drawn increasingly to Europe as the more promising place of the future, where both new forms of shared or limited sovereignty and new possibilities for hospitality seem, for the time being, to have a better chance of being invented than, for example, in the present-day US.

Nevertheless, despite all the obstacles he sees to enlightenment in America, I don't believe Jacques Derrida has ever been seriously tempted to abandon his ties to that place, and certainly not to all his friends there, anymore than to the places and friends who love him throughout the world. Derrida has kept his promise to go on criticizing and deconstructing America from wherever he might be, whether within America or elsewhere. Indeed, he has kept asking how one could even know today where America begins and ends. He might even say the same thing of himself, whose relation to America did not start the day he first set foot there and has not ended because he will never return there. A Frenchman, a European, a North African, an Algerian, Derrida is also none of the above, except formally. Not essentially. He is not even of the world, but has always belonged to what is coming not simply from but *as* the future.

Before Jacques died so suddenly, I had several conversations with him about the then-upcoming US presidential elections. He asked me more than once what I thought was going to happen. And I told him without hesitating and with conviction that President Bush's bid for re-election would be defeated. I believed it then, even if my belief bespoke sheer hope. But it was a hope that I thought reasonable and grounded. He never argued against this prediction and this hope, but only re-iterated it by saying 'I hope you are right'. On one occasion he added with emphasis '*Il faut*', 'It must be', 'It has to be', 'It is necessary', 'It is needed'. I don't know of course if he really shared my hope, or if thought it was as naïve as it proved to be several weeks later. But I do believe that had we been able to speak again after the hope was dashed he would have insisted that it remains necessary.

Notes

1. I am greatly indebted to Simon Glendinning for his transcription of the improvised remarks on which this essay is based.
2. See, most recently and most pertinently, Jacques Derrida, "'Justices'", trans. Peggy Kamuf, in *Critical Inquiry* 31, 3 (Spring 2005), an essay in honour of J. Hillis Miller: 'How does J. Hillis Miller *himself* feel when he says "je", "I" or when he has the feeling of "himself"? These borders of the I are vertiginous, but inevitable. We all rub up against them, make contact without contact, in particular as concerns our dearest friends. This is even what is astonishing about friendship, when it is somewhat alert. It is also vigilant friendship that startles us awake to this strange question: what does it mean, for an I *to feel itself*? "How does he *himself* feel, J. Hillis Miller? J. Hillis Miller *himself*, the other, the wholly other that he remains for me?"' (690).
3. Jacques Derrida, *Circonfession*, in Geoffrey Bennington and Derrida, *Jacques Derrida*, trans. G. Bennington (Chicago: University of Chicago Press, 1993), and 'A Silkworm of One's Own', in Hélène Cixous and Derrida, *Veils*, trans. G. Bennington (Stanford: Stanford University Press, 2001).
4. See, in particular, Derrida, 'The University Without Condition', in Derrida, *Without Alibi*, ed. and trans. Peggy Kamuf (Stanford: Stanford University Press, 2002), and *Who's Afraid of Philosophy?*, trans. Jan Plug (Stanford: Stanford University Press, 2002), which collects a number of Derrida's writings on the philosophical institution.
5. An important exception, one could argue, is 'Envois' in *The Post Card*, in which the author frequently depicts his – fictive, we should recall – letter-writer sending his post cards from New Haven, Connecticut, where indeed Derrida himself spent several weeks every year teaching at Yale University between 197? and 1987. But the condition of fiction has to forestall any simple assimilation of this character's 'experiences' to that of its author, even if the resemblance between them is remarkable. Another exception would have to be made for Counterpath: Traveling with Jacques Derrida, by Catherine Malabou and Jacques Derrida (trans. David Wills [Stanford: Stanford University Press, 2004]). This time, Derrida himself signs the post cards he sends to Malabou from his travel destinations, four of which are in the US (New York, Villanova Baltimore, Laguna Beach).
6. After shaking out, with an admirable analysis, the assumptions that structure and accompany the specific genre of the biography-of-the-philosopher, Geoffrey Bennington writes, in 1996: 'It is of course to be expected that Derrida will some day be the subject of biographical writing, and there is nothing to prevent this being of the most traditional kind.... I imagine that there are anecdotes to be told (probably mostly to do with cars and driving) and remarks to be reported (probably to do with other philosophers). But this type of complacent and recuperative writing would at some point have to encounter the fact that Derrida's work should at least have disturbed its presuppositions' ('A Life in Philosophy', in Bennington, *Other Analyses: Reading Philosophy* [pdf: 2004], p. 425). Complacency and recuperation are indeed what I would avoid, if possible, even though I do recount one anecdote having to do with cars and driving.
7. Derrida, *The Monolingualism of the Other, or the Prosthesis of Origin*, trans. Patrick Mensah (Stanford: Stanford University Press, 1998). This paradoxical double assertion has a particular status among Derrida's aphorisms or watchwords. What is remarkable about this refrain, which forms something like the swinging hinge in the text where it occurs, is that its provocation depends not on syntax or semantics of the French idiom, but purely, if that is possible, on the logical relations it installs between the two clauses, which are moreover separated only by a comma without coordinating or subordinating conjunction ('Je n'ai

qu'une langue, ce n'est pas la mienne'). Unlike, therefore, many other aphoristic formulations that Derrida has put forward, which will torment and incite translation from now on (e.g. 'Tout autre est tout autre'), this gem, this pearl, passes into translation seemingly without resistance, for example: 'I have only one tongue, it

is not mine', where the loss between one tongue and the other seems almost negligible. Its action is thus counter-Babelian, inasmuch as it points to the condition of a universal tongue, which is universally translatable because it cannot be appropriated by any 'mineness'.

8. Op. cit.
9. See Derrida, 'The "World" of the Enlightenment to Come (Exception, Calculation, and Sovereignty)', in *Rogues: Two Essays on Reason,* trans. Pascale-Anne Brault and Michael Naas (Stanford: Stanford University Press, 2005).
10. See in particular Derrida, *Rogues* (op. cit.) and 'Auto-Immunity: Real and Symbolic Suicides', trans. Pascale-Anne Brault and Michael Naas, in Giovanna Borradori, ed., *Philosophy in a Time of Terror: Dialogues with Jürgen Habermas and Jacques Derrida* (Chicago: University of Chicago Press, 2004).

Index

Related titles from Routledge

Culture and the Real
Theorizing Cultural Criticism
Catherine Belsey
New Accents

'Belsey is that rarest of birds, a tough-minded romantic, at once a close reader and a far-seeker. She has shown us all how it is possible to write with extraordinary methodological and theoretical sophistication, and at the same time to write clearly, gracefully, and simply. Belsey demonstrates by example that criticism can go about its academic business and still demand the critic to examine and take position on issues that affect our lives.'

Harry Berger, Professor of Literature and Art History, University of California, Santa Cruz

What makes us the people we are? Culture evidently plays a part, but how large a part? Is culture alone the source of our identities? Catherine Belsey calls for a more nuanced account of what it is to be human. In the light of a characteristically lucid account of their views, as well as their debt to Kant and Hegel, she takes issue with Jean-François Lyotard, Judith Butler, and Slavoj Zizek. Drawing examples from film and art, fiction and poetry, Professor Belsey builds on the insights of her influential *Critical Practice* to provide not only an accessible introduction to current debates, but a major new contribution to cultural criticism and theory.

ISBN 10: 0-415-25288-1 (hbk)
ISBN 10: 0-415-25289-X (pbk)

IBSN 13: 978-0-415-25288-1 (hbk)
ISBN 13: 978-0-415-25289-8 (pbk)
ISBN 13: 978-0-203-00144-8 (ebk)

Available at all good bookshops
For further information on our literature series, please visit
www.routledge.com/literature/series.asp

For ordering and further information please visit:
www.routledge.com

Related titles from Routledge

Jacques Derrida
Nicholas Royle

Routledge Critical Thinkers series

'Excellent, strong, clear and original'
Jacques Derrida

'A strong, inventive and daring book that does much more than most introductions are capable of dreaming'

Diane Elam, *Cardiff University*

'Readers couldn't ask for a more authoritative and knowledgeable guide. Although there is no playing down of the immensity of Derrida's work, Royle's direct and often funny mode of address will make it less threatening than it can often appear to beginners.'
Derek Attridge

There are few figures more important in literary and critical theory than Jacques Derrida. Whether lauded or condemned, his writing has had far-reaching ramifications, and his work on deconstruction cannot be ignored. Nicholas Royle's unique book, written in an innovative and original style, is an outstanding introduction to the methods and significance of Jacques Derrida.

ISBN10: 0-415-22930-8 (hbk)
ISBN10: 0-415-22931-6 (pbk)

ISBN13: 978-0-415-22930-2 (hbk)
ISBN13: 978-0-415-22931-9 (pbk)

Available at all good bookshops
For further information on our literature series, please visit
www.routledge.com/literature/series.asp
For ordering and further information please visit:
www.routledge.com